Studies
in
Romans 12

Studies in Romans 12

The Christian's Sacrifice and Service of Praise

Robert S. Candlish
Foreword by Cyril J. Barber

KREGEL PUBLICATIONS
Grand Rapids, Michigan 49501

Studies in Romans 12: The Christian's Sacrifice and Service of Praise, by Robert S. Candlish. Foreword by Cyril J. Barber. © 1989 by Kregel Publications, a division of Kregel, Inc. P. O. Box 2607, Grand Rapids, MI 49501. All rights reserved.

Cover Design: Don Ellens

Library of Congress Cataloging-in-Publication Data

Candlish, Robert S., 1806-1873.
  [Christian's sacrifice and service of praise]
  Studies in Romans 12: the Christian's sacrifice and service of praise / by Robert S. Candlish; foreword by Cyril J. Barber.
      p.   cm.
  Reprint. Originally published: The Christian's sacrifice and service of praise. Edinburgh: Adam and Charles Black, 1867.

  1. Bible. N.T. Romans XII—Criticism, interpretation, etc.
I. Title.
BS2665.C345   1989   227'.106—dc20   89-2660
                                             CIP

ISBN   0-8254-2332-5 (pbk.)

        1 2 3 4 5 Printing/Year 93 92 91 90 89

        Printed in the United States of America

CONTENTS

PART THREE
The Christian's Relationship to a Hostile World

FOREWORD

The documentary on television had already proved to be boring. Just as I was about to switch channels they began showing a spider building a nest of air underwater. I suddenly became intrigued. This air breathing insect had found a suitable leaf, and each time it went to the surface of the pond it would bring back an air bubble in the thick hairs of its abdomen. What impressed me so much was that this spider (called *Argyroneta aquatica* by biologists) lives in a hostile setting but carries with it an environment that enables it to survive.

As I watched it occurred to me I was witnessing a parallel between the natural and spiritual realms. We are *in Christ* while also *in the world*. The world is hostile toward us in much the same way that water is hostile to the general well-being of the spider, but we carry with us our own special "atmosphere" as *Argyroneta aquatica* carries with it an air bubble that enables it to breathe.

From this simple analogy in nature it is easier for us to consider the development of this theme in Scripture, for it is this truth Dr. Robert S. Candlish brings out so beautifully in his exposition of Romans 12. He commences by describing the Christian in relationship to God (12:1-2); then he discusses the Christian's relationship to other professing believers (12:3-13); and he concludes by providing valuable insights into how Christians should conduct themselves in relationship to the world.

Like the spider which must continually replenish its supply of air, so a believer must regularly fellowship with the Lord through meditation upon His word. A continuous transformation of the mind may then occur and he or she can come progressively to know and approve more and more of the good and acceptable and perfect will of the Father.

But God created us as relational beings. It is in our relationships with others, as Dr. Candlish shows, that love becomes the primary motivation. Candlish avoids becoming bogged down in theological debate. Instead, he focuses on the *quality* of the relationship that should characterize followers of Christ.

In the final part of his exposition, namely, "The Christian's Relationship to a Hostile World," the same judicious approach is seen. Candlish describes the way in which the Christian can bestow blessing rather than cursing, show mercy, and grow in knowledge of the truth.

There is a treasure trove of riches to be found in this book, and it would be tragic if Christians failed to be informed about that which a loving Father has made available to them. Robert Candlish's writing is neither trite nor superficial. Rather, it is an important discussion which skillfully applies sound theology to interpersonal relationships.

It is a pleasure to recommend this book to pastors and laypeople alike, trusting that each reader's life will be enriched as the words of this great man of God are carefully read and applied to a variety of individual situations.

CYRIL J. BARBER

INTRODUCTION

THE Twelfth Chapter of Paul's Epistle to the Romans is usually regarded as a section complete in itself. The thirteenth chapter, or at least the first ten verses of it, might perhaps be taken in as part of the section. The topic there discussed,—which is, the duty of Christians as members of civil society—the obedience which they owe to their civil rulers and the obligations under which they lie to their fellow-subjects,—fits in well enough to those which occupy the twelfth chapter. And the pithy and emphatic maxim about charity or love,—" Love worketh no ill to his neighbour; therefore love is the fulfilling of the law," —would form a not unsuitable close to a series of practical lessons which all turn on the cultivation of that grace or virtue of love, in the different forms or modifications of it which different relations and circumstances require. I am inclined, however, to adhere to what seems to be the ordinary opinion. The thirteenth and subsequent chapters embrace several questions of a somewhat casuistical nature, and of rather difficult solution, apt to arise in particular states of the Church and the world. The twelfth is quite general and comprehensive. It is not of course to be disconnected from the preceding and following portions of the Epistle,—especially from the preceding. But as a summary of Christian ethics, it is, when taken by itself, an entire whole ;—having, if I may so say, its own beginning, middle, and end.

Considered in that light, the summary has always commanded the warm admiration, not of divines only, but of moralists also ;—and is, indeed, rather a favourite with a class of persons who are fond of praising the preceptive part of Christianity at the expense of those peculiar dogmas which they regard as hard and mystical. Even Christian readers themselves, perhaps, have been apt to feel as if the moral beauty and simplicity of the exhortations of this chapter were a relief, after the more abstruse matters of doctrine which have strained and taxed their attention so severely in what goes before.

One object of the present volume is to modify any such impression, and to show how thoroughly the ethics of the Gospel are impregnated with the spirit of its theology. Not merely does the word of connection or inference in the first verse,—" therefore,"—warrant the general conclusion, that it is upon the views given in the previous chapters of the Divine Sovereignty, first in the grace of justification, and then in the grace of election, that the precepts of the present chapter all hang ;—but when these precepts come to be examined in detail, they are found, one and all of them, to embody the principle, that man's right conduct, in all the relations in which he is placed, consists essentially in his knowing, and believing,

and sympathizing with what may be called the conduct
of God ; insomuch that, in every instance, man feels and
acts rightly just in proportion as he understands, by
divine teaching, how God himself feels and acts in his
great plan of saving mercy. I believe that what is required of me, in every department of duty, is, that,
on the one hand, I apprehend God's sovereign grace,
in his justification of the unrighteous through faith in
the righteousness of his Son, and in his choice and calling of the unworthy and the unwilling according to his
own mere good pleasure ; and then, on the other hand,
that apprehending this sovereign grace in its immediate personal application to me, and as ruling God's
treatment of me, I enter into the spirit of it, and apply
it myself to all with whom I have anything to do, for
the ruling of my treatment of them. Now these are the
two themes which occupy the whole doctrinal part of the
Epistle ;—the sovereignty of God's grace in justification,
and the sovereignty of his grace in election and vocation;
—the one being discussed in the first eight chapters, and
the other in the ninth, tenth, and eleventh. I assume
the teaching of these chapters upon both of these views
of God's grace ; and I endeavour, with reference to the
twelfth chapter as a whole, and with reference to its precepts in detail, to bring out the amazing harmony and
identity that there are between that grace of God and
every duty which, on the ground of it, he requires of them
that believe.

The plan which I have adopted, dividing the chapter
into three parts, is explained and vindicated as I proceed

from verse to verse in my exposition.[1]   It is not necessary
to enter upon a formal defence of it beforehand; I trust
to its approving itself in the course of its detailed development.   I may observe, however, that down to the end
of the eighth verse, there is little or no room for doubt.
Believers are in the first place (ver. 1, 2), summoned to a
personal dealing, each for himself, directly and immediately
with God.   They are to consecrate themselves to God,
and separate themselves from the world, for the proving
of the will of God ; and this they are to do as individuals,
—not jointly, but severally.   Then, in the second place,
(ver. 3–8,) they form themselves, or find themselves
formed, into a collective body, in which they have all
their separate gifts, and functions, and offices ; while yet
such order and mutual subordination reign that they all
act in harmony,—not only severally, but jointly also.
Thus far, the arrangement is clear enough.   After the
eighth verse, however, there might at first sight seem to
be a mere miscellaneous string of good advices, some
having reference to the Christian's duty in the Church,
others to his duty towards the world, and others again
partly to both, but all mingled together, as one would
say, very much at random.   Thus the ninth verse brings
in the duty of universal charity, or love, in the midst of
precepts evidently bearing upon the fellowship of Chris-

---

[1] It is proper to explain that the Discourses on the first eight verses of the
chapter, occupying rather more than a hundred pages of the present volume
(pp. 11–126), appeared some years ago in a small volume, now out of print,
under the title of "The Christian's Sacrifice." They have been carefully revised,
and adapted to their position as part of the larger treatise, which I had then in
progress, and which, such as it is, I have now completed.

tians as such; whereas again in the fifteenth and sixteenth verses, or at all events in the latter, we have
what looks like a counsel of Christian brotherhood, while
both before and after the teaching refers to the treatment
of persecutors. Hence I believe the notion has come to
prevail, that beyond the first eight verses there is no
exact order to be traced in the chapter. I am persuaded
that this is a mistake, and that it has led to an inadequate interpretation, to say the least, of some of the
verses -in question. I have endeavoured to show how
the introduction of the general commandment of love
(ver. 9) qualifies the special commandment of brotherly
love (ver. 10); and also how the enjoining of sympathy
(ver. 15), and even apparently of unanimity (ver. 16), is
very much to the purpose in considering how a hostile
world is to be treated. I look at those precepts which
appear to be out of their place, and inquire what, supposing that they are in their place, is their bearing in
the connection in which they actually stand; and in doing
so, I begin to find in them a force and point not otherwise observed. I trace an orderly sequence in the whole
train of thought, as the writer would lead believers in
Jesus to apprehend what they are to God, as his peculiar
people; what they are in respect of their union among
themselves, and their organization into one body, for the
purposes of fellowship and of work; and what they are
in respect of their position in a hostile world, and the
duties which they owe to " them that are without."

It is this view that has reconciled me to the Title
suggested by a friend for my treatise. I do not profess

formally to discuss the "two great commandments" in connection with my theme. But having sought to enter into the meaning of Paul's ethical directory, without any immediate reference to the Lord's summary, I have noticed with much interest how the law or principle of love, given forth as a pure ray of light from the Sun of Righteousness, is as it were broken up in its application to the details of duty;—how, as if he were giving a practical commentary on his Master's saying, the Apostle brings out the working of supreme love to our God in self-consecration, transformation, and obedience; and brings out also the working of equal love to our neighbour,—our loving him as ourselves,—in Christian brotherhood among believers, and Christian humanity towards all men.

There is no attempt in this work to deal with the chapter critically, or even, in the strict sense, exegetically. If that had been my aim, I must have discussed some questions of interpretation which I have not even raised, and dwelt upon some sentences and clauses on which I have only slightly touched. It is to be remembered, however, that there are not any considerable critical or exegetical difficulties in the passage.

Of the various readings, two only are noticeable, not for any force of external evidence in their favour,—the weight of manuscript authority, both in quantity and in quality, being decidedly against them;—but because they illustrate the way in which alterations of the text have sometimes crept in, through the prejudice or erroneous judgment of transcribers. Thus in the thirteenth verse, some copies have, instead of distributing or ministering to the " necessities" of saints, ministering to their "memories" (μνείαις for χρείαις) ;—an alteration evidently savouring of that undue reverence for the departed which early began to prevail in the Church, and ultimately became worship. Again at verse eleventh, the clause, serving "the Lord," is in a considerable number of manuscripts, serving "the time," or "season" (καιρῷ for Κυρίῳ). The copyist apparently thought that the idea of "serving the Lord" was too general to come in among the specific directions with which it is joined, and therefore he made it "serving the time,"—that is, acting in conformity or in obedience to the time or season ; an injunction not very appropriate or emphatic, and not very much in accordance with what Paul elsewhere says about being diligent in season and out of season. That the received text, as it stands, has a relevant meaning, I have endeavoured to show.

Much has been made, in former times, by theologians, both Romanist and Protestant, of the expression in the sixth verse, "the proportion" or the analogy "of faith." It has been used, in fact, as a sort of proof text to support a principle of interpretation of very wide application, and requiring somewhat delicate handling. The principle is this,—that in fixing the meaning of any particular passage, regard is to be had to the general strain of the teaching of Scripture, and of the system of truth as understood and held by the Church Catholic. However sound the principle may be, within due limits, it derives no support from the passage now in question ; in which it cannot be an objective measure or standard of faith that is intended, but rather the inward, subjective kind,

or amount of conviction which a man has in himself.
Having formed that opinion, I have not deemed it needful
to dwell on the phrase, " the proportion of faith," or to
discuss the principle of interpretation which it has been
supposed to countenance ; since I take it to mean simply
that he who prophesies should in doing so go to the full
extent of the faith wrought in him, or, as I have expressed
it, should prophesy—" believing all that he says, and saying all that he believes" (see page 119). I am glad to
find that I may appeal in support of my opinion to so
high an authority as Alford.[1]

Had my plan been different from what it is, I must
have gone much more fully into the consideration of the
topic treated of in the fourth and following verses,
taken in connection with Paul's teaching in his First
Epistle to the Corinthians, (ch. xii.,) where the same subject is handled at greater length. I am aware that I
have thus been led to omit some topics of interest regarding the constitution and organization of the Church,
whether viewed as an unseen, spiritual fellowship, or as
an outstanding society in the world. But the discussion
of these topics would have drawn me away from the
more immediate design of the Apostle's discourse ; which
is not to lay down an ecclesiastical platform, but to enforce personal obligations.

For much the same reason, I have dealt somewhat
summarily with the phrase in the twentieth verse, " coals
of fire," or " burning coals ;" contenting myself with a

---

[1] Greek Testament, *in loco*, vol. ii. page 416, third edition.

single reference to the passage in the Old Testament which the Apostle manifestly has in view (Prov. xxv. 21, 22). Several other Old Testament texts[1] might have been exegetically examined, and might have been found very much to the purpose. An inquiry of deepest interest would thus have been opened up, into the harmony of the teaching of both Testaments, not only as to the penal justice of God, but as to the sentiments with which his saints regard the execution of its righteous awards. The inquiry, however, would demand, and deserve, a separate treatise. It would demolish, I am persuaded, the notion of there being any real difference between the Christian dispensation and those which preceded it, on the subject of God's treatment of his enemies and his people's acquiescence and sympathy therein ; and would make it clear, that, with all the fuller discoveries of his love which we have in the Gospel, we are called all the more on that account to realize, for ourselves and for others, the dark, overhanging cloud of ultimate retribution. But any such discussion as that would have led me away from the line I had prescribed to myself. Of the texts indicated, it is enough to say, that since they, one and all of them, apply the phrase exclusively to the infliction of judicial vengeance, for the vindication of the righteous and the punishment of the ungodly, they confirm the opinion that we cannot interpret the Apostle's precept (ver. 20) as if it contemplated only a good issue of kindness shown to an enemy ; that its meaning is not exhausted unless we hold

---

[1] Deut. xxxii. 24 (marginal reading) ; Ps. xviii. 12, 13 ; cxx. 4 ; cxl. 10 ; Ezek. x. 2 ; Hab. iii. 5.

it to have fully in view the possibility of the issue being exactly the reverse.

What I wish to be understood, in short, is, that the present treatise is entirely practical. The Discourses when preached were meant to be practical ; and they are published nearly as they were delivered. When I call them practical, however, I mean practical in an evangelical point of view. I endeavour, throughout, to carry the stream of sound doctrine through all the departments of duty that I have to survey. In particular, as the chapter begins with a pointed reference to Sacrifice, and ends with a very solemn appeal to Judgment, so I think there is a propriety in viewing the whole of this brief code of Christian ethics, as well as every part of it, in the light of those high attributes of the Divine character, and those great principles of the Divine government, of which the first and second advents of Christ may be said to be the exponents. I start with the assumption of the Atonement made by Christ at his first coming being a real satisfaction to Divine justice, through his real substitution of himself in the room of the guilty who are obnoxious to justice. And I can find no meaning in the very solemn closing verses of the chapter unless they involve the reality of wrath and retribution, to be consummated when the Lord cometh again. I solicit special attention, in this view, to the last two or three Discourses in the volume. For, however modern theological refinement may shrink from any notion of righteousness that is not remedial, and any notion of punishment that is not resolvable into correction, I am fully persuaded that it is fatal, not less to the high and healthy tone of Christian morals than to the living power and influence of Christian faith, to repudiate or keep in the back-ground the doctrine or fact of judicial retribution. That doctrine, or fact, I take to be the essence of law and government. Without it, neither the Divine sovereignty nor human responsibility,—neither the sovereignty which is God's prerogative as a moral ruler, nor the responsibility which is man's dignity as a free moral agent,—can, in my opinion, be safe. On any system which excludes that element, God is dishonoured, and man must in the long run be degraded. I recognise it alike in the theology and in the ethics of Paul.

PART ONE

THE CHRISTIAN'S RELATIONSHIP TO GOD (12:1, 2)

1

CONSECRATION TO GOD

"I beseech you, therefore, brethren, by the mercies of God, that ye present your bodies a living sacrifice, holy, acceptable unto God, which is your reasonable service." —Romans 12:1

BELIEVERS in Christ are consecrated to God. This is the first element in their relation to him; the second being separation from the world. They are addressed as priests; called to execute a priestly office,—to "present a sacrifice." And this implies consecration to God.

In one view, it is a high calling. "Ye are a royal priesthood," is the testimony of the Apostle Peter. "Thou hast redeemed us to God by thy blood," is the new song of the saved, "and hast made us unto our God kings and priests." In another view, it is a humble position. A priest is ordained to minister and serve at the altar. In this passage, it is not so much the high dignity of the priestly office as its humble ministry, that is brought out. Still it is, in every view of it, a sacred position; a position of consecration to God.

Paul has been touching some of those deep, dread mysteries which shroud in impenetrable gloom the eternal throne and the eternal world; mysteries which only thicken into darker midnight the more we try to pierce them. For the sovereignty of God, in its bearing on the ultimate issues of his providence, and on the final destinies of the creatures whom he has made intelligent and free, must ever be inscrutable. Paul, accordingly, closes the great argument which he has been maintaining for the Divine prerogative, with a solemn ejaculation, implying utter impotency and prostration : " O the depth of the riches both of the wisdom and knowledge of God ! how unsearchable are his judgments, and his ways past finding out !" (xi. 33).

To silence, however, where he cannot satisfy, he appeals abruptly to any who would still raise questions.

By what right, he asks, do you presume to judge or to interrogate the Supreme ? Have you been in his confidence from the first ? Or must he advise with you ? Or have you any such claim on him as to lay him under an obligation to give you satisfaction ? " For who hath known the mind of the Lord ? or who hath been his counsellor ? or who hath first given to him, and it shall be recompensed unto him again ?" (34, 35.) Are you the Lord's confidants ? Are you the Lord's councillors ? Are you the Lord's creditors ? If not, how are you entitled to pry into those " secret things" which " belong to the Lord your God ?" " The things which are revealed belong to you and to your children." But as to the secret things which belong to him, he is not in any way bound to you ; nor with reference to them can you demand that he should discover more of his plans to you than he sees fit ; " For of him,

and through him, and to him, are all things : to whom
be glory for ever. Amen." (36.)

Your becoming attitude is that of the Psalmist :
" Lord, my heart is not haughty, nor mine eyes lofty :
neither do I exercise myself in great matters, or in
things too high for me. Surely I have behaved and
quieted myself, as a child that is weaned of his mother :
my soul is even as a weaned child. Let Israel hope
in the Lord from henceforth and for ever " (Psalm
cxxxi.)

We are then in our right place, when, instead of aspiring to master, as critics, the whole mind and will of God,
we thankfully consent to learn, as children, what it is
his pleasure to teach. He is not dependent on us : he
is not indebted to us. The dependence and the debt
of obligation are all on our side. We are not competent
to dictate or give lessons to him. We are children and
scholars under his training.

And the training is for service. We are to be, not
advisers or judges, but ministers, servants, priests. " I
beseech you, therefore, brethren," instead of aspiring to
be the confidants, or the councillors, or the creditors of the
Lord, to assume the office and discharge the functions
of the priesthood.

For the priesthood is to be considered as a ministry
and service. It was so to Him with whom we are
associated in its exercise. " The Son of man came not
to be ministered unto, but to minister, and to give his
life a ransom for many." So he came to do the business of his priesthood. So we are summoned to do the

business of our priesthood. The business of his priesthood was to "give his life a ransom for many." The
business of our priesthood is to "present our bodies a
living sacrifice, holy, acceptable unto God, which is our
reasonable service."

From this general account of what Christians have to
do, as consecrated to God, in the character of priests, the
following particulars may be drawn out in detail:—

I. There is to be a sacrifice : " I beseech you, brethren,
that ye present a sacrifice."

II. It must be a sacrifice that fulfils two conditions :
it must be such as may righteously find acceptance in
the sight of God, and such as may reasonably be required
and expected at the hands of man : " I beseech you
that ye present a sacrifice;" such as shall, on the one
hand, be " acceptable to God;" and such as shall, on
the other hand, and on your part, be " a reasonable
service."

III. If it is to fulfil these two conditions, the sacrifice
must possess the two qualities of life and holiness : " I
beseech you that ye present a living sacrifice, holy ;"—for
such a sacrifice alone can be acceptable to God ; such a
sacrifice alone can be your reasonable service.

IV. The substance or matter of the sacrifice is indicated ; it is to consist of " your bodies," your persons,
yourselves: " I beseech you that ye present your bodies."

V. The motive also is indicated which is to prompt
the sacrifice : " I beseech you, brethren, by the mercies
of God."

Under these heads, the sacrifice which as Christians, bearing the character of priests, we have to present to God may be considered ; and the connection and correspondence, as well as the difference, between it and the sacrifice of Christ may be traced. The connection and correspondence will be found, if we rightly apprehend the Spirit's teaching, to be very close.

1. THE SACRIFICE: ITS NATURE

"I beseech you that ye present a sacrifice."   —*Romans 12:1*

There is to be a sacrifice. Priests are not to approach to God empty handed. " Bring an offering and come into his courts ;" so runs their summons.

This law applies to the High Priest as well as to ordinary priests. It applies pre-eminently to the High Priest. " Every high priest is ordained to offer gifts and sacrifices ; wherefore it is of necessity that this one," our great High Priest, Christ, " have somewhat also to offer " (Heb. viii. 3). So far, Christians who are priests, and Christ who alone is the High Priest, have this in common, that they as well as he have to present a sacrifice.

But there is a wide and essential distinction. Any sacrifice which we as priests can present, must be of an entirely different nature from what Christ, the High Priest, presents. His sacrifice is, in the strict and proper sense of the term, a sacrifice of atonement. His sacrifice alone can be so. Our sacrifice is a sacrifice of thanksgiving and praise.

This is a distinction recognised in the Levitical economy. In that economy, there were atoning sacrifices, designed to be effectual for the expiation of guilt and the reconciliation of offenders to God. Of this kind, in particular, were the sacrifices appointed for the great annual day of atonement, when the high priest entered within the veil with the blood of bulls and of goats, " which he offered for himself and for the errors of the people." The sacrifice of Christ is represented in the New Testament as exactly of the same character with these sacrifices, only infinitely more efficacious. Thus the Apostle writing to the Hebrews reasons : " If the blood of bulls and of goats, and the ashes of an heifer sprinkling the unclean, sanctifieth to the purifying of the flesh : how much more shall the blood of Christ, who through the eternal Spirit offered himself without spot to God, purge your conscience from dead works to serve the living God?" (ix. 13, 14.) In the offering of a sacrifice of this kind, Christ, our High Priest, stands alone. Into his ministry of atonement, his propitiatory work, we may not, as priests, intrude. But there were sacrifices of another kind under the law ; sacrifices of praise and thanksgiving, offered in acknowledgment of the sovereignty and bounty of God, and as pledges of dependence and gratitude. These sacrifices had nothing to do with the cancelling of guilt and the restoration of the guilty party to favour. They did not make peace. They proceeded on the faith of peace being otherwise made, by a previous sacrifice of atonement. They were, in fact, expressions of thankfulness on that account.

The sacrifice of Cain was a sacrifice of thanksgiving. And as a sacrifice of thanksgiving, it would have been legitimate and right, if it had been preceded by the ordained sacrifice of atonement. The sacrifice of Abel was a sacrifice of atonement. And undoubtedly, if his life had been spared, it would have been followed up by an appropriate sacrifice of praise. Having offered " of the firstlings of his flock and of the fat thereof;" and having evidence of the acceptance of his offering, in the " light of God's reconciled countenance lifted up upon him," and " the love of God shed abroad in his heart by the Holy Ghost being given to him;" he would gladly and gratefully have "brought of the fruit of the ground an offering" of thanksgiving and praise " to the Lord."

And this now is our ministry as priests. This is all our ministry. The ministry of atonement is not ours, either for others or for ourselves. That ministry Christ alone exercises. " He treads the wine-press alone," in his work of bloody propitiation, as well as in his work of bloody judgment, "and of the people there is none with him." All the more may the ministry of thankoffering be ours. For our pardon and peace, our acceptance and justification, we have nothing to offer, we have nothing to give. The Apostle calls for no sacrifice at our hands for the purpose of cleansing us from sin and restoring us to favour. So far as that matter is concerned, he uniformly points our view exclusively to the one only sacrifice of the one only High Priest: " We are ambassadors for Christ, as though God did beseech you by us: we pray you in Christ's stead, be ye reconciled to God. For he hath made him to be sin for us, who knew no sin; that we might be made the righteousness of God in him " (2 Cor. v. 20, 21). But now, upon the supposition that we are reconciled, freely, effectually, thoroughly reconciled, through faith in the great Atonement, the Apostle calls for some suitable offering of praise. He tells us that the atoning ministry of the High Priest, thus available on our behalf, opens the way for a graceful and grateful ministry of thanksgiving: " I beseech you, brethren, that ye present a sacrifice."

2. THE SACRIFICE: ITS CONDITIONS

"I beseech you, brethren, that ye present a sacrifice, acceptable to God, which is your reasonable service." —*Romans 12:1*

The nature of the sacrifice which, as priests, Christians are called to present, having been ascertained, the next point is to consider the general principles which ought to determine the character of the matter, or material, to be used in the sacrifice, or of which the sacrifice is to consist.

If there is to be a sacrifice of thanksgiving and praise, proceeding upon the faith of a sacrifice of atonement having been offered and accepted, let it be a suitable sacrifice. Let it be a sacrifice that fulfils these two indispensable conditions: let it be, as regards him to whom it is presented, "acceptable to God;" let it also be, as regards you who present it, "your reasonable service."

Of the sacrifice of atonement which our great High

Priest has to present, it may with equal justice be said that it must fulfil these two conditions. To that sacrifice also—to that sacrifice primarily—they apply, as conditions. When a ransom was to be found for sinful man, it was necessary on the one hand, that it should be such a ransom as it might be worthy of God to accept; and on the other hand, that it should be such a ransom as it might be reasonable to expect should be offered on behalf of reasonable creatures.

The character and nature of the offended party, God, the holy lawgiver and righteous judge; the character and nature of the offending party, man, a free and intelligent being, made in the image of God; and the relation between the parties, implying just condemnation on the one side and guilty enmity on the other; all must be taken into account. The sacrifice must bear some adequate proportion, or suitable relation, to the majesty of violated law and the unforced responsibility of its violators. It must have in it worth and value enough to meet the case of God's sovereign authority having been outraged, and to meet also the case of man's conscience having become burdened and defiled. It must be sufficient to satisfy Divine justice; and sufficient also to assuage the anguish of genuine remorse and shame.

Tried by this test, it is easy to see how the blood of bulls and of goats can never take away sin. The substitution of a senseless, unconsenting animal, as a victim or ransom, in the room and stead of a race which has intelligently and wilfully sinned, is felt to be, upon every principle of common sense and reason,

as well as of right religious feeling, an utterly
inadequate atonement. There is no propriety or suitableness in the idea of the death of such a substitute
being accepted as an equivalent for the execution
of the sentence upon the guilty. The law cannot
in that way be vindicated. The Lawgiver cannot on
that ground be warranted in treating offenders as if
they had never sinned ; or as if they had themselves
suffered the penalty, and come out from the suffering of
it, pure and upright. Nor can such a vicarious endurance
of my punishment, by a bull, or goat, or ram, or lamb,
held to represent me, satisfy my own conviction of right
and my own consciousness of wrong. Whatever may
come of my controversy with my Maker, I instinctively
feel that these animal sacrifices cannot avail for its settle-
ment ;—no ; nor any formal observances I may be
inclined to put in their place. " The blood of bulls
and of goats cannot take away sin." " None can by
any means redeem his brother," or ransom his own
soul.

The conditions which it was necessary that the High
Priest's sacrifice of atonement should fulfil must be fulfilled also by the sacrifice of praise which believers, as
priests, are to present. This sacrifice of theirs must be
in accordance with what God is, and with what they
are. In particular, it must be in accordance with what
God is to them, and with what they are to God.

Let it be remembered that we present our sacrifice of
praise, as priests, on the footing of the High Priest's sacrifice of atonement being on our behalf offered and ac-

cepted ; on the footing of our personal interest by faith in its efficacy and fruit.

Upon that footing, what is the idea which we are called to entertain of the God to whom we have to present our thank-offering ?   " God is a spirit ; and they that worship him must worship him in spirit and in truth.   The Father seeketh such to worship him."   He is weary and impatient of all other worship.   " My son, give me thy heart," is his demand.   That we may be in a condition, and may be made willing, to give him our heart,—he redeems us to himself by the blood of Christ, and renews us by the power of the Holy Ghost.   He, therefore, to whom we are to present our sacrifice is a spirit, requiring spiritual worship.   And we, who are to present the sacrifice, are spiritual men.   " Now he that is spiritual judgeth all things " (1 Cor. ii. 15). We can judge, therefore, what may be fairly regarded as our " reasonable service;" what is the sort of service that may be reasonably expected and required, as a sacrifice of praise, at our hands, if God is a spirit and we are spiritual men.

And this we may the rather do, when we consider the relation now subsisting—the relation which ought to subsist—between our God, who is a spirit, and ourselves who are spiritual men.   Through that one sacrifice of propitiation presented by the High Priest on our behalf, there is peace, friendship, reconciliation.   All our guilt is expiated : all our sin is purged.   We are no longer treated as guilty criminals under a respite.   We are accepted as righteous in the sight of God.   We are adopted as children in his Son : we receive "the Spirit of his Son into our hearts, crying, Abba, Father" (Gal. iv. 6).

Now it is as thus knowing God, who is a spirit ; knowing thus, also, ourselves as spiritual men ; and knowing, above all, the footing on which we stand with our God and Father ;—that we are called, as priests, to present a sacrifice of praise. May we not decide and determine for ourselves, according to these considerations, what sort of sacrifice is suitable and appropriate? what is worthy of God ? what is worthy of ourselves ? What sort of sacrifice may God be expected to accept? What sort of sacrifice, in the full view of all the circumstances, may be regarded as our "reasonable service ?"

At all events, tried by such a test, how miserably will many a sacrifice and service that we are apt to present to God fail and be found wanting ! Form, ceremony, routine; heartless prayers, however long ; ostentatious alms, however large ; bodily exercise, whether in the way of easy compliance with outward rites, or in the way of painful inward self-mortification ; enforced obedience ; reluctant abstinence from pleasure ; the cold and cheerless performance of duty; all or any of these kinds of worship—all similar methods of serving God— we can bring to this criterion. Is it such a sacrifice of praise and thanksgiving that a reconciled God and Father should in fairness be asked to accept? Is it such a sacrifice of praise and thanksgiving that we, his reconciled children, may be reasonably asked to offer? Is it such a sacrifice of praise and thanksgiving that should signalize and seal so thorough a repairing of the breach caused by sin between our God and us, as that which the High Priest's sacrifice of atonement effects? Surely, if it is felt by the universal moral instinct of all men to be true, that the blood of bulls and of goats cannot take away sin,—it must be felt also by the universal spiritual instinct of all those whose sins are taken away, by the blood of a better ransom, to be not less true, that formal worship, or obedience rendered in the spirit of bondage, is not the sacrifice which a redeeming God can worthily accept, and is not a " reasonable service" on the part of the people whom he redeems.

3.   THE SACRIFICE: ITS QUALITIES

"I beseech you that ye present a living sacrifice, holy."   *—Romans 12:1*

The sacrifice which Christians present, as priests, must possess two qualities which formal worship, or obedience rendered in the spirit of bondage, is sure to want.   It must possess the qualities of life and holiness. Without these qualities it cannot fulfil the two indispensable conditions ; it cannot be either an acceptable offering to God, or, on our part, a reasonable service.   The sacrifice must be living and holy: " I beseech you that ye present a living sacrifice, holy.''

It was necessary that the sacrifice of atonement which our High Priest was ordained to present should possess these two qualities.   It must be living and holy.   It must have in it life and holiness.

Life must belong to it.   And what life ?   Not merely animal life, the life that is common to all sentient and moving creatures; not merely, in addition to that, intelligent life, the life that characterizes all beings capable of thought and voluntary choice; but spiritual life: life in the highest sense; the very life which those on whose behalf the sacrifice of atonement is presented lost, when they fell into that state which makes a sacrifice of atonement necessary. If a ransom is to be found,—an adequate and suitable substitute for those who have ceased to live, as they were originally made and meant to live, in the favour and loving-kindness of God, and have become dead under his sentence of righteous condemnation,—it must be a ransom, a substitute, having the life which they once had; exempt and free from the death which they have incurred. A living sacrifice of atonement alone can suffice; a sacrifice of atonement having the quality of life; of that life which consists in a right standing with God; in complete exemption from his condemnation, and the complete enjoyment of his favour and loving-kindness.

And the sacrifice must be holy also. As it must have life forfeited by no guilt, liable to no sentence of death; so it must have holiness tainted by no corruption. Let either guilt or corruption—let either death or sin—belong, by whatever tenure, hereditary or personal, to the ransom or victim that is to be the atoning sacrifice presented by the High Priest on behalf of guilty sinners;— it is not such a sacrifice as God, the Lawgiver, can be justified in accepting as a compensation for the breaking of his law; it is not such a sacrifice as can be considered a reasonable service on behalf of the breakers of that

law,—if it is to exempt them from the penalty which
they have incurred, through the vicarious endurance of that
penalty by a worthy substitute in their stead. The dead and
unholy cannot be ransomed or redeemed, if the only sacrifice provided for that end is itself involved in their death
and unholiness. "Behold the Lamb of God that taketh
away the sin of the world," is a welcome call to sinners,
and to me, the chief of sinners. But if that very Lamb
of God that is to take away the sin of the world, is involved in that very sin of the world which is to be taken
away, where, alas ! is my hope ?

Thus the sacrifice of atonement presented by the High
Priest for us must be free alike from the condemnation
and from the corruption, from the death and from the
defilement, of our sin. It must be "a living sacrifice,
holy."

And so, also, must be the sacrifice of praise and thanksgiving which, as priests, we are to be always presenting ; it
must be "a living sacrifice, holy." It must partake of
the character of the sacrifice of atonement, in immediate
connection with which it is presented. It is by faith in
the sacrifice of atonement that we present the sacrifice of
praise. This last sacrifice is the fruit of the first; and
indeed, in some sense, a continuation of it. We enter into
the spirit, while we appropriate the efficacy, of our great
High Priest's sacrifice of atonement, as a living sacrifice
and holy. We become one, as priests, with him who, as
High Priest, presents it. We become one with him in his
presenting of it. And being one with him who is the
High Priest, we go on, as priests, to present our sacrifice

of praise. We cannot, in such circumstances, think of presenting any sacrifice of praise that is not in keeping and
in harmony with the High Priest's sacrifice of atonement.
We cannot ask God to accept, we cannot offer as our
reasonable service, any tribute of gratitude, any sacrifice
of thanksgiving, that does not possess the qualities which
impart worth and efficacy to the High Priest's great propitiation. Ours, like his, must be a sacrifice, living and
holy.

4. THE SACRIFICE: ITS MATTER

"I beseech you that ye present your bodies a sacrifice." —Romans 12:1

The nature of the sacrifice as a sacrifice of praise, as
well as the indispensable conditions and qualities of it,
having been considered, the next inquiry relates to the
substance or matter of the sacrifice. What shall it be?
Our bodies: " I beseech you that ye present your bodies
a sacrifice."

The same phraseology is used when it is the High
Priest's sacrifice of atonement that is in question. " We
are sanctified," it is said, we are cleansed from the guilt
of sin, " through the offering of the body of Jesus Christ
once for all" (Heb. x. 10). It is the entire person of
Christ that is there meant. He offered himself. That
was his sacrifice of atonement. The offering of ourselves
is our sacrifice of thanksgiving.

But how can there be any parallel or analogy here?
How can there be any correspondence, in respect of life
and holiness, between Christ's person, offered as a sacrifice
of atonement,—and mine, offered as a sacrifice of praise?

That Christ, the High Priest, may offer his body, or present himself, as a sacrifice of atonement, living and holy, I can understand.

As to his life, I read what his beloved disciple records as part of his teaching in his humiliation: " Therefore doth my Father love me, because I lay down my life, that I might take it again. No man taketh it from me, but I lay it down of myself. I have power to lay it down, and I have power to take it again. This commandment have I received of my Father" (John x. 17, 18). I read also what that same beloved disciple records as a voice from his beloved Master in his exaltation: "I am he that liveth, and was dead; and, behold, I am alive for evermore, Amen" (Rev. i. 18). He has life; life forfeited by no guilt, liable to no condemnation or death. When he offers, or presents, himself as a substitute for the dead, the guilty, the condemned, he offers, or presents, himself a living sacrifice. His life; his right to live, according to the highest idea of life; his prerogative of life in the favour of God, in the bosom of the Father;—cannot be challenged or impugned. He is not under any sentence of condemnation, he is not doomed to die a penal death on his own account. No fault, therefore, can be found with him on that score, when he offers himself as willing to be the substitute of the guilty.

Nor can any objection be taken on the score of his being one of our race, as if that involved any compromise or surrender of his essential holiness, or any participation in our sin. His holiness is still as untarnished, as his life is unforfeited and uncondemned. It was needful that he should become one of us, that he should become one with us, if he was to present himself as a sacrifice of atonement in our stead. And, without a miracle, there might be difficulty in his taking our nature, without taking also our corruption and criminality;—which if he had taken, his offering of himself in our stead would have been in vain. But it is miraculously otherwise arranged. He is essentially the living one, the holy one, in respect of his divine nature. And even when he associates the human nature with that divine nature, so as to constitute one person, Emmanuel, God with us, — the Word made flesh, — Jesus, saving his people from their sins,—he is still the living one and the holy one. A sacrifice of atonement is needed, a ransom to deliver from going down to the pit. The sacrifice or ransom, in order to fulfil the twofold condition of its being such as God may accept and such as may be a suitable and reasonable service of propitiation for man's sin, must be living and holy. It must possess the qualities of life and holiness; life in God's favour forfeited by no guilt; holiness unstained by any taint of pollution. Such a sacrifice of atonement is found in Christ. He is the living one. He " lays down his life of himself." He is " holy, harmless, undefiled, and separate from sinners." " He offers himself without spot to God " (John x. 18 ; Heb. vii. 26; ix. 14).

Now our sacrifice of praise must partake of the qualities of his sacrifice of atonement. It must be living and holy.

But how may that be, if it is our bodies, our persons, ourselves, that we are to present as the sacrifice?

'Woe is me!' some poor soul may be heard to cry out, 'I am asked to present a thank-offering and sacrifice of praise. It is a just demand; a gracious invitation. Fain would I comply with it.—But the sacrifice, I am told, must be living and holy.'—'Certainly,' I answer, 'it is most right and fitting that it should be so.'—'But I am further told that it must be myself; myself bodily; my very self.—Alas! alas! are life and holiness in me, that I should furnish in my own person the material of this sacrifice?—Life and holiness in me!—I am lost and dead in sin; I am carnal, sold under sin. In me, that is, in my flesh, dwelleth no good thing;—nothing but guilt weighing me down to utter destruction, and corruption defiling the whole inner man. For me, undone, unclean, to present myself a living and holy sacrifice!—it cannot be.'

Nay but, my brother, it must be. It is thyself that thy God will have thee to present as a thank-offering. He will accept no other thank-offering at thy hands : it is not reasonable that he should. Say not that there is no life in thee. Is not Christ in thee? "Thou art crucified with Christ, nevertheless thou livest; yet not thou; but Christ liveth in thee" (Gal. ii. 20). And for thine uncleanness—"what God hath cleansed, that call not thou common or unclean" (Acts x. 15).

Believers in Christ, called to be priests, present yourselves a sacrifice, as the great High Priest presents himself a sacrifice. Let your ministry and his be one. Are not

you and he now one,—intimately, inseparably one? When
you present yourselves a sacrifice, are you not presenting
him? Even as when he presents himself a sacrifice, is he not
presenting you? He presents himself as crucified for you;
he presents you as crucified with him. You now present
yourselves; yet not yourselves; it is Christ in you that
you present. The Spirit making you one with Christ by
faith, makes you partakers of Christ's life; the life which
he laid down that he might take it again,—the life which
he has as no more bearing guilt, but justified, accepted,
raised and glorified. The same Spirit, making you one
with Christ in nature, by the renewing of your mind,
makes you partakers of Christ's holiness. The Spirit
takes of what is Christ's, and shows it to you. And
when, through the Spirit, you present yourselves a sacrifice, he takes of what is Christ's in you, and shows it to
God. May not this be an acceptable thank-offering? Is
not this, ye redeemed and regenerated saints of God,—is
not this your reasonable service?

" I beseech you therefore, brethren, that ye present
yourselves a sacrifice." And let it be yourselves in
Christ; let it be Christ in you. For thus only can it be
a sacrifice " living and holy." When Christ presents
himself a sacrifice of atonement, be you one with him in
his doing so. When you present yourselves a sacrifice of
praise, let him be one with you in your doing so. Let
the two presentations be ever going on together, simulta-
neously, unitedly. The presentation by Christ of himself
as the sacrifice of atonement is always going on in the
sanctuary above. There, in the true holy place, he is

always ministering as your great High Priest, having his own blood to offer, ever freshly flowing, and freshly efficacious to cleanse from all sin. Enter, be always entering, within the veil, that you may associate and identify yourselves by faith, through the Spirit, with Christ, in what is there transacted for your peace. In a corresponding manner, let your presentation of yourselves, as a sacrifice of thanksgiving, be always going on in the sanctuary here below; the only sanctuary now owned on earth,—the deep and sacred shrine of a believing heart. And oh! let Christ be always entering in there, within the veil, and dwelling there, that he may associate and identify himself with you, in what is there transacted for God's praise. Thus it will be always Christ, and Christ alone ; yet always you in Christ, and Christ in you. In the sacrifice of atonement, it is Christ crucified for you, and you crucified with him. In the sacrifice of thankfulness, it is Christ living in you, and you become partakers of his holiness. It is the sacrifice of propitiation, living and holy, prolonging itself, in a manner most acceptable to God and most reasonable on your part, into a living and holy sacrifice of praise. There is the sin-offering of the living and holy body of Christ once for all; and there is the thank-offering of the living and holy Church, " which is his" mystical "body, the fulness of him who filleth all in all" (Eph. i. 23).

5.   THE SACRIFICE: ITS MOTIVE

"I beseech you, by the mercies of God."   —*Romans 12:1*

It now only remains for us to advert a little to the motive by which Christians are to be animated in their discharge of the office of their priesthood, for which they are consecrated to God.   As it is a sacrifice of praise and gratitude that they are to present, they are fitly adjured and implored to do so " by the mercies of God."

The adjuration, the entreaty, is very earnest. "I beseech you," says the Apostle.   I make it a matter of personal request, as if I were asking you to do me a personal favour.   I may well thus appeal to you; for the motive which I have to urge is one which I have had good reason myself personally to feel.   " The mercies of God " have been very abundant towards me.   But it is not from myself, or for myself, that I speak.   I speak as an ambassador of Christ.   I call to mind what these mercies of God were to Christ,—what they were in his eyes and in his esteem,—when, as the great High Priest, he went about the business of presenting his sacrifice of atonement.

What were they to him ? What were they in his eyes and in his esteem ?—These mercies of God ?

Go back in imagination, to the unfathomed depths of that unbroken eternity, before the world was, wherein the Son is alone, with the Spirit, in the bosom of the Father.   There are mercies in that bosom, throes of pity, yearnings of kindness and love unquenchable.   A guilty,

lost and ruined race is before him; a race of beings who
are miserably. to fall, under the temptation of an evil
spirit more powerful and more knowing than themselves.
The great Father's heart is moved; his bowels of compassion are stirred : his mercies are overflowing. But
alas! there is a barrier; a great rampart of righteousness ; a holy law; a righteous rule of government ;—that
keeps these mercies back ; pent up, barred, restrained ;
so that they can find no vent or channel through which
they may reach their miserable objects. Is the Father's
heart to hold these mercies in, through reverence of
sacred justice, until, if we may dare to say so, it shall
burst or break ?

Lo ! the Son, moved by these mercies thus struggling
to find a vent, comes forth, and by his own sacrifice of
himself, becomes himself their vent, the outlet and channel for their effusion. He opens a door, a door of righteousness, through which these floods of richest love may
freely flow, till they reach and revive and renovate even
the guiltiest of the guilty, the chief of sinners.

Now by these mercies, no longer pent up in the bosom
of the Father, but gushing in full stream through the
rent veil,—the veil rent by that offering of his body once
for all which the great High Priest makes,—and coming
in, through the Spirit opening the door of your hearts,
into the deepest recesses of your souls, and pouring life
and gladness, peace and hope, through your whole inner
man ;—by these mercies of God, thus issuing from the
bosom of the Father, thus coming home to your bosoms,
as you believe on Him who is the way, the truth, and

the life, "I beseech you, brethren, that ye present your bodies a living sacrifice, and holy, acceptable to God, which is your reasonable service."

Some practical applications of the views which have been given on the subject of the Christian's sacrifice of praise may be briefly stated:—

I. If any of you who are called to be priests feel that there is something vague and shadowy about the sacrifice of praise which you are here called to present, and that you would like to have materials more tangible to offer,— or at least to have some more definite instruction as to what is meant by offering yourselves,—will such scriptural intimations as these afford you any help?

First, hear what David says (Psalm li.), in the depths of his sorrow for his grievous sin, after he has sought an interest anew in the sacrifice of atonement, offering the prayer of faith, "Purge me with hyssop and I shall be clean," "Create in me a clean heart, O God." He looks about for a fitting sacrifice of praise, to seal and witness his appropriation of the sacrifice of atonement. And he finds it, not in any external acts of worship, but in his own sense and experience of the evil of his sin;— "For thou desirest not sacrifice; else would I give it: thou delightest not in burnt-offering. The sacrifices of God are a broken spirit: a broken and a contrite heart, O God, thou wilt not despise." Next, hear what the Lord himself testifies (Ps. l.) when he pleads with "his people, who have made a covenant with him by sacrifice,"—by faith in the sacrifice of atonement;—hear

what sort of sacrifice of praise the Lord desires ;—
" If I were hungry, I would not tell thee : for the world
is mine, and the fulness thereof. Will I eat the flesh of
bulls, or drink the blood of goats? Offer unto God
thanksgiving ; and pay thy vows unto the most High :
and call upon me in the day of trouble : I will deliver
thee, and thou shalt glorify me." Or again, hear the
words which the Lord so graciously puts into the mouth
of penitent Israel (Hosea xiv.) ;—" Take away all iniquity,
and receive us graciously : so will we render the calves
of our lips." Or once more, hear the exhortation of the
Apostle writing to the Hebrews (ch. xiii.), when, having
spoken of Jesus, who, that he might sanctify or cleanse
the people by his own blood, suffered without the gate,
he adds ;—" By him therefore let us offer the sacrifice of
praise to God continually, that is, the fruit of our lips
giving thanks to his name. But to do good and to com-
municate forget not : for with such sacrifices God is well
pleased."

Here is a choice of materials for a thank-offering ; a
broken spirit, a broken and a contrite heart ; the pay-
ment of your vows, calling upon God in the time of trouble ; the calves of your lips, the fruit of your lips, con-
fessing and praising the name of Jesus ; good deeds, good
gifts; all or any of these things may be sacrifices of praise.
And in fact, are they not all comprehended in your presenting yourselves a sacrifice ?

So Paul seems to teach when writing to the Corinthians (2 Cor. viii.), he stimulates their zeal by quoting
the example of the churches of Macedonia ;—" How that

in a great trial of affliction the abundance of their joy and their deep poverty abounded unto the riches of their liberality. For to their power, I bear record, yea, and beyond their power they were willing of themselves; praying us with much entreaty that we would receive the gift, and take upon us the fellowship of the ministering to the saints." A fact like this—such abundance of joy in great affliction, such abundance of liberality in deep poverty, requires explanation. The Apostle feels this, and accordingly he furnishes the explanation when he adds, "And this they did, not as we hoped; but first gave their own selves to the Lord."

THEY FIRST GAVE THEIR OWN SELVES TO THE LORD. Ah! this solves the riddle : this accounts for the mystery. No wonder their joy abounded in a great trial of affliction; no wonder the riches of their liberality abounded in deep poverty. And no wonder your joy in your religion is marred by gloom, and your liberality straitened by selfishness, if you do not first give your own selves to the Lord. That you may rejoice right heartily in God your Saviour, that you may be always abounding in the work of the Lord, "I beseech you, brethren," that you first give your own selves to the Lord ; "that ye present your bodies, a living sacrifice, and holy."

II. And let the deed of gift, the act of presentation, be thorough and unreserved. There is no reserve on the part of Christ, when he presents himself a sacrifice of atonement. Let there be no reserve on your part, when you present yourselves a sacrifice of praise. Let your surrender of yourselves be as complete as Christ's surrender of himself was. Through the Eternal Spirit, he offered himself to God; his whole self: himself whole and entire. Through the same Eternal Spirit, offer ye also yourselves to God; your whole selves: yourselves whole and entire: mind and body, heart and soul. That is what as Christians you profess to do: let it be what you really do. Sin not as Ananias and Sapphira sinned; when wishing it to be understood that they were giving their all, they kept back a part. Remember how it was not the amount withheld that was the measure of their guilt. Even their offering of what they gave was vitiated. They lied to the Holy Ghost. Grieve not thus the Spirit. Let no portion whatever of yourselves,—none of your affections, faculties, powers, energies, resources,—be held back from God. Be it ever so little, the holding back of anything mars your whole sacrifice; its life and holiness are gone; it is dead and dull; it is hollow and insincere; it is a cheerless, joyless, routine of duty; not a glad service of love. If that be your religion, it may well weary you and repel others: you neither glorify God, nor do good to man; no, nor even gain contentment for yourselves. Follow the Lord wholly; give your all to him; if you would be really Christians, and happy, as well as useful, in your Christianity.

III. Finally, let it be always by the mercies of God that you are moved to present yourselves a sacrifice of thanksgiving to him.

"The mercies of God!" How precious is the very phrase! How sweet its sound! "The mercies of God!" How great is their multitude! How manifold are they!

New every morning, fresh every moment, coming down as rain upon the mown grass, as showers that water the earth! Only let your eye be open to see them; your hand to take them; your mouth to sing of them all the day long; above all, your heart to keep them in its inmost shrine.

Thy mercies, Lord, in Christ, flowing in upon me through Christ,—if I would declare and speak of them, they are more than can be numbered. First and chiefest of them all is Christ himself, whom thou, O Father, givest to be mine; my Saviour, brother, friend. And in his train what troops of mercies!—mercies of all sorts, for soul, body, spirit: if I am weary, rest; if I sin, forgiveness; if I have sorrow, comfort; if I am weak, strength; if I am wayward, chastening; if I am dying, hope!—mercies for all times and places; songs in the night; a table spread in the wilderness; bread and water sure; oil to anoint the head; a cup running over!—mercies always, mercies everywhere! Thy tender mercies, Lord, are great: thou crownest me with lovingkindness and tender mercies. What shall I render to thee for them all? Wilt thou take myself, O Lord? Wilt thou suffer me to give myself to thee? Wilt thou enable me to give myself to thee? Wilt thou make me thine? thine alone, thine altogether, thine for ever?

But what if thou art disqualified, O sinner, for presenting a sacrifice of praise at all? And art thou not disqualified if thou hast not embraced the appointed sacrifice of propitiation? In such a state, unbelieving, unforgiven, think not that any offering of thine can avail thee with God. I move, for thee, the previous question. I beseech thee, brother, to let Christ wash thee in his blood, and present thee to his Father. Think not that whilst thou continuest in thy present state, thou canst bring into God's house any offering that he will accept as thy reasonable service. Thou art dead ; thou art unclean. Thou canst not present any service or sacrifice that will at all avail thee for averting the Divine wrath or winning the Divine favour. But see, O Sinner, there is a sin-offering lying at thy door. And it is thine, if thou wilt but have it to be thine. Why shouldst thou continue in so sad a condition as to be debarred from offering songs of praise to thy God ? Nay, it is a condition which, if thou continuest in it, must extort from thee, ere long, instead of songs of praise, weeping and wailing and gnashing of teeth ! But thou needst not continue in it, no, not for an hour. Accept now in faith the sacrifice of atonement, and thereupon present the sacrifice of praise. First, be reconciled to thy God ; then come and offer thy gift.

2

SEPARATION FROM THE WORLD

"And be not conformed to this world; but be transformed by the renewing of your mind, that ye may prove what is that good, and acceptable, and perfect will of God."   —*Romans 12:2*

THE change which takes place in our relation to God, when, through faith in the High Priest's sacrifice of propitiation, we, as priests, present ourselves a sacrifice of praise, implies a corresponding change in our relation to that system of things—that course and current of thought and feeling—which, in scriptural language, is the world. It implies,—and this is the second element in the Christian's relation to God,—separation from the world.

That separation is described in this verse as a trans formation. And it may be viewed in three practical lights—with reference, I. To what it puts off;—" Be not conformed to this world." II. To what it is in itself;—" Be ye transformed by the renewing of your mind." And III. To what it aims at accomplishing;— " That ye may prove what is that good, and acceptable, and perfect will of God."

1. NONCONFORMITY—"BE NOT CONFORMED TO THIS WORLD."

The antagonism or opposition between God and the world is strongly asserted in the word. Thus John, the beloved disciple, speaks, "Love not the world, neither the things that are in the world. If any man love the world, the love of the Father is not in him. For all that is in the world, the lust of the flesh, and the lust of the eyes, and the pride of life, is not of the Father, but is of the world. And the world passeth away, and the lust thereof : but he that doeth the will of God abideth for ever."

John, it will be observed, fastens upon one feature as characteristic of the world, whose friendship, as another Apostle testifies (James iv. 4), is "enmity with God :" " The world passeth away, and the lust thereof." The Apostle Paul, also, singles out the same feature, in summing up his argument as to the bearing of Christian faith on the relations and arrangements of the world : " But this I say, brethren, the time is short : it remaineth, that both they that have wives be as though they had none ; and they that weep, as though they wept not ; and they that rejoice, as though they rejoiced not ; and they that buy, as though they possessed not ; and they that use this world, as not abusing it : for the fashion of this world passeth away " (1 Cor. vii. 29–31).

" The fashion of this world passeth away ;"—" Be not conformed to this world ;"—the statement and the exhortation are intimately connected. The verb, " be not conformed," is a derivative of the noun, " the fashion." The admonition literally is,—Be not co-fashioned with this world ; take not the fashion of this world ; the fashion which passeth away.

In this view, the warnings of the Divine word, as

to nonconformity with the world, may be regarded as having a distinctness and definite precision not always apprehended.

Whatever passeth away, is the fashion of this world. Whatever is permanently abiding, and always the same, is not the fashion of this world. In so far as our hearts and minds take the character, the stamp or impress, the form or fashion, of what is transitory in this present state of things, we are conformed to this world. And in so far as we are in that sense conformed to this world, we are unfitted and disabled for presenting ourselves a sacrifice of praise to God.

Plainly therefore, in reference to every institution, every pursuit, every work, every pleasure, every company or companionship, of which this world is the scene, the question arises, Is there in it and about it anything,—and, if so, what is there in it and about it,—that is not fleeting and fickle, but lasting and unchanging? Has it, in short, a fashion,—and if so, what fashion has it,—that does not pass away?

If it has nothing in it or about it that can fairly be held entitled to that character,—if it has no fashion that does not pass away,—there is no practical difficulty in deciding how you are to deal with it, if you would not be conformed to this world, but would present yourselves a sacrifice, living and holy.

But there is scarcely anything in this world, not in itself sinful, which can be said to partake exclusively of the fashion which passes away; scarcely anything which has in it no germ or element of what is abiding, what is permanent and unchanging. In so far as what you come in contact with in this world has in it any such germ or element, conformity of spirit with it is not forbidden. It is only in so far as its fashion is a fashion which passeth away, that you can apply with reference to it the maxim, "Be not conformed to this world."

Perhaps I may best illustrate what I mean by taking the particular instances which the Apostle, writing to the Corinthians, specifies, in the passage already quoted.

He names two social institutions—marriage, and trade or business;—he names also two social affections, weeping and rejoicing;—as proper to our social state. He specifies those who marry and those who buy; he specifies also those who rejoice and those who mourn;—and so he suggests a double lesson of nonconformity to the world; 1. In its institutions; and 2. In its events.

a. Nonconformity to the World's Institutions

Let us, in the first place, take the two social institutions, marriage and commerce. Let us ask what it is, with a special application to them, not to be conformed to this world, in respect of the fashion of this world which passeth away? "It remaineth that both they who have wives be as though they had none, ... and they who buy as though they possessed not."

I. Marriage, and the relations of which marriage is the source and centre, are not permanent ordinances of God. They are, when considered in the light of eternity, temporary and provisional arrangements. In heaven they "neither marry nor are given in marriage; neither can they die any more; for they are equal unto the angels; and are the children of God, being the children of the resurrection." And in heaven there will be realized among the redeemed that equal fellowship, superseding all family distinctions, which the Lord Jesus recognised on earth when he stretched forth his hand toward his disciples and said, "Behold my mother and my brethren; for whosoever shall do the will of my Father which is in heaven, the same is my brother, and sister, and mother."

It might seem, therefore, that marriage, and its attendant and accompanying relationships in this world, have stamped upon them essentially the brand of that fashion of this world which passeth away. This world's fleeting fashion is theirs. It is but a little while, and there shall be but one family; the family of which the Apostle speaks when he says, "I bow the knee to the Father of our Lord Jesus Christ, of whom the whole family in heaven and earth is named."

But is there nothing in these relationships, or about them, that will abide, even when the fashion of them passes away? Is there not a living spirit enshrined and embodied in every one of them, which will survive when its mere outward earthly tabernacle is dissolved? Conformity to that living and abiding spirit is not forbidden, but only conformity to the passing form or fashion in which, as in a husk, for a season it lives and grows.

A searching practical question may here be raised and pressed home with a special application to every one of the institutions of domestic and social life—every relation which any one of us occupies, as spouse, parent, child, brother, neighbour, citizen, friend, lover. What, with reference to that particular relation,—what is it for me to be conformed to this world?

The answer may be found in the putting of another question—What is it, in that particular relation, that I chiefly regard? What is it that I have habitually at heart? Is it what pertains to the form or fashion of it which passes away? Or is it what breathes, or may breathe, into it a living and, therefore, an abiding spirit?

Try by this test your walk at home, in your family, among your kinsmen and familiars. You form no alliance or connection that can be called sinful. All your fellow-ships are in themselves lawful and right. And you are faithful, upright, and exemplary in them all. No wilful or customary breaking of any of these ties or relations of private life can be laid to your charge. So far good. But what, after all, is it in these relations that you feel to be congenial? What is there in common between them and you?

Is it their adaptation to your mere animal desires and wants, whether of a higher or of a lower sort? Is it their fitness to minister to your bodily or mental contentment, and make the time you have to spend in this world pass the more easily and the more pleasantly? Is it for their convenience to you in your journey of life, their advantageous bearing on your comfort, your credit, your advancement and success, that you use and value them? Or is it for their capacity of being turned to

far higher and more lasting account that you prize them?
Do you, as with a spiritual instinct, seize that in them
which can be made available for eternity ;—that which
will live and fructify when the fashion of them, with the
fashion of this world, passeth away?

As husbands and wives, are you walking together as
heirs of the grace of life, that your prayers may not be
hindered ?   Are you helpers of one another's faith, hope,
love and labour, as well as sharers of one another's joy and
grief ?   As parents, are you training your children in the
Lord ?   Are you training them for the Lord ?—not provoking them to anger by caprice or passion : not making mere
playthings of them, or slaves, or helps and conveniences in
your business, or in your idleness, or in your pleasure, or in
your sin ; but treating them reasonably, reverentially, affectionately, as belonging to the Lord, and placed under your
guardianship by the Lord?   As children, are you obeying
your parents in the Lord, and through obedience to them,
exercising yourselves in obedience to the Lord? As brothers
and friends, are you not merely amusing one another,
instructing one another, showing kindness to one another;
—but praying for one another, praying with one another,
seeking the Lord and serving the Lord together ?   As
masters and servants, are you owning a common Master
in heaven, and a common service to him on earth ?   And
generally, in all the cares and crosses, as well as in all
the endearments, joys and comforts of society and of
home,—what tastes are you cultivating by means of
them ?   What affections are you cherishing?   What
habits are you forming ?   Are they tastes, affections,

habits of regardless selfishness, as if you had a right to consult for your own ease alone, and to expect that all around you should minister to your pleasure or your peace? That surely is the fashion of this world. When you use these blessed institutions and arrangements for ends and purposes thus transitory and fleeting, are you not conformed to this world in the using of them? But on the other hand, are they tastes, affections, habits of another kind altogether that you are exercising? Are they tastes, affections, habits of unselfish, disinterested, generous, and self-denying kindness,—mutual forbearance,— mutual tenderness and truth? Are they tastes, affections, habits of pure and benign, Christ-like and God-like, charity? These will bear to be transplanted into the soil of heaven. They do not partake of any fashion of this world that passeth away. They will live and thrive in the new heavens and the new earth wherein dwelleth righteousness ;—in the recovered and regained paradise of God ;—where all is light and all is love.

Thus with reference to the social institutions, the domestic and social relationships of life, represented by marriage,—the origin at once and cement of them all,— and thus only,—we comply with the precept, " Be not conformed to this world ; " not by disparaging or disowning them ; not by withdrawing from them and evading them ; but by seeing to it, and making conscience of it, that it is not in what about them is fleeting and transient that we rest with complacency, but in the more abiding good which they may be made to minister to us as pilgrims, declaring plainly that " we seek a country."

II. So also with reference to the other class of institutions, or operations, specified by the Apostle—those connected with property and the transfer of property, represented by the instance of buying—exactly the same principle may be applied.

We may speak here comprehensively of the whole business of life ; the transactions of the farm, the counting-house, the market-place, the exchange, the bar, the court, the senate, the camp ; whatever work a man has to do, whatever bargain he has to make, in any lawful calling, any honest trade, any honourable profession, or in the preparation for any of them.   These surely are things of which the fashion wholly passeth away, with the passing fashion of this world.   What room in heaven for money-changing, for buying and selling, any more than for marrying and giving in marriage ?   Is not my strenuous application to such pursuits as these, necessarily, so far as it goes, conformity to this world ?

Yes, if I contemplate merely what in them and about them is temporary and passeth away ; whether it be the mere pleasure of present occupation and excitement, or the chance of speedy gain ; whether it be the daily pittance that I get for myself and those whom I love, with such weary, drudging toil, or the wealth which I am beginning to accumulate and lay up, or the character for sober industry that I am so steadily maintaining.   If these, and such as these, are the considerations connected with my calling, which alone come home to me—which alone have power to touch me, and move me to discontent or to hope —too plainly the point of contact, the bond of sympathy, between them and me, partakes exclusively of that fashion of the world which passeth away. This is to be conformed to the world in these things.

But I do not mend the matter by ceasing to buy, to sell, to work. While the hands are idle, the heart may all the more be drawn to what is of most fugitive interest in the pursuits and affairs of time. And so on the other hand, attention, diligence, activity, and if you will, ambition, in all the laudable pursuits of busy life, may be entirely compatible with a state of mind quite otherwise fashioned than according to the passing fashion of this world. What binds me to them, what moves me in them, may be no mere delight or complacency in what is manifestly transitory and fleeting about them, but a view of something, nay, of much, in every one of them, that for myself or for my fellow-mortals may be made available for eternity.

Art thou condemned to tread the incessant round of never-varying, never-advancing routine ; paying thy day's task for thy day's food ; paying often, not only in the sweat of thy brow, but almost in the blood of thy heart; and getting less than thou wouldst call thy daily bread for what thou payest ? Be not conformed to this world. Fasten not, in thy musings, on those incidents of thy hard fate of which the fashion will pass away with the fashion of this world. Grasp, as a Christian man, what, even in thy dreary monotony of thankless toil, may ally thee, and those dear to thee, to eternity and the Eternal ; its lesson of obedience in suffering, of faith hoping against hope, of love not to be quenched even by the waters of despair.

Art thou chained, like a galley-slave, to thy desk, all the live-long day, and often also through the sleepless hours of the night? Is thy business anxious, engrossing, uninterruptedly importunate in its demands? Give thy mind to it, brother; but be not conformed to this world in it. Only be sure, by God's grace, that what fastens thee to thy work is no mere regard to any fruit of it that must pass away with the fashion of this world, but some sight, such as faith can give thee, of its bearing on eternity, and on thy relation to the Eternal.

Art thou plunged into the conduct of a hot and bloody war,—immersed in the calculations of an inextricable campaign,—or rushing up the heights to storm the ramparts of the foe? Let there be no misgiving, no shrinking from thine occupation, dark and bloody as it is. But be not conformed to this world in it. Ask the Lord to give thee his Spirit, that what nerves thee for the strife of death, may be no sympathy with the fierce passions which rage furiously for an hour of battle, and pass away when the stern crisis is over,—nor any mere lust of plunder or of fame,—but some insight into the mind of that great God and Saviour, who maketh the wrath of man to praise him, and who still, in all the march and movements of time, is consulting for the issues of eternity.

Thus human society, in its mutual relations and in its necessary avocations, is consistent with divine Christianity. Thus it is possible for a man to marry and to buy—to be a father or member of a family, and a trader in the business of life—yet not conformed to this world.

The secret lies in that faith which, wherever it is, and whatever it is doing, looks "not to the things which are seen, but to the things which are not seen; for the things which are seen are temporal, but the things which are not seen are eternal."

b. *Nonconformity to the World's Events*

From the institutions of society and the occupations of busy life,—from marriage and merchandise, let us now turn to the events and occasions in the world which cause either weeping or joy; as these two affections are named by the Apostle,—"And they that weep, as though they wept not; and they that rejoice, as though they rejoiced not."

Now the events and occasions in the world which cause either weeping or rejoicing may be of two kinds; either such as in the providence of God seek and find us; or such as we, at our discretion, seek and find for ourselves. Let us consider both kinds.

I. The dealings and dispensations of providence move us to tears or to gladness ; and with reference to them and their effects, the exhortation is to be applied, " Be not conformed to this world."

And here again the same test as before may be used. Whatever befalls us, whether joyous or grievous, has a double character, a double aspect or bearing. It partakes of the fleeting and shadowy nature of the world whose "fashion passeth away." But it has in it and about it that also which touches eternity, and may be turned to account for eternity. After which of these two forms or moulds into which it may be cast is our mind, when we come in contact with it, fashioned?

Do we take to what is merely transient and temporary in the occurrence? Is that the bent and bias of our mind? Is it exclusively or chiefly in that direction that we find ourselves moved? Or is it rather in the light of eternity that what has happened presents itself to us? Is it there, in the light of eternity, that the point of assimilation, if I may so speak, between the event and us, is to be discerned? Do we, not as by an effort, but as it were instinctively, seize it, and make it our own, on that side of it which looks towards eternity? That, I would say, is, in reference to that matter, not being conformed to this world.

You weep, for some calamity has overtaken you. You have lost some cherished comfort, some favourite possession, some beloved friend. You are in poverty, in distress, in pain, in bitter grief. That you are so, does not necessarily imply that you are conformed to this world. It did not in the case of Jesus. "Jesus groaned." "Jesus wept." And he surely was not conformed to this world. Nor need you, in your groanings, in your weeping, be so either.

But your sorrow and its cause are in themselves transitory; the fashion of them passes away. The calamity presses sore upon you for a season. You feel as if you did well, as if you had a right, to be angry because your pleasant gourd is withered. There is fond complaining, peevish melancholy, wailing lamentation.

Gradually, however, your passion expends itself. The trial is over. And you resume your activity as if nothing had been afflicting you. Or, if you do carry with you, as you may ever after, a settled despondency and gloom, it is because to your apprehension there is a fixed dark cloud over your path and your prospects, and the world is become to you all dark and dreary.

Such effects and fruits of your suffering too plainly indicate that you are conformed to this world ; that your minds are fashioned according to that fashion of the world which passes away. It is in its aspect towards what is transient and fleeting in time that the suffering affects you, not in its aspect towards what is permanent and unchanging in eternity.

For if it were so, your grief in your suffering, your consolation in your grief, and the issue of all the three—your suffering, your grief, your consolation—in a calm and trustful peace, would all possess a character harmonizing with the solemn realities of eternity. Your grief would be neither discontent, nor despondency, nor defiance, nor despair, but the humbling of yourselves under the hands of the Eternal God. Your consolation would be neither apathy nor oblivion, but your taking to yourselves the sure and free love of the Eternal Father. And the issue would be the peaceable fruit of righteousness to the praise of the Eternal Father's glory, in the Eternal Son, and by the Eternal Spirit.

Again, you rejoice. You have good cause to rejoice. You eat your pleasant food. You live in a quiet habitation. You dwell among your own people. You have quiet nights and comfortable days: loving children, troops of friends. And from time to time events occur to cheer you. Good news reaches you from a far country. Your lost and banished ones are restored to you. Unlooked-for prosperity comes to you. Surely you do well to rejoice for these things, and such things as these: to be grateful, to be cheerful.

But be not conformed to this world in them. These benefits and blessings partake very largely of the fashion of this world which passes away. And there is a strong tendency in your hearts to rest in them and rejoice in them under that aspect. In their immediate bearing on this transitory scene, they are but too congenial to you. Learn to regard them in another light. View them as fitted to feed and cherish gracious, loving, kindly feelings —benignant and benevolent affections—feelings and affections not tainted with the vice of the world's transitoriness, but destined and fitted to endure for ever. And above all, unite with your enjoyment of them all, that submission to the will of the Eternal God, which animated the bosom of the Eternal Son when he " rejoiced in the Spirit," and said, " Even so, Father, for so it seemed good in thy sight." They who thus rejoice, in the same Spirit in whom he rejoiced—the babes to whom is revealed what is hid from the wise and prudent—they who echo the Saviour's own words, whether the Lord gives or takes away, " Even so, Father, for so it seemed good in thy sight,"—they assuredly are not conformed to this world in their joy. They enter into the joy of their Lord.

II. There is another class of events and occasions productive of weeping or of joy, with reference to which the exhortation is to be applied,—" Be not conformed to this world." These are not such as in the providence of God seek and find us, but such as we, at our discretion, seek and find for ourselves. In regard to them, we have evidently much more liberty and power of choice, and therefore, of course, a much more immediate and direct responsibility.

Our voluntary pursuits and pleasures ; our studies, our relaxations, our amusements ; our places of resort, our companionships and associations ;—these are all to a large extent under our own control. And two questions evidently present themselves here: Are they such as I ought to countenance and frequent at all ? And if so, how am I to use them, if in the using of them I would not be conformed to this world ?

As to the first question, let it be honestly and fairly met, in the spirit of the Apostle's test or criterion, honestly and fairly understood. And there will be an end of not a little special pleading and partial counsel.

May I go into a certain company ? May I attend a certain spectacle or show ? May I read a certain kind of literature ? That is the question. In reply, let it be asked—What is the fashion of it ? Is its fashion the passing fashion of this world, and nothing more ? Is it altogether cast into the mould of what is as fleeting and transitory as is the present state of things ? Are the feelings which it moves, the emotions which it calls forth, the impulses which it prompts, the principles which it enforces, such as will pass away with the fashion of this world—the fashion of its lust, the fashion of its sentiment, the fashion of its romance, the fashion of its vain pomp and pride? Should not that, if it be so, be enough to decide your judgment, and determine your conduct? On that supposition, is not the line of duty clear?

Or, since we are now in the region of what is matter of discretion and voluntary choice, let the determination turn on the influence actually exercised, and the effect actually produced upon yourselves. Does the practice in question tend to move you rather according to the fashion of the world, which passes away, than according to the fashion of the heavenly state, which endures for ever? Are you conscious that when you are engrossed in the gay party, or entranced by the sweet music, or absorbed in the fascinating scene, or possessed by the spell of the resistless eloquence or pathos of the book,—there steals over you a disposition to rest with fond complacency on the shadows of time, and to recoil from the realities of eternity ; insomuch that when you are interrupted in your grief or joy, or when the exciting cause is over, you have more difficulty than before in adjusting your thoughts and affections for the fellowships of eternity, and more ease than before in squaring them with the conversations of time? Should not this be enough for you?

Judge not others. Judge not by others. Judge not for others. Judge and act for yourselves. And if there be a pursuit or a pleasure which you find from sad experience has a tendency to unfit you for the closet or the sanctuary, to make you weary of the Bible and heartless in secret prayer, to mould you, in short, after the fashion of things seen and temporal, rather than after the fashion of things unseen and eternal,—for your soul's sake, be firm. Let there be no wavering. " Be not conformed to this world."

And then, secondly, as to the other question—How, if you do find the pursuit or the pleasure to be one which you may countenance,—how you are to be safe in countenancing it?—let the same principle be scrupulously applied. Let it be applied with peculiar delicacy, with peculiar and very sensitive jealousy. For the danger is peculiarly great when you are satisfied that you may,—when you are convinced even that you should,—take a part in studies and occupations and recreations, which have in themselves scarcely anything of the element of heaven's perpetuity; being of the earth, earthy; fashioned after the fashion of the world which passeth away. It may be that you are right in what you are doing : that you can do it safely ; that you could scarcely do otherwise. But it can do no harm to suggest, in the first place, that your warrant should be very clear, that your call should be very strong ; and above all, that your conscience should be void of offence in regard to it. What you do with a misgiving ; what you allow yourself with hesitation ; however lawful it may be, is not expedient. Be fully persuaded in your own minds. Then, secondly, go into the scene, or company, or occupation, with prayer and pains ; prayer that God may show you—pains that you may discover—some way of glorifying him in it. Not that you are to do so artificially : as if by a forced

effort, felt out of place, out of keeping, out of season. If
it is only by outraging the proprieties of any meeting,
that you can do good, is not that a hint to you to be
away from it? If your Christianity is not at home and
at ease in it, surely you had better be elsewhere. But
with all simplicity, with the gracefulness and graciousness
which singleness of eye bestows, move freely among the
elements of time, with a heart still full of eternity. And
you will find none of them altogether barren of what
may be turned to account for something better than the
fashion of this world which passeth away ;—none of
them that may not be made to minister to that habit
of obedience which the Apostle John commends, when
he says : " The world passeth away, and the lust
thereof : but he that doeth the will of God abideth for
ever." This doing of the will of God is not the
fashion of this world ; neither is it a fashion that passeth
away.

2. THE RENEWING OF THE MIND

"Be ye transformed, by the renewing of your mind."   *—Romans 12:2*

The Christian's sacrifice of praise and thanksgiving is to
be himself. It is to be himself living and holy : living,
yet not himself living, but Christ living in him : holy,
as being a partaker of Christ's holiness. If he is to be in
a position to present his body thus, " a living sacrifice,
holy," he must not only cast off the fashion of this world;
he must assume a fashion of an entirely opposite character. The negative prohibition, accordingly, " Be not con-

formed," is followed up by the positive commandment, " Be ye transformed."

This word—transform—occurs elsewhere in the New Testament on two occasions. It is the word used to denote the Lord's transfiguration (Matt. xvii. 2 ; Mark ix. 2). And it is the word employed by Paul to describe that growing conformity to the likeness of the Lord, which results from the contemplation of his excellency : " We all, with open face beholding as in a glass the glory of the Lord, are changed"—transformed or transfigured —"into the same image from glory to glory, even as by the Spirit of the Lord" (2 Cor. iii. 18).

In his transfiguration, the Lord's mortal body was seen invested with the glory in which he is to appear at his second coming. So the Apostle Peter expressly testifies, when he says concerning himself and the other apostles present at that scene, " We were eye-witnesses of his majesty"—the very majesty which is to mark his coming in power (2 Peter i. 16). They saw him then transfigured, or transformed. But it was only in appearance, and only for a few moments. His real transfiguration, his actual transformation, did not take place till that mortal body of his passed through death, and the resurrection from the dead, into the heavenly glory. We are to see him thus really transfigured, thus actually transformed. And we are to be partakers of the transformation: " For our conversation is in heaven; from whence also we look for the Saviour, the Lord Jesus Christ; who shall change our vile body, that it may be fashioned"—formed, figured—" like unto his glorious body, according to the working whereby he is able even to subdue all things unto himself " (Phil. iii. 20, 21).

That transformation is for the life to come. But there is a transformation in the life that now is. This also is a transformation into the image or likeness of the Lord. And therefore it is a transformation into glory,—"from glory to glory." The glory, however, is not what was seen on the mount of transfiguration, but what was seen in the manger at Bethlehem, in the wilderness of Judea, beside the lake of Galilee, along the streets of Jerusalem, in the garden of Gethsemane, and on the cross. Beholding that glory we are changed into the same image ;— not suddenly and completely, all at once, as beholding the other glory, we shall be changed into the same image with it, when this corruptible shall put on incorruption, and this mortal shall put on immortality—but by a gradual and ever brightening progress, "from glory to glory." And not as it will be then, without our concurrence and co-operation, is the transformation to be effected, but by means of it. For while in that Second Epistle to the Corinthians it is announced as a natural consèquence, or a gracious promise, or both, that beholding the glory of the Lord we are transformed into the same image—here, the matter is put upon the footing of a peremptory command, " Be ye transformed."

The manner of this transformation is indicated ; it is by "the renewing of your mind." And the end of it also is indicated ; it is " that ye may prove what is that good, and acceptable, and perfect will of God." You are to prove this, as the Lord himself did. You are to be changed into his likeness as proving it. For this is his glory in his humiliation,—and it is into his glory in his humiliation, and into that alone, that you are now to be transfigured and transformed,—he " proves what is that good, and acceptable, and perfect will of God."

For this end there was needed in his case a previous transformation ; a transformation, as to the manner of it, analogous to ours ; not indeed by the renewing of his mind, but by what may be viewed as the type and model of the renewing of our mind, his receiving a new nature and entering into a new state. His transformation, in the sense now indicated,—as being not his ultimate transformation, upon his work being finished, but his preliminary transformation, for the doing of his work,—is his being made of a woman, made under the law. He is transformed, when, being the Son of God, he becomes man, in order that in his experience, as a man, he may " prove what is that good, and acceptable, and perfect will of God." "The renewing of our mind," our being born again, our being created anew, is our corresponding transformation. And in our case as in his, the transformation is in order that "we may prove what is that good, and acceptable, and perfect will of God."

Thus, as to the manner of it, our transformation consists in " the renewing of our mind." And as to the end or design of it, it is developed and unfolded, it grows and makes progress, in our " proving what is that good, and acceptable, and perfect will of God." In both of these points of view we are to be transformed into the image of Christ.

The end of this transformation will afterwards be considered. Let us meanwhile advert to the manner of it.

The source and essence of the transformation in our case is the renewing of our mind. In the case of Christ, it was his receiving a new nature. He was transformed by becoming man. We are transformed by becoming new men in him. The renewing of our mind, when we become new men, is our being brought to have the same mind which Christ had when he became man. And what mind was that? Let Christ himself reply, speaking by the mouth of the Psalmist (Ps. xl. 7, 8; Heb. x. 5), " Then said I, Lo I come; in the volume of the book it is written of me, I delight to do thy will, O my God; yea, thy law is within my heart." To be renewed in the spirit of our mind, is to have "the same mind in us which was also in Christ Jesus, who, being in the form of God, thought it not robbery to be equal with God, but made himself of no reputation and took upon him the form of a servant, and was made in the likeness of men." (Phil. ii. 5-7.)

"I come, to do thy will, O God," is the language of the Saviour, in the very act of taking the new nature, the new position, of a creature and servant. The renewing of our mind is, our making that language our own. There is a new nature, there is a new position, in our case also, when we do so. For we are made partakers of the Divine nature; and we receive the adoption of sons.

How close the analogy is, how intimate and vital the connection, between Christ's being transformed by a body being prepared for him, a new and holy human frame, and our being transformed by the renewing of our mind,—the consideration of a few particular points of resemblance may suffice to show.

In the first place, the agency is the same—the agency of the Holy Ghost. It is he alone who can make the Son partaker of our human nature, really,—and yet without making him to be as fallen man. It is he alone who can make us partakers of the Son's divine nature, really,—and yet without making us to be as God. Born of the Spirit, the Son comes into the world, one with us indeed in nature, yet not involved in our natural vileness. Born again of the same Spirit, we enter into the kingdom of God, one with the Son indeed in nature, yet not exalted or aspiring to his essential majesty. When our human nature and condition was to become his, could this be, without its radical vice becoming his also? When his divine nature and condition, as the Son, is to become ours, can this be, without its incommunicable sovereignty becoming ours also? Could he become what we are, as the fallen children of men, without being a sharer in our apostasy and rebellion? Can we become what he is, as the beloved Son of God, without being sharers in his everlasting Godhead itself? These are questions to which, in both instances, the fact of the agency of the Holy Ghost furnishes an answer—a satisfactory answer —and it may be confidently said, the only possible answer.

Thus, on the part of Christ, his supernatural birth, by the power of the Holy Ghost, secures his exemption and

immunity from all participation in what sinks and de-
grades our nature to the level of that which the fallen
angels now own. And so also our being supernaturally
born of the Spirit, provides for our being partakers of the
divine nature of the Son, without intruding into that
essential divinity which is indefeasibly the prerogative of
the one only God, Father, Son, and Holy Ghost. It is
the same Spirit who enables the Son to become a servant,
as we are, without prejudice to his holy character and
high standing as the Son,—who also enables us to become
sons, as he is, without any abandonment of our place and
position as servants.

In the second place, these two operations of the Spirit
admirably fit into one another : the one effecting that
supernatural birth by which the Son becomes a servant ;
the other, that supernatural new birth by which the servants become sons. The new creation by which the Son
becomes partaker of our human nature, has for its
counterpart the new creation by which we become
partakers of his divine nature. The one transformation is the cause of the other. It is so, not only as
being that without which the other could not have
been, but also as being that by means of which the other
is wrought.

But for the Son being transformed into our likeness,
we could never have been transformed into his. And it
is through our believing, apprehending, laying hold of,
and appropriating, his transformation, that we are ourselves transformed. For the transformation, in either case,
is a union. His being transformed, is his being united,

by a new creation, to us. Our being transformed, is our being united, by a new creation, to him. The Spirit makes him one, in his birth, with us. The same Spirit also makes us one, in our new birth, with him. This, in point of fact, is the renewing of our mind. It is our being one with the Son, really and intimately one with the Son; in his entrance, through a new and unprecedented birth, into a state of subjection, as a servant, but still the Son, to the Father.

In the third place, it is a transformation "by the renewing of our mind." To the Son himself, his being born of the Spirit brought a new mind. It was a new thing for him to have the mind of a servant; to be minded, as the Father's servant, to say,—" I come to do thy will, O my God; yea, thy law is within my heart." This was to him, the Eternal Son, a new mind.

And is it not a new mind in us, when we are minded, as sons, to say the same? Truly this is a great change, a thorough transformation. Naturally, self-will is the ruling principle of our mind. We aspire to a liberty of independence. We would fain be our own masters. "Our lips are our own, who is lord over us?" "Who is the Almighty that we should serve him? Or what profit shall we have if we bow down to him?" Insubordination to God is the characteristic of fallen man; the setting of his own will against the will of God. This is that fashion of this world which passeth away. It must pass away. For there is nothing stable, nothing permanent in the world, but the will of God. What the

creature wills,—what the world wills,—the works it wills
to have done,—the customs it wills to have established,
—the conventional rules of convenience and expediency
it wills to have observed,—can endure but for a season.
It is what the will of God ordains that alone can stand.
Therefore " be not conformed to this world, but be ye
transformed by the renewing of your mind." Be
changed into the same image with the Lord, " from
glory to glory." For it was his glory as well as his
meat to do the will of Him that sent him. There
was glory in his saying, " I come to do thy will, O
my God."

Finally, in the fourth place, observe the imperative
way in which this transformation is enjoined : " Be ye
transformed by the renewing of your mind." It is a command addressed to us. And it is rightly so. For the
transformation, by the renewing of our mind, is with our
own consent. Otherwise it could have no worth or value
in the sight of God. It could not really be a renewing
of the mind.

The transformation in the case of Christ, when he
humbled himself to do the will of God, was voluntary on
his part ; he himself consented to it. Otherwise his
humiliation, with all his subsequent obedience unto death,
could have had no efficacy, either as satisfactory to God
or as available for us. Equally voluntary—as thoroughly
an act of our own will—must be the transformation on
our part. We are not passive, but active, when we are
transformed into the same image with the Lord, and say,
with renewed minds, entering into his mind, " I come to

do thy will, O my God." It is true, that in order to our thus acting, we must be acted upon by the Holy Ghost. In that sense we may be said to be passive in our renewal or regeneration, and in that sense only,—that we are acted upon. But we are not acted upon as inert matter, or as an unintelligent living creature, may be acted upon. We are acted upon as beings who, strictly speaking, never can be passive, whose wills ever are, and ever must be, active. We are so acted upon that our own active consent is ultimately and effectually secured. And therefore, in entire consistency with the statement of the great fact or doctrine that we are saved by the renewing of the Holy Ghost, the peremptory command is to be urged, " Be ye renewed in the spirit of your mind." It is by the Spirit of the Lord that we are changed into the same image with the Lord. All the more on that account does the exhortation apply to us, " Be ye transformed by the renewing of your mind ; "—just as the Apostle puts the matter, with reference to our sanctification, " Work out your own salvation with fear and trembling. For it is God which worketh in you both to will and to do of his good pleasure " (Phil. ii. 12, 13).

Such is the manner of our transformation. It is by the renewing of our mind ; that renewal being exactly analogous to the new creation that there was when the Eternal Son was transformed into the condition, and took the character, of a servant.

Two practical applications here suggest themselves as appropriate.

I. If it be so—if the transformation in us is thus

like the transformation in Him—let the transformation be complete ; let the renewal be thorough. It
was so in the case of Christ. It must be so in our
case.

Let us meditate on the humiliation of our Lord, in the
very first act or instance of it, his assuming our nature
and condition, being made of a woman, made under the
law, with this language on his lips, or rather in his heart,
" I come to do thy will, O my God." What an unquali-
fied surrender of himself! What a transformation!
What a change ! He who, as the Son, is from everlasting
the heir of all things—he who claims the homage and
obedience of all creation—he whose will is the law of the
universe,—becomes the servant of the Father;—subject to
him as the holy Lawgiver and righteous Judge;—bound
to do his will, whatever to him in that character his will
may be ;—consenting, ah ! how willingly, how cordially,
how absolutely and without reserve, to do it ! And let
us remember, that this transformation, and nothing short
of it, is to be the type, and model, and standard of ours.
" Be ye " thus " transformed."

Be ye transformed, by the renewing of your mind, into
the attitude and frame of mind in which the Son consented so unreservedly to do the will of God. He made
himself of no reputation. He emptied himself. Do you
also empty yourselves. He laid aside his natural position
of equality with God ; he did not eagerly retain it ;
when he was willing to take upon himself the form of a
servant. Do you lay aside your assumed and usurped
position,—alas ! now your natural position,—of seeking

to be equal with God, presuming to make terms with
God, venturing either to set him at defiance, or to think
that you may capitulate upon conditions. Grasp not,
retain not, a position in your case so impious. Empty
yourselves. Empty yourselves of all self-complacency,
self-confidence, self-will. Take at once, and out and out,
the form of a servant. Say, as Christ the Son says, " I
come to do thy will, O my God." "Be ye" thus "transformed by the renewing of your mind."

II. That it may be so,—that you may be thus
thoroughly transformed into the image of your Lord,—
apprehend and appropriate, as available for you, your
Lord's transformation into your image, into your likeness.
It was for your sakes, it was in your stead and on your
behalf, that he humbled himself to become obedient. All
the benefit of his being transformed,—from his being the
Son only, to his becoming the servant also,—is yours.
It is the beginning, it is the essence, of his offering
himself for you. Consider it in that light. Behold him
thus transformed for you. And be ye, after a corre
sponding manner, transformed in him.

The correspondence, the mutual adaptation, between
his being transformed for you, and your being transformed
in him, is very gracious, nay, very glorious. The Eternal Son, the Father's fellow, becomes one of you, one
with you, taking your place under the law of God, to
fulfil all its obligations,—nay, to meet all its responsi-
bilities and all its threatenings,—in your stead and on
your account, as you were bound to do, but could not.
All this is implied in his being transformed, by his taking

what to him was the new nature of man, and the new
position of a servant. Receive him, welcome him,
embrace him, cleave to him, be one with him, in this
surrender of himself,—this giving of himself up to do the
will of God for you. Then will you be transformed by
the renewing of your mind. You will find yourselves,
being one with him, already surrendered, already given
up, to do the will of God in him. You will apprehend
your being so. You will consent to your being so. Let
Christ, in his being transformed, become yours ; and you
are in him yourselves transformed, by the renewing of
your mind.

You are transformed into his position, as he is transformed into yours. He becomes a servant for you, continuing still to be the Son. You become sons in him,
feeling yourselves now more than ever,—now for the first
time,—to be really servants. He, being the Son, comes
to do the will of God as a servant. You, being servants,
come to do the will of God as sons. You become one
with Christ in the filial love and filial submission with
which he said—" I come to do thy will, O my God."

3. PROVING THE WILL OF GOD

"That ye may prove what is that good, and acceptable, and perfect will of God."　　　　　　　　　　　　　　　　　　　*—Romans 12:2*

The believer's transformation, by the renewing of his
mind, is not the ultimate end which the Holy Spirit seeks
in his regenerating and renovating work. It is the
immediate and primary design of that work, in one

sense. We are created anew in Christ Jesus. That new creation is what the Holy Spirit first aims at and effects. But "we are created in Christ Jesus unto good works, which God hath before ordained that we should walk in them" (Eph. ii. 10). The essence of a good work is the doing of the will of God. The proving of the will of God, therefore, is a fitting sequel of our "being transformed by the renewing of our mind."

Now here, in the first place, let it be noted that the will of God requires to be proved. It can be known only by trial. Its nature and qualities can be discovered and ascertained only by experiment.

This, it would seem, is a universal law or principle of created intelligence ; a truth applicable to every order of mind in the universe which God has made. No one who is partaker of a finite nature, and who occupies the position of a subject or servant, under the authority of God,—under his law,—can understand what, or of what sort, the will of God is, otherwise than through actual experience. You cannot explain to him beforehand what the will of God is, and what are its attributes or characteristics. He must learn this for himself. And he must learn it experimentally. He must prove, in his own person, and in his own personal history, what is the will of God—"that good, and acceptable, and perfect will of God."

How it should be so,—why it should be necessary for created beings thus to learn the will of their Creator by reducing it to practice, and impossible for them really to apprehend or appreciate it in any other way,—is a question which might open up a field of thought deeply and richly valuable. The nature of God, and the authority of God,—the one, the nature of God, as determining the essence of his will ; the other, the authority of God, as determining the form of it,—would need to be considered. Essentially, the will of God is and must be the expression of his nature. Formally, it is the assertion of his authority. Whatever God wills, he wills in accordance with what he is in himself. He wills it authoritatively, because he reigns supremely. But the nature of God far transcends the comprehension of finite minds ; and therefore his will, as the expression of his nature, may well be expected to be incomprehensible too. God himself cannot be grasped in the understanding ; and therefore neither can his will. Hence, in its first announcement to the creature, antecedently to experience, the will of the Creator presents itself rather in its formal aspect, as the assertion of his authority, than in its essential character, as the expression of his nature. But in that formal aspect of it, as the assertion of the authority of God, let his will be put to the test of actual trial. Then will its real character, as the expression of his nature, come out. For while neither God himself, nor his will, can be grasped in the speculative understanding,—both he and it can be grasped in the obedient and loving heart.

But apart from any inquiry into the reason of it, the fact may be assumed to be as it has been stated. And it is a fact pregnant with not a few important doctrinal and practical consequences.

For one thing, it may be noted, in the second place, this fact,—that the will of God needs thus to be proved, —partly explains the economy of probation. It makes it cease, at all events, to appear very startling or surprising that every new order of free and intelligent minds, called into existence by the Creator, should have to stand a trial. Nay more, it tends to show how the trial, in every instance, must be both summary and decisive. It must be summary ;—that it may be ascertained at once, and once for all, whether the authority of God, which his will formally asserts, is to be acknowledged or disowned. And it must be decisive ;—for if his will, as the assertion of his authority, is acknowledged, the way is open for proving it, as the expression of his nature, to be good, and acceptable, and perfect ;—whereas, if, in its form of an assertion of his authority, the will of God is disowned, all opportunity of testing and knowing its real character, as the expression of his nature, is hopelessly and for ever cut off.

Let actual instances of probation be contemplated in this light.

I. The probation of the angels is a fact revealed in Scripture, though the manner of it is not fully explained. These bright and blessed spirits had to stand a trial. The will of God was revealed to them in an authoritative form. What precise commandment issued from the eternal throne, is not expressly said. It may have been— in all likelihood it was—the command to worship the Son. " When he bringeth in the First-begotten into the

world, he saith, And let all the angels of God worship
him" (Heb. i. 6);—"Worship him all ye gods" (Ps.
xcvii. 7).

But whatever it was, the will of God, as communicated to them, did not beforehand commend itself to
them as in itself, in its nature—in the matter or substance of it—good, and acceptable, and perfect. On the
contrary, too many of their number took exceptions to
it, deemed it unreasonable, if not unrighteous; unwel-
come, if not unfair; and were on that account offended.
Even those who willingly complied, did so most probably
very much in the dark. They acted under a just sense
of the Almighty Father's sovereignty;—but certainly
with very little apprehension of all the beauty, all the
glory, all the joy, to be found in that worship of the
Son, which it was the will of God to demand. This they
have been learning ever since. This they are learning
still. For they have not yet half proved—no, nor
throughout eternity will they ever have fully proved—
" what is that good, and acceptable, and perfect will of
God;"—that will of God the Father that his Son
should be worshipped;—that all created intelligences
should "honour the Son even as they honour the
Father!"

Alas! alas! for those who missed the first step in this
high training of the sons of God.

II. The probation of man, in the temptation of the
first Adam, is more circumstantially recorded than that of
the blessed angels. But it is substantially of the same

kind. He too was tried upon this very point,—his willingness to put the will of God to the proof.

Without actual trial and proof, the will of God, as it was barely, and without explanation, announced in paradise, was not such as to command either approbation, or consent, or satisfied acquiescence and rest, on the part of our first parents. On the contrary, it was capable of being insidiously misrepresented to them, and fatally misapprehended by them. The command, not to eat of the fruit of the tree,—which was to them, as they were then situated, the testing will of God,—did not naturally and obviously commend itself as good, and acceptable, and perfect.

Doubtless, if they had kept it, they would have proved it to be so. In the first place, they would have found by experience that what God announced to them as his will was really in itself, as the seal of his previous covenant of life, and as the preparation for the unfolding of his higher providence, fair, reasonable, good. Secondly, they would have learned experimentally that it was suited to their case and circumstances ; deserving of their acceptance ; sure to become more and more well pleasing, as they entered more and more into its spirit, and became more and more thoroughly reconciled to the quiet simplicity of submission which it fostered. And thirdly, they would have ascertained by time that it was the only sort of formal expression of his will that could consistently uphold the perfection of the Creator, and ultimately secure the perfection of the creature. For it would have been made clear to them that thus only could the perfection of the Creator be vindicated :—the perfection of his character and authority, the perfection of his intolerance of evil, the perfection and completeness of his sovereign right to rule ; and also, that thus only could the perfection of the creature be wrought out, in an onward and upward path of confidence, loyalty, and love.

All this, and far more, our first parents would have learned concerning the will of God, if they had consented to prove it.

But they would not prove it. They formed an opinion of it, they passed judgment upon it, unproved. They refused to give it a fair trial. They chose to make the opposite experiment. And they have left that sad experiment, with its issue, as their legacy and inheritance to all the race.

For how, ever since, have men, left to themselves, been occupied ? Not in proving what is that will of God; how good, how acceptable, how perfect ;—but in proving what is the fashion of this world, and how they may be so conformed to it as to make the most of it ;—proving, in short, what is the will of this world, and of this world's god ! (Eph. ii. 2.)

III. The probation of Christ, the second Adam, the second representative of mankind, proceeds also upon this principle. In consenting to do the will of God, he undertook to prove it.

That will of God, in his case, had little in it at any time that, in the anticipation of it, could be attractive or well-pleasing to him.

Behold him, the man Christ Jesus, come in the flesh to do the will of God !

First, see him in the wilderness, tempted by the Devil. He is there tried as the first Adam was tried. And he is tried upon the same issue,—his willingness to prove the will of God. In his case also, as in Adam's, the will of God which he has to do may be so presented to his human soul as to appear neither reasonable, nor expedient, nor desirable, but the very opposite. In such a light, accordingly, Satan tries to put it before him. The privations and pains ; the shame and obloquy ; the protracted service of toil, and weariness, and blood ; awaiting him in the course he has to finish, if he is to do the will of God ;—all these hard conditions the tempter contrasts with the simpler, brighter, shorter road to glory which he would have him to take. But the second Adam will not, like the first, accept Satan's representation of the will of God. He will prove it for himself. And so he goes on to do. " He learns obedience by the things which he suffers" (Heb. v. 8).

Behold him thus learning obedience ! See him proving the will of God in his own experience ; proving what and of what sort it is to him ; to him, the surety of the guilty !

All throughout he needed to prove it. It was only by proving it that he could find it to be good, and acceptable, and perfect. It was not so to him beforehand. It did not so commend itself to him beforehand. He must prove it to be so.

Look at him as he sits at the well of Samaria. He is

weary, hungry, faint. To his human frame, what could be more welcome, what more necessary, than repose ; the repose of an hour's solitary meditation, while his disciples are gone into the city to buy bread. The interruption may well be felt to be irksome and vexatious, when the woman comes to draw water ; all the more when, as it appears, he has to deal with the perversity of an unintelligent, and apparently impracticable, mind. It may be the will of God that his rest should be thus broken, and that his spirit should be chafed by the necessity of what might seem an unseasonable and unprofitable conversation. Flesh and blood may feel it to be hard. But he proves the will of God in this instance,—to see what it is. He makes trial of it. And in the proving and actual trial of it, he finds it to be good, and acceptable, and perfect. His soul is refreshed by seeing the pleasure of the Lord prospering in his hands. The opening of the woman's understanding, the softening of her heart, her going to bring her countrymen, are his immediate and present reward. This will of God, that might seem at first anything but reasonable or agreeable, turns out to be like a savoury banquet to him. " My meat," he cries, " is to do the will of him that sent me, and to finish his work."

Ah ! there was much in that will of God which he had to do on earth that might have made the Holy Jesus shrink back from it at every step. The acute and tender sensibilities of his bodily frame, the pure tastes and heavenly affections of his spotless soul, must have recoiled with poignant and nervous sensitiveness from the rude shocks and collisions which the will of God required him to be ever sustaining, as he went on enduring such contradiction of sinners against himself. It must have been, it often was, with him, a struggle—an effort—to do the will of God. It was not easy, it was not pleasant. It was self-denial, self-sacrifice, self-crucifixion throughout. It was repulsive to the highest and holiest instincts of his pure humanity. It laid upon him most oppressive burdens ; it brought him into most distressing scenes ; it involved him in ceaseless, often thankless, toil; it exposed him to all sorts of uncongenial encounters with evil men and evil angels. But he proved it. And in the proving of it, and as he was proving it, he found it to be good, and acceptable, and perfect.

Yes ! he was reconciled to the will of God in the doing of it. He tasted the delight of obedience, as "he learned obedience by the things which he suffered." He "rejoiced in spirit" as he found the work advancing, and the meek, and poor, and guilty, receiving gladly what the rich and righteous cast away. He rejoiced in proving what is that good, and acceptable, and perfect will of God, when he said, "I thank thee, O Father, Lord of heaven and earth, that thou hast hid these things from the wise and prudent, and hast revealed them unto babes. Even so, Father ; for so it seemed good in thy sight."

Need I point to that crowning instance of his willingness to prove the will of God,—his unknown agony in the garden of Gethsemane ? What then presented itself to him as the will of God ? The cup to be drunk,—the cross to be borne,—the Father's sword of justice to be

sheathed in his bosom,—the shame, the sting, the curse
of death,—the endurance of the law's awful sentence of
condemnation,—the hiding of his Father's countenance
from him as he was to be made sin for us. The will of
God then, in that garden, wore a dark and terrible aspect
before the soul of Jesus ;—witness the bloody sweat, and
the cry of bitter anguish, " Father, if it be possible, let
this cup pass from me." " Nevertheless," he adds, " not
as I will, but as thou wilt." He consents to prove this
will of God, all dark and terrible as it is. And he does
prove it. And in the very proving of it, he finds it to
be good, and acceptable, and perfect. Yes ! In the very
proving of it. For does not the penitent's prayer, " Lord,
remember me when thou comest into thy kingdom," pour
into his spirit some sweet, consoling balm, in the very
moment of his utmost pain ;—making him feel that the
will of God which he is so fearfully proving, is indeed
good, and acceptable, and perfect ;—causing him already
to " see of the travail of his soul and be satisfied?" And
is not his latest utterance the expression of that satisfaction,—" Father, into thy hands I commend my
spirit ?"

IV. Now it is into this image,—into the image and
likeness of Jesus, thus proving what is that good, and
acceptable, and perfect will of God,—that you are to be
transformed, by the renewing of your mind. This is
that glory of the Lord which you are to " behold as in
a glass, that you may be changed into the same image,
from glory to glory, even as by the Spirit of the Lord."

You are to prove for yourselves, as Christ did, "what is that good, and acceptable, and perfect will of God." You are to put it fairly to the test. You are honestly to give it a trial.

In the first place, You are to prove for yourselves what is that good, and acceptable, and perfect will of God,—in what must always be the first act of your obedience ;— your believing on Him whom God has sent. For this is his commandment, " that you should believe on the name of the Lord Jesus Christ." This is his will. It is declared to you authoritatively and peremptorily. And as an assertion of his authority, it binds you to instant compliance with it. What this will of God is, as an expression of his nature, you cannot really or fully know until you prove it. How good, and acceptable, and perfect it is, you can find out only experimentally, by actual personal trial. You must " taste and see that God is good, and that the man is blessed that trusteth in him." You must put the gospel to the proof of actual trial. This is the inexorable law of the obedience of faith.

You would fain have it otherwise. You would fain have all made clear to you ; you would have all made bright and satisfying to you ; you would have a perfect and complete understanding of the whole matter;—before you surrender yourself to the call of the Gospel, and consent to be reconciled to your God. Not only so. You stand aloof, and start objections, and raise difficulties. You do not see how this aspect of the gospel system may be compatible with that. You cannot harmonize its sovereignty and its freeness ; the secret decree of election and the open proclamation of mercy. You cannot see how an extreme case such as yours is to be met. You cannot get rid of doubts and misgivings besetting you on every side.

Nay, but, is it not enough for you that this is the will of God, that you should believe and embrace Christ as your Saviour? Will you not prove it? Be very sure that in the proving of it, and not before, all about it will be cleared up, and it will be found by you to be good, and acceptable, and perfect. Try this dipping in the Jordan seven times. It may seem an unlikely mode of cure; it does not commend itself to you; you have grave scruples about it. But at anyrate try it. Prove it and see if it will not turn out to be the good, and acceptable, and perfect will of God.

Yes! You will have cause to exclaim, The saying which I have heard is good. "It is a faithful saying, and worthy of all acceptation, that Jesus Christ came into the world to save sinners, of whom I am chief." Yes! "The law of the Lord is perfect, converting the soul." "As for God, his way is perfect. The word of the Lord is tried. He is a buckler to all them that trust in him."

So also, in the next place, all along the path of your new obedience, you are to be proving what is that good, and acceptable, and perfect, will of God. At every step it will be a trial to you; often a trial most severe. It may be very hard sometimes to believe that the will of God concerning you is good, and acceptable, and perfect;—very hard even in little matters; when you have to bear the disappointment of an anticipated pleasure, or to yield your own way to the unreasonable pertinacity of a companion, or to suffer some wrong you may not resent, or to return good for evil, kindness for injury ;— very hard, when you have to forego some indulgence you can scarcely see to be wrong, or to go through some task and toil that seems to be quite unprofitable ;—very hard, when you have to deny yourself, and take up your cross, and brave the frowns of the world, and the estrangement of friends, the ridicule of singularity, the coldness of suspicion, the imputation of insincerity ;—very hard, when you have to cultivate unwonted tastes and overcome besetting sins ;—very hard, when you have to endure the loss of all things, to bear suffering, sorrow, bereavement, death. But prove what the will of God is in every such instance ; give it a trial. Make full proof of it. Let it have a fair trial. Accommodate yourselves to the will of God in it. Accommodate yourselves to God himself in it. Go through with whatever may be the will of God, in whatever circumstances you may be placed. And assuredly you will find, that in the very keeping of his commandments there is a great reward.

The waters of Marah may be bitter. But the Lord shows you a tree, which when you have cast into the waters, they are made sweet. There he makes with you a statute and an ordinance, and there he proves you, and says,—" If thou wilt diligently hearken to the voice of the Lord thy God, and wilt do that which is right in his sight, and will give ear to his commandments, and keep all his statutes, I will put none of these diseases upon thee which I have brought upon the Egyptians ; for I am the Lord that healeth thee."

May not this word sweeten any waters ;—" I am the Lord that healeth thee ?"

Let a brief practical appeal be suffered, upon this whole subject of nonconformity to the world, transformation by the renewing of the mind, and proving what is that good and acceptable, and perfect, will of God.

I. Mark how opposite to one another are the two habits, or frames of mind, indicated ; the one, in the pro- hibition, " Be not conformed to this world ;" and the other in the command, " Be ye transformed by the re- newing of your mind, that ye may prove what is that good, and acceptable, and perfect will of God."

There are here two types, of one or other of which you must take the fashion : the world—and the will of God. You must either be conformed to the one,—or trans- formed into the proving of the other. The fashion of the world : the fashion of the Divine will : one or other of these you must adopt. To adopt the fashion of the world—to be conformed to the world, is to take things as they are and make the best of them ; to consider what is, and accommodate yourself to what is. The opposite habit is to try things as they should be : to ascertain what ought to be, and put that to the proof. There is all the difference between floating down the current and making head against it ; between acquiescence and resistance ; between a surrender of yourselves to the ungodly spirit of earth, and an emphatic protest against it, in the name and on behalf of the God of heaven.

II. Mark how complete the transformation by the renewing of your mind must be, if you are to acquire and cultivate this latter habit; if, instead of being conformed to this world, you are to prove what is that good, and acceptable, and perfect will of God. For the trial must be a fair one. And in order to its being so, your compliance with the will of God must be sincere, willing, cordial. You must make full proof of it. But that you cannot do, if you give merely a grudging, reluctant, and enforced submission. A son, yielding obedience to his father's will in such an ungracious spirit, never will, he never can, become acquainted with its true character and blessedness. But let him throw himself heart and soul into the doing of it. Then, and then only, will he prove it,—of what sort it is. So you must prove the will of God. And to have the mind so to prove it ;—to be willing so to prove it ;—in the way of a cheerful, ready, honest, out and out conformity to it ;—this implies a great change, a new creation, a new heart, the renewing of the mind.

III. Mark also how, so long as the fashion of this world lasts, and so long as that second transformation which awaits you is postponed, this proving of the will of God must all throughout be more or less an effort ; often an effort both difficult and painful. But take courage. The fashion of this world is not to last always. It passes away. You look for new heavens and a new earth, wherein dwelleth righteousness. And you yourselves are to be changed at the coming of the Lord. For " as you have borne the image of the earthy, you are to bear the image of the heavenly."

Ah ! well may you long for that coming of the Lord ! —for the time of the restitution of all things ! Then the fashion of that new world, and the fashion of the will of God, will no more be opposed to one another. They coincide ; they are in harmony. The proving of the will of God then, in that world, with body as well as soul renovated and transformed,—your whole nature changed into the image of the heavenly ;—ah ! what a joyous exercise of liberty and love will it be ! No more complaining of " the law in your members warring against the law of your mind "—" the flesh lusting against the Spirit, and the Spirit against the flesh." No more,—" I would do good ; but evil is present with me." Well may you long for the appearing of the Lord, which is to harmonize all, within and without, in you and around you ;—and to bring about a state of things in which God shall be all in all.

IV. Meanwhile mark the encouragement which you have to struggle on, here and now. Mark in particular one point of contrast between the two types, or fashions, to one or other of which you must be conformed.

Of the fashion of the world, it may be truly said that the more you try it, the less you find it to be satisfying. It looks well, it looks fair, at first. But who that has lived long has not found it to be vanity at last ?

It is altogether otherwise with the will of God. That often looks worst at the beginning. It seems hard and dark. But on. On with you in the proving of it. Prove it patiently, perseveringly, with prayer and pains, And you will get growing clearness, light, enlargement, joy. You will more and more find that "the path of the just is as the shining light, that shineth more and more unto the perfect day." For "Wisdom's ways are ways of pleasantness, and all her paths are peace." "The judgments of the Lord are true and righteous altogether. More to be desired are they than gold, yea, than much fine gold ; sweeter also than honey, and the honeycomb. Moreover by them is thy servant warned ; and in keeping of them there is great reward."

PART TWO

THE CHRISTIAN'S RELATIONSHIP
TO THE CHURCH
(12:3-13)

3

QUALIFICATION FOR MEMBERSHIP:
SELF-ESTIMATION

"For I say, through the grace given unto me, to every man that is among you, not to think of himself more highly than he ought to think; but to think soberly, according as God hath dealt to every man the measure of faith. For as we have many members in one body, and all members have not the same office; so we, being many, are one body in Christ, and every one members one of another."

—Romans 12:3-5

THE form of this exhortation to think soberly is remarkable. The Apostle gives it very authoritatively. And those to whom it is addressed are singled out individually, one by one, to receive it: " I say, through the grace given to me—to every man that is among you."

The Apostle assumes a high tone: " I say, through the grace given unto me." He speaks as one entitled to issue an order and insist on its being obeyed. He takes his stand upon the grace given unto him. That grace, in his case, reached not merely to his being converted, and united to Christ for his own personal salvation, but to his being invested with the apostolic office, and called, as an apostle, to rule in the Church. Thus, elsewhere, he speaks of his having "received grace and apostleship" (Rom. i. 5), and of his being made a minister of the gospel, "according to the gift of the grace of God given unto him, by the effectual working of his power" (Eph. iii. 7 ; see also Rom. xv. 15, 16).

"Through the grace thus given to me,"—the grace, or favour, or mere good pleasure of God, to which I owe it that I am myself a believer, and to which I also owe it that I have a commission to speak and act as an apostle, —"I say unto you."

Evidently this manner of introducing the exhortation which he is about to give, must have a meaning. It indicates the importance which he attaches to it. But it indicates, also, that he applies it and takes it home to himself. He would have all the members of the Church to know, each his proper gift or calling, his proper place, his proper work ; and he sets the example by showing that he knows this himself. He is not now dealing with Christians generally and indiscriminately, in the mass, considered simply as converted and believing men, having a common character, and lying under a common obligation to give themselves up to God, to separate themselves from the world, to be transformed by the renewing of their minds, to prove what is that good, and acceptable, and perfect will of God. He is proceeding to deal with them as associated together in a community or organized body, and to enforce the essential principles and conditions of good order and good working in such a fellowship. Of these the very first is, that every member shall fall into his right rank,—as I, the Apostle virtually says, fall into mine when I say, "through the grace given unto me, to every man that is among you, not to think of himself more highly than he ought to think ; but to think soberly, according as God hath dealt to every man the measure of faith."

I say this "to every man who is among you." For manifestly in this matter every man must judge for himself. In fact he has to judge himself. He has to form an opinion, to make an estimate, of what he is, what he is fit for, what he is intended for. This he must do in the exercise of his own individual discretion ; and, therefore, what I have now to say, I say, not to your society as a whole, but to every man who is among you, individually.

The exhortation itself, thus authoritatively introduced, and thus individually addressed, is connected with what goes before, as well as with what follows.

Its connection with what goes before is indicated by the particle "For." It is brought in, apparently, as a reason for your "not being conformed to the world, but transformed by the renewing of your mind, that ye may prove what is that good, and acceptable, and perfect will of God." It is doubly so. You need to be no longer conformed to this world, but transformed by the renewing of your mind, because the injunction which I have to give as to your thinking soberly is one which you cannot otherwise obey ;—that sobriety of thought which I enjoin,

being a habit very foreign to the world's way of thinking, and very characteristic of the new mind. Again, you
may well hope and expect, being transformed by the renewing of your mind, to prove what is that good, and
acceptable, and perfect will of God, because the state of
mind which I desire you to cultivate is peculiarly favourable to your doing so; your thinking soberly of yourselves being the best preparation for your practically and
experimentally learning the nature and the excellency of
the will of God which you have to prove. Thus the
exhortation is connected with what goes before.

Its connection with what follows appears in the fourth
and fifth verses. There the duty of thinking soberly is
enforced by the consideration of the great law or principle
of unity in diversity, which prevails in the Church as the
body of Christ ;—" For as we have many members in one
body, and all members have not the same office :—so we,
being many, are one body in Christ, and every one members one of another."

Such being the manner in which the exhortation is
introduced, and such the connection in which it stands, a
few words may suffice to illustrate its meaning.

In itself, the Apostle's command or counsel would be
very vague and indefinite, but for the concluding clause—
" According as God hath dealt to every man the measure
of faith." A general advice, to the effect that you should
not think too highly of yourselves, but should think
soberly, might be very edifying as a commonplace, or trite
topic, in morals. It rebukes self-conceit. It commends

modesty. But as addressed to the members of a body which ought to be intensely active,—it is desirable that it should be made more specific.

There is a spurious sort of modesty, of a negative or passive character, which hinders combined effort, and paralyzes activity. It takes the form of shyness, bashfulness, diffidence, reserve. It interprets an admonition of this sort against self-conceit,—a mere general exhortation to think soberly,—as if it were a reason for evading responsibility,—an excuse and apology for indolence or sloth, for indifference or unconcern, for cowardice or treachery. It settles down, under the cover of meek self-distrust, into tame pusillanimity. But all pretence for thus construing the precept is obviated and done away, when there is given, not a negative warning merely, but a positive command :—to think soberly—" according as God hath dealt to every man the measure of faith."

Now the measure of faith, as the phrase is here used, must mean the measure of faith considered as working ;— using the gifts, and employing the talents, conferred by the Great Head of the Church upon its several members. For faith has a double function ; it has two offices to discharge. On the one hand, it is receptive of Christ. On the other hand, it is energetic from Christ and for Christ. When the question of one's acceptance in the sight of God is raised, faith is receiving and resting upon Christ, embracing Christ, coming to Christ, closing with Christ, feeding upon Christ, abiding in Christ, being shut up into Christ, and growing up more and more into Christ. But the question of acceptance being settled, and in a sense set aside, another question arises as to what follows and flows from acceptance. And then faith takes the character of an impulse, a power, a principle of activity. As a lost and guilty sinner, I am moved by the Holy Ghost, and under his movement constrained by the sense of my own need, and drawn by the sight of Christ's glorious excellency and gracious suitableness and sufficiency, to receive and welcome him, for the saving of my soul. He is the Saviour of sinners, and, the Lord, the Spirit, enabling me, I take him to be my Saviour. I acquiesce in, I approve of, the whole arrangement according to which God "sent forth his Son, made of a woman, made under the law, to redeem them that were under the law, that we might receive the adoption of sons." Thus believing, I live in and with Christ: "Christ liveth in me." And now, believing, I live for Christ, and to Christ. "The life which I now live in the flesh I live by the faith of the Son of God, who loved me, and gave himself for me" (Gal. ii. 20). "I live, not unto myself, but unto him who died for me, and rose again" (2 Cor. v. 15).

Faith makes me one with Christ, as to my personal standing before God. It does so, as the hand laying hold of Christ. Faith makes me, as being one with Christ, a fellow-labourer with him. It does so, as the hand not now withered, but healed with his own health, strengthened with his own strength, nerved with his own life, and therefore fitted for working in his name and on his behalf.

In both of these aspects of it, faith admits of degrees;

and we may speak of the measure or degree of faith.
There are different degrees, or measures, or proportions of
faith, considered as appropriating Christ. There are also
different degrees, or measures, or proportions of faith,
considered as acting and working for Christ, and with
Christ, and in Christ.

But the measure of faith which the Apostle has in
view when he issues the precept to think soberly, can
scarcely be understood as having reference to the degree
or amount of faith which each man has subjectively in
himself. It rather points to an objective standard of faith.

In this view, the precept is applicable only to that
exercise of faith which wields and works the power of
Christ, for usefulness in his Church and in the world. It
cannot apply to the other act or exercise of faith, which
appropriates the grace of Christ for one's own salvation.
For, in this last case, there is no thinking of one's self at
all ; there is thinking of Christ alone. When I believe
on Christ for the pardon of my sin, for my peace with
God, for reconciliation and renewal, I go out of myself.
I lose myself in him. I am nothing, He is all in all.
There is no occasion, therefore,—there is no room, for the
adjustment of any measure or proportion of faith here.
The object of my faith is without measure. It is the
Father's measureless love ;—it is the Son's measureless
fulness of grace and truth. To speak of a measure of
faith with reference to such an object, as if different sorts
of minds were to acquiesce in different proportions of
faith, is neither reasonable nor safe. The measure of
faith equally for all alike,—the one standard to which

all alike should reach, " is the fulness of the blessing of the gospel of Christ."

But it is otherwise when faith is summoned to the exercise, not of appropriating Christ for one's own salvation, but of working with Christ and for Christ, in the discipline of new obedience,—in the labour of love. Here faith has to deal, not, if I may so speak, with a fixed quantity, the same for all; but with what is variable, and different in different believers. For it has to use the powers, the gifts and endowments, the means, occasions, and opportunities, which Christ distributes to every man, severally as he will.

When, therefore, I am called to this exercise of faith, I must form my judgment as to the measure of it, upon a right estimate of the spiritual capacity or ability which Christ is pleased to bestow upon me. My gift, whatever it may be, is to me the measure of faith. It may be the gift of prophecy, or the gift of ministering, or teaching, or exhorting, or giving, or ruling, or showing mercy. Whatever it may be, let me ascertain the gift that I have, according to the grace of God that is given to me ; and let me " think soberly, according as God hath dealt to me that measure of faith." Such, generally, is the import of the exhortation.

It is an exhortation which receives its best practical illustration and application in the directory for work in the Church which the Apostle gives in the verses that follow. In the meantime, two brief observations, suggested by the place which it occupies in the chapter, may suffice to show its importance.

In the first place, the relation in which we stand to God, to whom we present ourselves a sacrifice, enforces the admonition, both in its negative and in its positive form. If we present ourselves a sacrifice of praise, on the footing and in the spirit of Christ's presenting of himself a sacrifice of propitiation, we can scarcely be in much danger of thinking more highly of ourselves than we ought to think. We present ourselves, indeed. And in one view that might seem to afford ground for self-complacency. But it is ourselves in Christ, it is Christ in us, that we present. What a death-blow to all inordinate self-esteem! And yet, on the other hand, a fair and sober self-estimate cannot be evaded. If it is ourselves in Christ,—if it is Christ in us,—that we present, we cannot get rid of the obligation and responsibility of ascertaining, or doing our best to ascertain, what it is that we have to present. We must think, soberly, indeed, but still we must think, we must consider, what is fairly implied in our giving ourselves to God as a sacrifice of praise,—what it is precisely that we have to give. For this end, we must know ourselves. In a high and holy sense, for a high and holy purpose, we must seek to attain to this sober self-knowledge.

And, secondly, the relation in which we stand to one another, in consequence of our presenting our bodies a living and holy sacrifice to God, precludes all undue magnifying of ourselves, in rivalry with one another. In presenting our bodies, we present ourselves jointly as well as severally—we collectively present ourselves as the one mystical body of Christ. In such an act, there is no room for anything like our having separate interests, or advancing antagonist claims to superiority. Nor is there room for anything like our shrinking from the recognition of what is to every one of us the measure of faith. The gifts severally bestowed on us by the sovereign grace of our common Head, are for our mutual edification in Christ, and our unitedly growing up to the measure of the stature of perfect manhood in him. They are not, therefore, the ministers of strife and vain-glory; although they may afford fitting occasions for our " considering one another, to provoke unto love and to good works." For we must ever remember, as a motive at once to humility, to charity, and to activity, that " as we have many members in one body, and all members have not the same office ; so we, being many, are one body in Christ, and every one members one of another." We must needs, therefore, in the view of our being all members of one body, and members of one another in that one body,—if the body is to thrive well and work usefully,—ascertain our several faculties and functions, and take our several offices accordingly ; none of us thinking more highly of himself than he ought to think ; every one of us thinking soberly, according as God hath dealt to him the measure of faith. Otherwise there must ensue disorder and disunion,—and ultimately, if grace prevent not, the dissolution of the body.

4

DIVERSITY OF GIFTS AND
OFFICES AMONG THE MEMBERS

"Having then gifts differing according to the grace that is given to us, whether prophecy, let us prophesy according to the proportion of faith:" —Romans 12:6

LET us use our several gifts in their appropriate offices. Such, in a general sense, is the import of the Apostle's words in the sixth and two following verses, whether we understand him as giving a description or as issuing an order. For there is room for doubt. The italics used in our translation show that the imperative mood, or form of command, into which the discourse is here thrown, has not the express warrant of the original. In fact, this whole passage, down to the thirteenth verse, might be viewed as descriptive, rather than hortatory; forming a continuation or enlargement of the brief picture given in the fourth and fifth verses.

The Christian society or congregation is represented as one body, with many limbs or members, discharging different offices or functions. The figure is expanded and applied. The diversity is first illustrated, and then the unity : " We, being many, are one body in Christ, and every one members one of another ; but having gifts differing according to the grace that is given to us ; such as either the gift of prophecy, for our prophesying accord-

ing to the proportion of faith ; or the gift of ministering
or serving, for service ; the teaching brother occupied in
his vocation of teaching, the exhorting brother in his
vocation of exhortation ; he who gives, doing so in simplicity ; he who rules or presides, using diligence ; he who
shows mercy, being cheerful." We are members one of
another, having thus different gifts and offices ; and yet
really all one ; of one mind and of one heart : " our love
unfeigned ; all alike abhorring evil and cleaving to good ;
kindly affectioned one to another with brotherly love ; in
honour preferring one another ; not slothful in business ;
fervent in spirit ; serving the Lord ; rejoicing in hope ;
patient in tribulation ; continuing instant in prayer ; distributing to the necessity of saints ; given to hospitality."

The difference is not material between such a rendering of the passage and that preferred by our translators.
Whether it be the descriptive or the imperative form
that is adopted is of little consequence. What was true,
as a matter of fact, of the early Christians ; of those, for
example, who after the day of Pentecost lived together
so harmoniously and so holily in Jerusalem ;—is binding
as a matter of obligation on all societies gathered into
one in the name of Jesus. The diversities among the
members are to be observed, and turned to account ;
while the essential principles of the unity are to be
sacredly fostered.

It is with the diversities, as indicated in the sixth
and two following verses, that we are now, in the first
instance, specially concerned.

There are several different works specified. They are

all of them necessary works in the Church of Christ;—
in every branch and in every section of it. They must
all be done, if there are to be health and vigour, life and
energy, in the Christian body. No society or congregation,
formed and organized in the name of Christ, can be complete, unless it has in it the means, the agency, the instrumentality, for doing all these works. There must be
found among its members persons fitted, qualified, and
inclined, to do them.

This implies, however, a division of the labour, and an
orderly distribution of it. For the works differ widely
from one another in their character, and in the kind of
qualification required for the doing of them. And in
regard to every one of them, whatever the qualification
may be that is required, it is the gift of the Lord.

The division of the labour, therefore, the distribution
of the works among the members of the body, belongs
properly to the Lord alone. It is his grace—free, sovereign, and discretionary,—which imparts, as a gift, to
any one, the qualification needed for any work. And
whatever qualification any one has got, for whatever
work, it must be understood to be the mind of the Lord
that he should undertake that work. It is the work
assigned to him. It belongs to him. It becomes his
proper function, his office. Therefore says the Apostle,
" Having gifts, differing according to the grace that is
given to us," let us be about the several works for which
our several gifts are bestowed.

This rule applies, this exhortation is addressed, to all
the members of the body; to all alike and indiscriminately,

and to every one in particular. It is not intended for officials, as such. It does not concern any one class in a Christian community more than another; the man more than the woman; the scholar more than the peasant; the eloquent and elegant orator more than him who is slow of speech and of feeble presence; the rich and influential more than the humble poor. The call is to one and all of you, to stir up the gift that is in you, whatever that gift may be.

For this end you must first ascertain what gift you have, and within what sphere it may be best exercised. And then, secondly, you must make conscience of occupying the place, and doing the work, whatever it may be, which the gift points out as yours.

I. The gift which you have, according to the grace that is given to you, is the index of the function or office which He who bestows it would have you to undertake. How important, therefore, how indispensable is it, that you know what the gift is!

And here, you are required to be very faithful. You are to be very jealous over yourselves; and very conscientious as regards Him whose servants and stewards you are; " not thinking of yourselves more highly than you ought to think," as regards your gifts; but yet " thinking soberly" and seriously; forming a just estimate of what you are and what you can do, " according as God hath dealt to every one of you the measure of faith," or " according to the grace that is given unto you."

Observe particularly what sort of gift is here meant.

It is the gift which you have for the Church's work. There are gifts of another kind which you must possess, and ascertain that you possess :—gifts, the possession of which must be admitted to be even of prior urgency and necessity, in comparison with this gift of which I now speak.

Thus, in the first place, there is the gift whereby you are enabled to believe to the saving of your own souls. For "by grace are ye saved through faith ; and that not of yourselves, it is the gift of God." The question about your possessing that gift must always be first and paramount with you. The inquiry, " What must I do to be saved ? " can never, at any time, be evaded or postponed. Always, and above all things else, let it be your chief concern to have the answer to that inquiry fulfilled in your experience and consciousness;—" Believe on the Lord Jesus Christ, and thou shalt be saved."

To receive the gift of saving faith : to be ever freshly and anew receiving it : to have grace given you to lay hold of Christ, to keep hold of Christ, to recover hold of Christ : to have the Holy Spirit ever shutting you up into Christ : to have an assured confidence that he, the only and all-sufficient Saviour, saves you the chief of sinners : that he firmly holds you : that none is able to pluck you out of his hands :—that is the gift to which you must ever give your first and most earnest heed.

Again, secondly, there is the gift whereby you are enabled to "grow in grace, and in the knowledge of our Lord Jesus Christ." Your progressive personal sanctification is the gift of God. Faith working by love, faith purifying the heart, faith overcoming the world, is as much the gift of God as faith apprehending and appropriating pardon, peace, righteousness, and the love of God in Christ Jesus your Lord. About your receiving and possessing this gift also, you are ever to be above all things anxious. You are to "work out your own salvation with fear and trembling, because it is God who worketh in you both to will and to do." You are to "give diligence to make your calling and election sure." You are to give earnest heed that "the God of peace, who brought again from the dead our Lord Jesus Christ, that great Shepherd of the sheep, through the blood of the everlasting covenant, may make you perfect in every good work to do his will; working in you that which is well-pleasing in his sight, through Jesus Christ, to whom be glory for ever and ever, Amen."

Once more, in the third place, there is the gift whereby you are enabled to behave yourselves wisely in a perfect way: to keep yourselves unspotted from the world: to guide your affairs with discretion: to steer a safe, prudent, consistent, and honourable course, through the manifold temptations and snares of ordinary social life: amid the entanglements of business, the allurements of pleasure, the worrying, petty cares and irksome provocations of your common household drudgery and routine. It is a gift, and a great gift, to have your minds rightly exercised amid these distracting and disturbing influences, in patience, meekness, charity: tempering zeal with knowledge; decision with sympathy; opposition to sin with kindness to sinners; being wise as serpents and harmless as doves. You do well to seek and covet, to prize and cultivate, this most excellent gift, that you may put on "the ornament of a meek and quiet spirit, which in the sight of God is of great price."

But, in the fourth place, the gift to which Paul here refers is something different from all these : it is something to be superadded, over and above them all. It is the qualification or endowment, whatever it may be, that fits you for taking a part, and being useful, in one or other of the Church's proper works. What these are, will be considered presently. In the meantime it is enough to say that they are works implying direct personal exertion and sacrifice in the line of Christian usefulness. They are essays or efforts to do good.

Have you a gift for any of these works ? For which of them is it that you have a gift ? Is there any department of the Church's business, whether connected with her own edification or with the discharge of her duty as Christ's witness in the world and Christ's missionary to the world, for which you have a taste—a turn—a faculty?

Have you considered such questions as these, seriously, soberly? Have you put them to your own conscience ? Have you put them conscientiously to your God ? Or do you think it enough if you take heed to yourselves, to your own interest in Christ, the sanctifying of your own hearts, and your safe preservation from the evil that is in the world ?

It is as much as you can do, you say, to look after the welfare of your own souls. As to your being expected to

take an active share in managing the affairs of the Church,
or to offer yourselves as agents in the carrying out of her
plans—it is not your province, it is not what you are
cut out for. You leave all that to others who have the
time, the talent, the inclination. For yourselves, it is
enough if, in your own poor way, you are enabled, in
such a world as you have to live in, to mind the things
which belong to your peace, and give no occasion to the
enemy to speak reproachfully.

But think for a moment, before you acquiesce in such
a timid policy, or make a merit of such false modesty as
that. Consider first your position, as members of a body
organized for work. What right have you, as one of a
band of brothers, to decline your share of the business
for the transacting of which the brotherhood exists?
Consider next the account which you have to give of
every talent your Lord bestows. You may hide your
one talent in a napkin. Will you venture, with the
hidden talent in your hand, to meet your Lord? Consider, again, the wrong that you do to Him whose gift you
refuse to stir up. Your capacity, your opportunity, whatever it may be, is the gift of God—of the Lord the Spirit.
It is not your own power or ability that you are trifling
with, but the gift of God. And once more, consider the
wrong which you do to yourselves. You hinder your
own souls from prospering; for it is mere idle folly to
imagine that your own faith, and hope, and love, can be
strong and healthy, while the common weal, and the
common woe, and the common work, are disregarded.
The arm cannot thrive, let it be held ever so devoutly

high, that refuses to do its office in the body; it shrinks, and shrivels, and dies. You miss also a great recompense of reward. You deny yourself a present pleasure. You run the risk of coming short of much glory in that day when "they that are wise shall shine as the brightness of the firmament; and they that turn many to righteousness as the stars for ever and ever."

And be not in haste to conclude that you have no gift, or scarcely any, that may be available for the Church's work,—or rather for the work of the Church's Lord. Every one has something in his power; and if he will but begin to try, he will discover that he can do a good deal more than he thought. Every one, if once he sets himself seriously to look out for business of this sort, will find his proper business laid to his hand.

Only let him not go in search of it to the ends of the earth. Let him not fancy that the gift which he has, according to the grace that is given to him, is a gift which he could exercise in some other sphere than that which he now occupies. Look not abroad, look not above, for the office you ought to fill, and the function you ought to discharge. Look at home: look at your own very door. Look within. Form a just and sober estimate of yourselves as you now are, and your position as it now is, "according to the grace that is" now "given to you."

Is there nothing that,—being what you now are, by the mercy of God, and placed where you now are, in the providence of God,—you can now be doing for his beloved Son, your beloved Lord, of whose living body

you are called to be the living members? Is there
nothing the Lord would have you to do for him? Is
there no walk of Christian usefulness inviting you to
enter on it? Is there no department of Christian charity
waiting for you to undertake it? Is there no vacant
place for you among any of the regiments of Christ's
army that go to fight against ignorance, and ungodliness,
and crime, and disease, and misery, and death? Oh!
surely, if only you are willing to use any gift, however
poor, in any sphere, however low; if—all false pride,
false shame, false delicacy, false modesty and humility
apart—you are ready, whatsoever your hand findeth to
do, to do it with your might;—" not thinking of yourself
more highly than you ought to think, but thinking
soberly, according as God has given to you the measure
of faith;"—you will not be long at a loss to know what
is your gift, what your calling, what your office, what
your work : not at least if yours is the experience, if
yours is the heart of him, the deeply abased and graciously
revived prophet of the Lord, who heard a voice saying,
" Whom shall I send, and who will go for us?" and
lost not a moment in sending heavenwards the unreserved and unambitious and unconditional reply, " Here
am I, send me."

II. But this is not all. Not only must you thus
ascertain the gift which you have, and the work to which
it points,—you are also to make conscience of the work,
as being your work. It is your business; it is your
office. Whatever you undertake, you are to make con-

science of undertaking it, with as deep a feeling of obligation and responsibility, as if you were solemnly ordained to it by the laying on of hands. This is plainly implied in what the Apostle says : "Having then gifts differing according to the grace that is given unto us," let us take our several places, let us assume our several offices, let us discharge our several functions, accordingly.

In this view, most truly and emphatically, all the members of Christ's Church are office-bearers. All belonging to the communion of any Christian society are virtually and really office-bearers in that society. You, my friend, whoever you are, who come to worship with us from Sabbath to Sabbath,—you who sit with us at the table of the Lord,—you become one of us ; a member of our body : and for accomplishing the ends and fulfilling the purposes of its organization, the body has a right, the Lord who made the body and is its head has a right, to the services of every member.

What, then, is your gift, Brother ? What can you do, as one of us, for advancing our common cause,—the cause of our common Lord ? What will you become ? To which of our different staffs of labourers will you join yourself ? Which of our various plans of usefulness will you patronize ? Will you be a teacher of the young on the Sabbath? or a week-day visitor from house to house ? or a collector of two or three together for prayer ? A fighter ? or a holder up of the hands of those who fight ? An active agent in the field ? or, if so the Lord will, a sympathizing sufferer, looking on from a sick-bed and interceding for a blessing ? Use your discretion. Make your election. Judge for yourself what is your calling. Only be something. Undertake something. You must have an office ; the office that best suits your gift : but an office of some sort you must have.

And you must regard it as an office. You must make conscience of so regarding it. You must go about it with the same preparation, the same punctuality, the same prayerfulness, that you would feel to be incumbent upon you, if the gift that is in you had been given you " by prophecy with the laying on of the hands of the presbytery" (1 Tim. iv. 14). Beware of the notion which is apt to insinuate itself into the minds of some workers in the Lord's cause, that because the task or duty you have got on hand is one which you assume spontaneously, and discharge gratuitously, therefore you may take it, sometimes, somewhat more easily than you would consider yourselves entitled to do, if it were the life-business to which you had been set apart by a special call, and for which you received stipend, wages, or pay. True, you offer yourselves willingly at first for the service ; it is of your own mere good pleasure ; and it is of your own good pleasure that you continue to render the service. But while in the service, you are to regard yourselves as ordained to it, and bound to it : ordained to it as solemnly as I am ordained to the ministry of the word and the cure of souls ; bound to it as sacredly as the enlisted recruit is bound to his Queen's and his country's work of arms when he has sworn the military oath.

The Lord, the King, delights in volunteers. His people are to be all volunteers in the day of his power.

He holds out a flag of invitation for volunteers. Who is on the Lord's side—who? Who will go up to the battle? Whom shall I send on my errand? Choose your rank, take your place, anywhere you please, so as only it be where you have some work to do that you may fairly think the Spirit has given you ability to do. And once in your place, remember that you are there by appointment of the Holy Ghost. For it is " according to the grace given to you" that you have the gift which you are now called to use. Use it faithfully, in prayer, perseverance, patience. Stir up the gift that is in you. It is the gift of God.

5

DISTRIBUTION OF OFFICES AND
WORKS AMONG THE MEMBERS

"Whether prophecy, let us prophesy according to the proportion of faith; or ministry, let us wait on our ministering: or he that teacheth, on teaching; or he that exhorteth, on exhortation: he that giveth, let him do it with simplicity; he that ruleth, with diligence; he that showeth mercy, with cheerfulness."   —Romans 12:6-8

THE general principle upon which the distribution of the Church's necessary works among the members is to proceed, is, that every man, " not thinking of himself more highly than he ought to think, but thinking soberly, according as God hath dealt to every man the measure of faith," should form an estimate of the gift, whatever it may be, which he has received, " according to the grace that is given to him," and should take the place, and hold himself responsible for the service, for which his gift may seem best to qualify him.   In illustration of this general principle, and with a view to its application, the Apostle enters somewhat into detail.

The works to be undertaken are enumerated.   They are seven.   They may be miscellaneous specimens merely, strung together at random ; or they may be exhaustive heads, embracing the classes to which all Christian enterprises and movements may ultimately be reduced.   This last is the more probable view.

For one thing, the bringing together of the first two of these seven works is remarkable. The second is unlike the first. Ministry differs from prophecy. And it comes in between the first,—prophecy,—and the third and fourth,—teaching and exhorting,—which are congenial to the first. The fifth, sixth, and seventh, again,—ruling, giving, showing mercy,—are evidently more akin to the second,—ministry, than to the first,—prophecy. They partake of the nature of a ministry or service, more than of the nature of prophesying.

No doubt all the functions mentioned after the second may fall under the general category of ministering, or serving ; for to teach, or to exhort, is a ministry, or service, in the Christian Church, in which there are no lords over men's consciences ;—in which even Apostles must say, " We preach not ourselves, but Christ Jesus the Lord, and ourselves, your servants, for Jesus' sake." But then, for the same reason, prophesying also must come under the head of ministering, or serving.

On the whole, it seems to be the most natural conclusion as to this enumeration, that here, as elsewhere (1 Cor. xii. 4), Paul adopts an orderly arrangement, and, in particular, that he puts first his general heads, and then brings in the particulars into which they respectively branch out.

The works, then, are twofold ; prophesying and ministering ; prophetical and diaconal. And both of them admit of expansion or sub-division. Prophesying includes teaching and exhorting. Ministering includes giving, ruling, and showing mercy.

I. There is a grand general division. To prophesy, to minister; these are the two great functions of the Church of Christ on earth, of all its branches, and of all its members.

They were the two great functions of her Head when he was on earth. He prophesied. He ministered. He prophesied; not merely in the sense of foretelling future events, but in the sense of revealing the whole counsel of God. He ministered; for " the Son of man came not to be ministered unto, but to minister, and to give his life a ransom for many." He was a prophet, opening up and unfolding the heart of God. He was a deacon, ministering to the service of man.

His Church is like himself. It is, in fact, himself. It has the same double office that he has. It prophesies, and it ministers. It is at once a seer and a servant; God's seer and man's servant. It is God's seer, as having, by revelation, an insight into the mind of God, and, by express authority, a commission to declare that mind. It is man's servant, as ordained for his good, appointed to be the instrument, the means and minister of his salvation.

For both of these offices the Church, which is Christ's body, needs and calls for the agency of her members. Whatever gifts they have, according to the grace that is given to them, they are to bring to the Church's help, or rather to the help of her Lord against the mighty, under one or other of these two departments of labour, prophesying or ministering.

Even the extraordinary and miraculous endowments of apostolic times fell under these two heads. The most gifted man was either a prophet, having in greater or less perfection the faculty of understanding God, and helping others to understand God ; or else he was a minister, servant, deacon, dispensing manifold relief and comfort, to meet the manifold wants and woes of suffering men.

All the supernatural manifestations of wisdom and power in the early Church might be thus classed. The highest inspiration, by which men spoke and wrote as the oracles of God, and the gift of tongues, by which men found access to their fellows of all nations ;—the faculty of supernatural insight, and the faculty of supernatural utterance ;—belonged to the function of prophesying. The miraculous healing of the sick, the raising of the dead, the casting out of devils, were acts of ministry or service. They were the extraordinary signs and tokens of the honour of the deaconship.

And so still,—whatever gifts we severally have, as members of Christ and of his Church, we may exercise in one or other of these two ways. Does our gift lie in the direction of insight or of utterance? Is it spiritual discernment, or enlargement and liberty of speech ? Is either of these attainments our forte, if I may so call it, or our faculty? Then our call is to prophesying. But failing that, we have another resource. " Whether prophecy, let us prophesy;"—or if " ministry," rather than prophecy, be our function, for which we are fitted, let us be content and thankful to have it so ; " let us wait on our ministering."

II. Under this general division of all the Church's

work into the two great heads of prophesying and ministering, there are particulars specified.

1. Thus belonging to prophecy, we have teaching and
exhorting. If you cannot prophesy, in the highest sense
of that term;—which we may now, in the absence of
miraculous endowments, be warranted in applying to the
preaching of the word ;—if you have not the leisure, the
learning, the cultivated talent and fluency of speech, the
sanctified genius and eloquence, which—instead of inspiration and the gift of tongues—might qualify you for being
a prophet of the Lord, a herald of the cross ;—you may
yet have it in your power to do something in that line.

You may be apt to "teach." You may have a facility
in so dealing with the understandings of men or of children, as to get them to open to the apprehension of the
truth. With no pretension to the gift of discovering new
truth, or even to the gift of presenting old truth in a new
light, and enforcing it with new strength,—you may be
skilful in carefully breaking up the truth, and affectionately training the raw and rude intellect for its reception.

Or you may have a power of direct appeal to the
conscience and the heart. Yours may be the gift which
many prophets and preachers have coveted in vain, and
in which many plain and simple believers have excelled,
—the gift of speaking right home to the convictions
and feelings of your neighbours.

To "exhort;"—to warn, entreat, invite; to use all the
weapons of direct, straight-forward expostulation and persuasion ; to tell a neighbour in a kindly way, that as a
fellow-sinner he is lost, as you were : to bid him repent

and believe, that he may be saved by the same grace by which you hope to be saved yourselves; simply to reason with him, as you would reason with a drowning man when you held out to him a rope to rescue him;—that may be your province; that may be your gift and calling. And when you go, in the exercise of that gift and calling, to remonstrate with an ungodly family; to plead with a backsliding professor; to speak a word in season to a weary soul:—brother! you are doing a prophet's office: brother! you are winning a prophet's reward.

Only see to it that when you thus "prophesy, or teach, or exhort,"—and so far as you thus "prophesy, or teach, or exhort,"—you make conscience of doing so, strictly, and out and out, "according to the proportion of faith." Speak because you believe. Speak as you believe. Whether in the higher office of prophetic preaching, or in the lower, or at least humbler, departments of teaching and exhorting, be sure that you speak out clearly, fully, unreservedly, all that you have to say of God, all that you have to say for God, to your fellow-man,—to this your brother whom you are teaching and exhorting in particular,—according to the full measure of your own light and your own convictions. Shun not to declare the whole counsel of God. Prophesy, teach, exhort; believing all that you say, and saying all that you believe. That I take to be in substance and spirit, and to all practical intents and purposes, what Paul means by prophesying "according to the proportion of faith."

2. And if you cannot prophesy, you can minister. If you cannot preach, or teach, or exhort, as a seer, you

can serve as a deacon. And the diaconate in Christ's Church is very honourable. There is variety enough in it also. There is room for the exercise of gifts, differing according to the grace that is given to you.

There are the three departments of giving, ruling, showing mercy. There is the ministry of giving; whether of your own substance, or as gathering in and applying the gifts of others. There is the ministry of ruling; superintending and directing plans of usefulness; presiding over holy and charitable movements; helping to manage the Church's affairs, and to carry on her government. There is the ministry of showing mercy; the blessed task and office of manifesting the divine compassion, as it flows from the heart of God, through the hearts of his believing and sympathizing people, into all the channels of human experience, and all the chequered vicissitudes of human affairs.

Have you means at your disposal, your own means or the means of others, so that you may go forth, full-handed, a giver of good things to those who need them? It is a good and grateful ministry, if only you go about it "in simplicity;" with singleness of eye; not seeking applause, or even thanks; not yielding to caprice or impulse; but with large mind and loving heart, devising liberal things, that by liberal things you may stand.

But perhaps it is not yours to give. You may have to say, with Peter at the Beautiful gate of the Temple, "Silver and gold have I none:" and to say it, alas! without having that to bestow which he had when he added, "Such as I have give I thee." You may have no alms or offerings, your own or the Church's, to dispense. But may you not lend a helping hand in managing some one or other of her pious and charitable undertakings? May you not assist in ruling, directing, actively conducting and carrying out some one or other of her practical plans and measures for glorifying God and doing good to men? Your "diligence" in any such business will surely not be in vain.

And even if you are shut out both from the ministry of giving and from the ministry of ruling; even if you can neither be an almoner nor a manager : if you have no bounty in your hand for charitable distribution, and no counsel in your head for the conduct of affairs,—you have mercy, pity, love in your heart. And with a hand empty of gifts, and a head incapable of ruling, if only you have a heart that is merciful, that pities, that loves, you have a ministry which you may exercise "cheerfully."

Cheerfully—oh! how cheerfully! For it is a ministry void of risk, and void of care. He who giveth, let him give ever so "simply," ever so disinterestedly, ever so unselfishly, has yet an anxious task upon his hands. He must be cautious, he must discriminate, he must suspect, he must inquire, he must often pause and restrain himself, and do violence to the best feelings of his nature, if he would not be the instrument of evil rather than good. He who rules, he who manages, he who takes a responsible part in any work or business of the Church, be he ever so "diligent," may have an anxious time of it also. Many things occur to embarrass and disconcert him. He is often perplexed, wearied, vexed, under a

sense of the load he has to bear, and the difficulties he
has to meet.   But with light heart and open brow may
the merciful man pay his welcome visits of mere kindness and goodwill among the families around his dwelling.
With a smile for the glad, a sigh and a tear for the
afflicted, a patient ear for the complaint of injury, an eye
of quick intelligence for the mute glance of unutterable
woe, a hand to lift the fallen, feet swift to run to the
relief of the poor, and a word in season to all that are
weary;—he goes about showing mercy, like his Master;
and like his Master also, he " showeth mercy with cheerfulness."

Now if this is the divine ideal of the Church as the
body of Christ;—if the picture which this inspired apostle
draws, whether by description or by exhortation, is the
picture of a rightly organized Christian society;—what a
melancholy shortcoming must be noted in the actual
Christianity both of past and of present times !
.How influential might a congregation be if, in terms
of the Apostle's representation, all its members were found
exercising their several gifts in appropriate offices of zeal
and love !   What a hive would it be of busy bees! flying
all abroad, over the waste wilderness as well as the
garden enclosed ! kissing into life and pure love many a
wild or wanton flower ! and bringing back to the central
hive, and for all its inmates, loads of sweetest blessings !
Such a flock would scarcely need pastor, or elders, or
deacons.   It might almost dispense with office-bearers,
whether for teaching or for ruling, for prophesying or

for ministering. In point of fact it is the necessity, and not the glory, of the Church on earth, that she must have her office-bearers. The Friends, the Plymouth Brethren, are so far in the right. That system of theirs which sets aside official distinctions, were it only practicable, would be the beau-ideal, the perfection, of Christian association and organization. " I would that all the Lord's people were prophets," must be the longing of every earnest heart, as it was the longing of the heart of Moses. But the Lord, as we believe, has not judged it safe to rely altogether on such a general and spontaneous alacrity and ability as that arrangement would imply; and we admire his wisdom, as well as his grace and condescension, in the setting apart of special functionaries, that so these necessary works may be laid as a special charge on parties specially responsible. In this very passage, accordingly, we are accustomed to trace the outline of the directory which the Lord would have his Church to observe in the appointment of her officers, as well as in the distribution or division of the labour among them.

Surely, however, it is an ungrateful abuse of this provision, if the members leave all to their officials. It was not so of old. Paul speaks of " Phœbe, our sister, who has been a succourer of many, and of myself also :" of " Priscilla and Aquila, my helpers in Christ Jesus :" of " Mary, who bestowed much labour upon us :" of " Urbane, our helper in Christ:" of "Tryphena and Tryphosa, who labour in the Lord :" of " Persis, which laboured much in the Lord :" and again, " of those women which laboured with me in the gospel, with Clement also, and other my fellow-labourers, whose names are written in the Lamb's book of Life." (Rom. xvi. ; Phil. iv.)

Why may it not now be as it has been ?

It is a step, at least, in the right direction, when a congregation throws itself heart and hand into some one definite undertaking,—some enterprise having for its object the social and Christian amelioration of a neighbourhood affording scope for its liberality and activity. To a congregation so engaged, who would not heartily bid God-speed? who would not rejoice in the opportunity of giving, not merely encouraging words of sympathy, but substantial aid? Let its members be thus stirred up and stimulated, one and all of them, to direct personal effort, with prayer and pains, in the good work to which as a congregation they stand pledged.

And now, in fine, let the honest language of every soul be, " Lord, what wouldst thou have me to do ?"

Art thou on the way to Damascus? Art thou going on in sin? Art thou wounding Christ, in his cause, his people, his gospel? Seest thou not that bright light from heaven ? Hearest thou not that voice,—" Saul, Saul, why persecutest thou me? It is hard for thee to kick against the pricks." Me thou canst not hurt : my purpose thou canst not hinder. But thyself—ah! what ruin is before thee ! At this sight, at this voice, be humbled. Fall on thy face before Him whom thou art piercing, and cry to him, " Lord, what wouldst thou have me to do ?" And be sure to go where he bids thee ; to wait on his guidance. Go, guided by his Word and Spirit; follow on to know him and his will. Resist not. Delay not. Be up and doing. "Now in the day of thy merciful visitation, mind the things that belong to thy peace, ere they be for ever hid from thine eyes." "Seek the Lord while he may be found."

Art thou trembling like that Philippian gaoler of old! Is there an earthquake, if not in thy prison-house, yet in thy heart? Is thy sin finding thee out? And as thou hearest songs of praise rising from the cell where some saint of God is pining, does thy heart misgive thee lest soon thou shouldst be hearing only weeping, and wailing, and gnashing of teeth? "Lord, what wouldst thou have me to do?" "What must I do to be saved?" Let that be thy cry, thine earnest cry, now. And hark! Hear the gracious, welcome response : "Believe—only believe —on the Lord Jesus Christ, and thou shalt be saved." Hear this, thou anxious, sin-stricken soul! Hear thy Lord himself,—"If thou canst believe; all things are possible to him that believeth." Hear; and let thy prompt and eager appropriation of this wonderful word be,—"Lord, I believe; help thou mine unbelief."

Art thou hesitating, halting, miserably at fault and at a loss for the way of peace and holiness and joy? Art thou ill at ease, not seeing thy signs,—before thee a pathless ocean, behind thee a frowning foe? Still let thy cry be, "Lord, what wouldst thou have me to do?" And hark, again! Listen to the stirring message which God gives through Moses : "Speak unto the children of Israel that they go forward." On, on : "My grace is sufficient for thee ; for my strength is made perfect in weakness."

And thou, whosoever thou art, who hast found grace in the Lord's sight, does thy warm heart move thee to long for some way of proving thy love to Him who has first loved thee ? Ask himself, and keep on asking himself, "Lord, what wouldst thou have me to do?" Confer not with flesh and blood. Go always to himself. He, if thou wilt hear his voice in his word, and see his hand in providence—and if thou grieve not his Spirit moving thee,—he will open to thee a door. He will show thee a way; he will prepare for thee a way. He who leadeth the blind by a way that they know not,—he who went before his people, as they marched through the wilderness, guiding them by the glorious symbol of his presence,—will make a plain path for thy feet. He will cause thee to know when he would have thee to move and when to rest. He will assign to thee thy task, thy toil, thy work and warfare ; thy seasons also of stillness, and intervals of repose ; and at last thy bright recompense of reward in the land whither thou art going to possess it.

6

CHARACTERISTICS OF ACTIVE MEMBER-SHIP: LOVE AND BROTHERLY LOVE

"Let love be without dissimulation. Abhor that which is evil; cleave to that which is good. Be kindly affectioned one to another with brotherly love; in honor preferring one another."

—*Romans 12:9, 10*

OF the two virtues, or graces, spoken of in these verses, love and brotherly love, the one, love, is more general, having for its objects all sentient and intelligent beings within the range of our acquaintance; the other again, brotherly love, is more limited, embracing those only who are one with us in Christ. In the connection in which they here stand, love, the wider affection, is to be considered chiefly in its relation to the more particular affection of brotherly love. It is brotherly love that properly fits into the Apostle's line of thought.

He is still, at this stage, addressing you as believers; organized into one body, having one common Head, but differing from one another, in respect of gifts, offices and functions, as the members of the natural body do. He is speaking to you on the subject of your internal relations to God and to one another. It is not till the thirteenth verse that he comes to speak of your relations to them that are without—outside of the Church or kingdom of Christ.

Up to that point, his exhortations seem to be, all of them, meant to bear upon your standing and your duties within its pale. It is, if we may so speak, the home administration of the kingdom that is here discussed. Its foreign policy does not come up till afterwards.

You have been marshalled, you have been endeavouring to marshal yourselves, as officers and officials in the kingdom, according to the general order:—" Having then gifts differing according to the grace that is given to us, whether prophecy, let us prophesy according to the proportion of faith ; or ministry, let us wait on our ministering : or he that teacheth, on teaching ; or he that exhorteth, on exhortation : he that giveth, let him do it with simplicity; he that ruleth, with diligence; he that sheweth mercy, with cheerfulness." You are all now, it is to be presumed, in your proper places ; the right men, and the right women too, in the right places. You have your several works assigned to you. You go about your several callings, you separate to ply your several tasks, in the one household of faith of which you are all members.

Is not the house then divided ? Practically is not this the upshot ? True, you tell us that, "as we have many members in one body, and all the members have not the same office ; so we, being many, are one body in Christ, and every one members one of another." And this ideal of unity in diversity may be a fine theory. But in point of fact, we find ourselves, in the actual business of the church, in congregational arrangements—even in the labours of love to which we are set, wide as the poles asunder. We scarcely ever come in contact with one another, or cross one another's path. Is not our oneness, then, as a body, a mere name? To all intents and purposes, in our outer Christian walk and work, as well as in our inner Christian life, are we not isolated, individualized; each doing the best he can for himself, feeling very much as if he were left alone, and must get on as he best may alone? Or if I am thrown into closer fellowship with some one or two stray followers of Christ, is it not, as I may say, by accident, by force of circumstances, congeniality of temper, similarity of situation, or some cause, at all events, quite independent of this fair vision of the one body with the many members—the many members in the one body?

It may be so. To a large extent perhaps it is so. Alas! that it should be so. The church-tie, the congregational-tie, the closer spiritual tie of a common interest in Christ and a common call to work for Christ,—potent as they are in theory,—are all apt at all times, and now probably as much as ever, to be practically weak; too weak to resist the influences at work, even within their range, to occasion separation and disunion. The moving bodies around the central Sun are ever tending, in their movements, to fly off from him and from one another. The attractive power must be strong that is to resist and overcome the tendency. And so it is. For it is love; and what is stronger than love, especially if it be true and holy? "Let love be without dissimulation. Abhor that which is evil; cleave to that which is good." Nay more, it is not love in general merely, but brotherly love; and what closer bond of union can there be than the genial and simple-hearted sympathy of a common home ? " Be kindly affectioned one to another with brotherly love ; in honour preferring one another."

Taking this view of the connection in which these two verses stand, we may, in the first place, consider generally the relation of love to brotherly love. And then, secondly, we may examine the particular attributes or features which they must have respectively, if they are to serve the purpose contemplated : the purpose, namely, of keeping the unity of the Spirit in the bond of peace. The love must be, on the one hand, unfeigned, —" without dissimulation ;" and, on the other hand, discriminating,—" abhor that which is evil, cleave to that which is good." The brotherly love again must be, on the one hand, hearty,—" be kindly affectioned one to another ;" and it must be, on the other hand, humble,— " in honour preferring one another."

I. Let us consider generally, in view of the connection in which they stand in the passage before us, the relation of love to brotherly love.

Charity, or love, in its widest sense, has been defined the love of being, of being as such, of all being. Or lest that should seem too abstract and transcendental a notion, it has been said to be the love of living, sentient, intelligences ; the love of beings possessed of proper personality. In a believer's heart, this love is sympathy with God. " Love is of God ; and every one that loveth is born of God, and knoweth God. He that loveth not, knoweth not God ; for God is love " (1 John iv. 7, 8). The affection of love, as it exists in the mind or heart of God, and is indeed the essential characteristic of his nature, is transferred or transplanted into your bosom, when you believe. For your believing is your grasping this love of God; apprehending and appropriating it;—not the fruit or effect of this love, but the love itself. " We have known and believed the love that God hath to us" (1 John iv. 16); the love which is manifested in "the sending of his only-begotten Son into the world, that we might live through him." "Herein is love, not that we loved God, but that he loved us, and sent his Son to be the propitiation for our sins." This love, this God who thus is love, you lay hold of as your own, when you receive his testimony concerning his Son. The Holy Spirit gives you an eye to perceive and a heart to welcome this very love, this very God who is love, as your own. And now you love him because he first loved you. You love, because you know and believe his love. His love to you reproduces, as it were, itself in you. Hence there results a certain harmony of sentiment, a certain union of nature, very imperfect indeed, but yet real so far as it goes, in virtue of which you see as God sees, and feel as God feels. Thus love, known and believed, begets love, in its own likeness.

Now this love, thus begotten in you, through your knowing and believing the love that God has to you, is not only an affection of a wider range, as to its objects, than brotherly love;—it is of a higher nature, a more heavenly origin. It has its seat in the bosom of God, where there is, where there can be, no room for the other.

Brotherly love is essentially the affection of a creature;

it is an affection of which a creature alone is capable. The Creator is incapable of it; he cannot exercise or feel it. There may be brotherly love among the angels. There may be brotherly love among men. Ultimately, there may be brotherly love among angels and men indiscriminately. But there can be no brotherly love in God. For there can be no brotherhood between him and any other. Love alone is of God. For God is love alone. Hence love, divine love, because it is divine or God-like, must take precedence, in your hearts, of brotherly love, which is an affection simply human. And indeed, if it is to be of the right sort, brotherly love must itself be a mode, or modification, of that higher love. It must be founded on that love ; it must flow from it.

For, apart from love, brotherly love in itself and by itself is not necessarily a virtue. Nay, it may be sin. It degenerates into sectarianism, partisanship, and the poor *esprit de corps* of a school, a class, a clan, a coterie. It worships idols of the tribe, the palace, the theatre, the cave. You love as brethren those who happen to agree with you in holding certain opinions, cultivating certain tastes, pursuing certain ends. You love them as brethren merely on the ground of that agreement. You draw together ; you club together ; you frequent one another's company; you take pleasure in associating with one another, in helping one another, and in serving one another. This is quite natural, and so far, all right. Congeniality of disposition, similarity of pursuits, obviously tend to create intimacy ; and within due limits, that tendency is safe and good. But if that is all—if the bond of

brotherhood is thus merely natural and human—if your
unity is simply the result of your unanimity—if it springs
out of yourselves, and, as it is almost sure to do, centres
in yourselves ; it may make you strong as an ecclesiastical corporation ; it may make you proud and happy as a
more choice and select spiritual company, dwelling apart,
nearer the throne than many.   But it does not enlarge
or elevate the heart.   Nor does it free the soul from the
yoke of self.   It is itself, in fact, little better than a sort
of enlarged selfishness.   It does not ascend heavenward.
It draws down earthward what is heavenly.   It is of the
earth, earthy.   It breeds earthly passions,—censoriousness,
superciliousness, moroseness ;—the fanatic's heroic rage,
the bigot's mean intolerance.   Such brotherly love has
been the bane and curse of the Church in all ages, the
scandal of Christianity, the fruitful mother of strife
among its professors, the world's too plausible apology
for not knowing and not believing the love which God
hath to us.

Very different was the brotherly love of Christ as it
was manifested when he lived among men.   As God he
was capable of love alone.   But as man, the man Christ
Jesus, he was capable of brotherly love as well.

And oh ! what brotherly love was his !   He loved his
own which were in the world ; he loved them well ; he
loved them to the end.   Never heart beat, true and tender, with a brother's love, as did the heart of Jesus
towards his chosen friends.   He had them always with
him.   He told them all that he was doing.   He had no
reserve in talking to them.   He was never weary of

talking with them. He could have talked on without limit, without end, if only they could have followed him. "I have many things to say unto you, but you cannot bear them now." He would fain have said more and more, but he will not speak to them too soon of what could only vex and sadden,without really doing them good. It is a brother's frank and open candour, only tempered by a brother's tender concern. He was their Master and Lord. But he was their brother too ; their elder brother. They lived with him on terms of intimate brotherly familiarity. He had a brother's patience for their waywardness ; a brother's pity for their weakness; a brother's tears for their sorrow. It was on a brother's breast that John leaned at supper (John xiii. 23). It was a brother's eye that looked on Peter (Luke xxii. 61). It was a brother's voice that so affectionately commended to the Father's love the little ones whom the Father had given him, and whom he was leaving desolate in a hostile world, (John xvii.)

And yet special and peculiar as was his brotherly love to his own, how free, how entirely free, was it from any element that could make it appear to be a love to them merely because they were his own ; because they belonged to him ; because they followed him ! It was with no selfish love that he loved them ; no love of selfish complacency, or as some might call it, just pride ; such love as one might feel when he looked round on a circle of devoted men whom he had won to be his sworn comrades and his brethren in council or in arms. The brotherly love of Jesus was of a higher tone ; it was of a more heavenly type. It was brotherly love indeed, such as man feels. It was real human brotherly love ; the brotherly love of a genuine human heart, true to all the instincts and all the sympathies of humanity. But it was welded into that other love which is of God. It took the character of that love which is in God ; that love, which God is.

Take as an instance the farewell prayer, and especially the close of it : " Father, I will that they also whom thou hast given me be with me where I am ; that they may behold my glory, which thou hast given me : for thou lovedst me before the foundation of the world. O righteous Father, the world hath not known thee : but I have known thee, and these have known that thou hast sent me. And I have declared unto them thy name, and will declare it ; that the love wherewith thou hast loved me may be in them, and I in them" (John xvii. 24-26).

Here truly is brotherly love. The Elder Brother is presenting to his Father and theirs, the children, the little ones, whom the Father hath given him to be his brethren. But what a constant reference has he to the Father ! What love to God the Father pervades, and animates, and elevates, this brotherly love of Jesus !

Why, let us ask, according to these wondrous words of his, does the Lord Jesus specially love his own ? For what reasons, and on what grounds ? In the first place, they are given to him by the Father. And, secondly, they receive him as sent by the Father ; and while the world knows not the Father, they receive the knowledge of the Father which the Son imparts, and the love of the Father which the Son conveys. Then again, let us further ask, for what end does the Elder Brother, with such tender importunity of brotherly love, commend his own to the Father ? That the Father may love them as he loveth him, and glorify them as he glorifies him : that he and they may be one in the Father.

Thus all this love is of God. Jesus, the Elder Brother, regards the little ones whom he loves as brethren, from the Father's point of view in heaven, as well as from his own point of view on earth. The love of Jesus to his own is sympathy with the Father in his love to them. It is sympathy with them as the objects of the Father's love. And so, in virtue of that twofold sympathy, it is welded into the Father's love itself.

Thus brotherly love is lifted up, from being a human, into becoming a divine affection. It is not now a self-originated, closet combination ; as when men come together, and finding themselves of one mind, resolve to act together. It is an integral part and portion of that great fountain of love which is in the bosom of God. Absorbed into this higher love, purified and hallowed by it, brotherly love issues forth anew. It selects its congenial company of believing friends. It finds itself at home among them. Yet still always it retains its identity and sympathy with that love in God, so wide, free, generous, unselfish, which embodies and expresses itself in the gracious mission of his Son.

My love to the brethren is thus like my Father's love to them. He loves them with a peculiar affection. And so do I. But it is an affection in him, and through his

grace, in me also, altogether beyond the imputation or suspicion of anything like mere favouritism, or partiality, or
party spirit. It is not respect of persons. It is not mere
selfish reciprocity; the owning of those who own me. It
is genuine love ; the love of the true, the good, for the
sake of their truth and goodness. My love to the brethren is thus, like God's love to them, not merely the love of
natural, human fellow-feeling,—but the love of divine benevolence ; of that divine benevolence which looks on all
out of itself with an equal eye, and has pity, mercy, complacency, for all;—pity, mercy, on the one hand, for all alike
of the lost family of man ; and on the other hand, holy
complacency for all alike who, in the Son, are created
anew unto holiness.

To love the brethren thus, is not to shut myself up
among a knot of devotees, in the cells and cloisters of an
exclusive monasticism. Nor is it to bind myself hand
and foot to a party organization like that of Loyola.
The brotherly love of the friar's convent, or of the Jesuit's
college, is not for me, if I am to be like-minded, like-
hearted, with Christ. No. Nor the brotherly love of
the sect, the party, the conclave, or the inner circle of
those who, hugging themselves in their own self-satisfac-
tion, bid all others stand aside. Let mine be the brotherly love of Him who was meek and lowly in heart ;
who did not cry, nor lift up, nor cause his voice to be
heard in the streets ; who did not break the bruised reed
nor quench the smoking flax ;—of Him whose advent
the angels hailed, when they sang, "Glory to God in the
highest, on earth peace, good-will toward men."

There, in that good-will toward men, is love; the love of God, wide, universal, free. It is goodwill to men; to men as such; to all men. This is the love of Him who would have all men to be saved, and to come to the knowledge of the truth. Let this love be in your hearts, as it was in the heart of Christ. Be ye philanthropists as he was. Be ye, like him, first and primarily, lovers of men. This Christ-like, God-like philanthropy, and this alone, will make your brotherly love Christ-like and God-like too.

II. Such generally being the nature of love and of brotherly love, and such their right relation to one another, let us now inquire what are the particular attributes or features which they must possess respectively, if they are to serve the purpose contemplated; the purpose, namely, of keeping the unity of the Spirit in the bond of peace.

In the first place, Love, if it is to inspire brotherly love of the right sort, must be of the right sort itself;—" Let love be without dissimulation; abhor that which is evil; cleave to that which is good." And, secondly, Brotherly love, if it is to claim kindred with such love as that, must make good its claim by its character;—" Be kindly affectioned one to another with brotherly love; in honour preferring one another." The love, and the brotherly love, must be of genuine quality.

1. The love must be unfeigned; "without dissimulation." And it must be discriminating; "abhor that which is evil; cleave to that which is good." In fact

it must be discriminating that it may be unfeigned. The love that does not discriminate, will invariably be found to be a love that dissembles.

Look, for example, at the easy sort of good-nature which passes current largely in the world for that good-will towards men which the angels welcomed in the birth of Christ. It is not certainly very discriminating. Is it very sincere? Are those who practise it remarkable for their freedom from dissimulation? Do they say the same things of one another that they say to one another? They are lax and easy enough in drawing the line between good and evil. There is not with them any very indignant or very repugnant abhorrence of what is evil; no very keen resentment of wrong; no vehement recoil from sin. Nor is there much of a " cleaving to that which is good." They may have good movements, and good impressions, by fits and starts, as it were, or upon random impulses. And if it comes to their hand naturally, and easily, they may have no objection to do good. They will themselves, however, be the first to confess that they are not too scrupulous or sensitive on that head. They are sincere so far as they go, but they are not straitlaced.

But are they really sincere? They say so. That is their boast. And they venture to think that this their sincerity may avail them before God as well as before men. They may not be altogether such as they should be; abhorring as they ought that which is evil, and cleaving as they ought to that which is good. They acknowledge that they do not always draw the line very carefully. But they are at any rate no dissemblers.

Is it so? Is it not on the contrary notorious, that those who are the least fastidious in open intercourse with doubtful company, are the most unscrupulous in their comments and commentaries behind backs? It has been happily and wittily said of those once famous Letters in which a worldly-wise father[1] sought to make his son as perfect in the world's wisdom and in the world's wickedness as himself, that whereas Paul's maxim is—Love without dissimulation, in his hands it might be read the reverse way—Dissimulation without love. This witness is true. The peace, and decency, and good order, of worldly society to a large extent depend on there being a common understanding on all sides, that what might be unpleasant shall be coloured, or shall be covered ; and that many things bordering on vice or folly shall be allowed to pass under some plausible disguise.

Would that we could limit this charge exclusively to worldly men ! to those who make no profession of evangelical holiness or evangelical love ! But alas ! even you who may be presumed to know something of that love of God to which your love ought to be conformed, are apt practically to lose sight of the unfeigned truth and the uncompromising holiness that it demands.

When you go among your fellow-men, when you mingle in society, you do not adopt the world's good-natured fashion of toying with what is evil and making light of what is good. You do not practise the world's convenient art of keeping up appearances with bright smiles

---

[1] Lord Chesterfield's Letters to his Son.

and honeyed words of feigned courtesy, covering and dissembling the real passions of the heart. In your presence, what is evil may not be obtruded offensively ; what is good may not be openly disparaged. So far your love may seem to be, and may really be, discriminating.

Again, when you speak, you do not actually say what you do not think ; you do not wilfully profess more than you feel, or anything else than you feel. So far your love may be allowed to be without dissimulation.

But as regards the first of these admissions, might it not be sometimes asked—When you return home from a social meeting, whether for business or for pleasure, would those you have been dealing or conversing with, gather from your demeanour while you were with them, that you abhor that which is evil, and cleave to that which is good ? Nay, might not their impression on the contrary be, that your abhorrence of evil is not very vehement, and your cleaving to good not very earnest ? There may be nothing tangible to which they can point. They cannot charge you with any one decided instance of compromise. They may even be forced to own that your presence did impose a restraint upon the company and the conversation ; that every approach to impropriety was checked and frowned down ; that much of what went on was even fitted to be useful. Still somehow, from your whole way of conducting yourself, they have taken up the idea, that while you must, for consistency's sake, be somewhat strict and grave, yet after all, you do not take things quite so seriously as they thought.

Ah! my Christian friends, beware of that facile and false kindness which is apt to usurp the place of love in your intercourse with the immortal beings around you. Yes; it is a false kindness, if when you go among them, you suffer them to get the notion that the difference between a state of sin and a state of grace is not so very decided as you would have them to believe ; that you do not think so badly of their case ; that the ways of godliness are not so very good, nor the ways of the ungodly world so very evil, even in your judgment, as they once imagined.

You may disguise your weakness under many plausible pleas. You would not take too much upon you. You do not like to be always thrusting forward your own peculiar views. It is harsh and unfeeling to be for ever finding fault. You must occasionally shut your eyes to some things, if you would get through the world peaceably. You cannot bear to be for ever damping gaiety and marring mirth. You need not be always wearing a solemn face, and uttering weighty sentences of wisdom. You may surely sometimes unbend, and be simply a man among your fellow-men, not everlastingly on your guard, but as it were standing at ease, and letting your Christian principles and punctilios for a season take care of themselves.

But will these, and such poor platitudes and truisms as these, avail to undo the evil influence that in a single instance may flow from your trumpet giving an uncertain sound? If your love is of such a sort as this, is it—let me now further ask—is it indeed without dissimulation ?

Without dissimulation !—Are you not dissembling your Christianity? Are you not dissembling your fixed

moral convictions, your deep religious faith? Are you
not dissembling your belief that the wages of sin is
death ; that sin is an abomination in the sight of God;
that the world lieth in wickedness; that the wicked
shall be turned into hell; that men must be born again ;
that if any man be in Christ he is a new creature ; that
without holiness no man can see the Lord ; that every
unconverted man is on the way to inevitable and eternal
ruin ; that for every idle word that men speak they must
give an account ; that it is a fearful thing to fall into
the hands of the living God ;—but that, on the other
hand, grace is sweet ; and God's favour is good ; and his
service is freedom ; and wisdom's ways alone are ways
of pleasantness, and her paths alone are peace ;—are
you not, I say, dissembling your belief of these things,
when you so live with your fellow-men, as to lead them
to ask, Would you live so if you believed them ?

And is that love? If the tender mercies of the wicked
are cruel, what shall we say of love like that in one calling himself a child of God?

A child of God! Is your Father's love of such a sort as
yours? Can any one doubt what He thinks of evil?
what He thinks of good? Can any one charge Him with
dissembling the truth, out of weak facility or false tenderness to the objects of his love? Ah ! His love is love
indeed, because it is so holy, and so true. A love indif-
ferent to the interests of holiness, a love keeping back
or compromising truth, would not be love at all. God
is love, because God is light. The light of inviolable
holiness, the light of eternal truth, sheds its highest glory

on the love of God; chiefly in that manifestation of
it through the faith of which you learn to love as
He loves. Behold the Father giving up his Son to die!
What abhorrence of evil is revealed in that act! what
cleaving to that which is good! How intolerable is sin
seen to be! and how inflexible righteousness! There is
no mincing of the matter in that Cross, no prophesying of
smooth things, no soft shading of realities too stern. That
Cross speaks very plainly. It dissembles nothing. It tells
the whole truth. And if on that account it be an offence
it is not so intended. For it tells the truth in love.

And you, brethren, have the same truth to tell; and in
the same love. This, which is the characteristic of the love
of God, must be the characteristic of your love too. Your
lips, your life, like that Cross, must reveal abhorrence of
evil, and a fast cleaving to that which is good. Your lips,
your life, like that Cross, must vindicate the claims of
righteousness, and stamp with righteous reprobation the
dark malignity of sin. Your lips, your life, like that Cross,
must be to all men an open exhibition of the truth. Your
lips, your life, like that Cross, must speak, and speak
plainly, of guilt and wrath, as well as of peace and joy.
Otherwise your love is false and wicked. It is man's
love ;—such love as may visit the breast of fallen man,
who cares little for truth, and less, if possible, for holiness. It is not the love that dwells in the bosom of the
true and holy God ;—of him who, when truth and holiness
seemed to be opposed to love, that he might blend the
three in one, spared not his only-begotten Son, but gave
him up to the death for us all!

2. Love, a love thus undissembled and undissembling, abhorring evil and cleaving to good, is the fit mother of a brotherly love, at once affectionate and humble, kind to others, lowly in its own esteem ;—" Be kindly affectioned one to another with brotherly love ; in honour preferring one another" (ver. 10).

Observe how such love as I have been attempting to describe may be traced as it passes into brotherly love. It goes forth, this love, honest and true, hating evil, cleaving to good ; or you, possessed by this love, go forth among your fellow-men. Your love embraces them all ; it longs for a response of sympathy from them all. But, alas ! too generally, it longs in vain. You come in contact, however, with some whom that love possesses, as it possesses you. They and you compare notes. You exchange with one another your thoughts and feelings. A new emotion springs up within you ; a new affection is generated. It is not an emotion of admiration merely, or of sudden surprise, as when a bright form of beauty first meets the eye. It is like that deep sense of home which fills the hearts of the children of one household, when, after long years spent apart, they find themselves together again in a foreign land. The thought of a home of love, and of a loving father there, whose image they all bear, whose love they all share, is freshly present to their minds. They feel themselves at home once more. This home-feeling, in a far country, among you who are the children of God, is brotherly love. The spirit of your home of love, which is heaven; the spirit of your loving Father, who dwells there ; is in you all.

Is it needful, let me ask in the first place,—is it not, on the contrary, almost a work of supererogation to exhort you, in such brotherly love as that, to be kindly affectioned one to another?

The brethren of Joseph were in a conspiracy of evil, held together by the tie, not of a common love, but of a common hatred. There was nothing in the feeling which made them one, fitted to soften or melt their hearts into any genial flow of kindness. For jealousy or envy is a cold, hard passion. It shuts up the bowels of compassion. To those who have been thus united, the admonition is far from being superfluous: " See that ye fall not out by the way." And if your Christian brotherhood is of this sort; if it is a union cemented rather by the spirit of human rivalry or resentment, than by the spirit of divine love ; the chances are that you will find yourselves agreeing better in the feelings which you indulge towards others, than in the feelings which you cherish among yourselves.

But your fellowship is not thus one of malice or ill-will, or a harsh judging of your neighbours. It is a fellowship of love in the Lord. And therefore you are called to put on bowels of mercies and kindness to one another. For the home feeling in a far country makes the children's hearts very tender ; so tender, that neither memory of old grudges, nor apprehension of new offences, can be suffered to part love again. It has a marvellous power to pull out every old root of bitterness, and to keep out every new one,—every new seed of irritation or estrangement. Cherish, then, ye children of your Father in

heaven, this home feeling, that ye may be " kindly affectioned one to another in brotherly love."

And that you may make sure of this, let me say to
you further, in the second place, see to it that your
brotherly love be as humble as it is kindly affectioned.
With bowels of mercies and kindness to one another, put
on also meekness; " in honour preferring one another."
" Let nothing be done through strife or vain-glory; but, in
lowliness of mind, let each esteem others better than himself " (Phil. ii. 3).

There was strife once in the little company of the
twelve as they followed Jesus on the earth.   They
disputed among themselves who should be the greatest.
This was at the time when they knew and believed
comparatively little of the love of God; when their
brotherly love, such as it was, had little or nothing in
common with that divine love ; but was, in fact, simply
earthly and human ; springing wholly out of the feeling
of their being pledged to a common Master and a common
cause; engaged in a common enterprise. So long as that
is their only bond of union, it is quite natural that, on
the one hand, they should rebuke those, however worthy,
who follow not with them ; and, on the other hand, that
they should dispute among themselves who should be the
greatest.   Accordingly, it has been always found that all
ecclesiastical combinations, whether churches, or sects, or
religious orders, formed upon this principle, have in them
the elements of these two sore evils, intolerance and ambition.   In any society of men, brought together and kept
together thus, as partisans, embodied to serve a purpose,

to gain an end, there must necessarily be the feeling that
all who are not with them are against them; and the honour
of taking the lead will be coveted and grasped as a lawful
prize.

It will not be so, when the Christian brotherhood is
felt to be, not an artificial organization of earth, but the
living spirit of love coming down from heaven ; the love
which dwells in the heart of God, reproduced in the heart
of a believing man, and recognising itself as reproduced
also in the hearts of other believers.

In a brotherhood thus created and born ;—for it is a
new creation, and a new birth ; a birth from above ; a
birth of the Spirit ;—in such a brotherhood there can be
no room, no place, for such merely human feelings as either
hostile suspicion of all who follow not with us, or eager
egotistic questioning as to who shall be the greatest. That
home feeling in the far country gives the death-blow to
self. We are all one. Which of us is above the rest, or
which beneath, is a small matter. We love one another as
brethren, for our Father's love that is in us, and our
Father's likeness that is upon us.

And for my part, each will say, I see more of that love
and of that likeness in my brethren, in the very least of
them, than in my best state I can find in myself.
I care not what his place and function, in the body,
may be ; or what mine may be, as contrasted with his.
He may be the door-keeper; I the priest. He may serve,
and I may rule. He may be a mere minister ; I, a
teacher and exhorter. Still, if he is a child of God, and
if I am one ; conscious as I am of sad shortcomings and

sins, I see my Father's love and my Father's likeness in
him, more than in myself.—As doubtless he, on the other
hand, having experience of his own infirmities, and not
of mine, giving me credit also—alas! how often too
credulously—for all that my office implies, thinks of me
far more highly than he ought ; and emptying himself, is
disposed to sit at my feet, who, alas! have too good
reason to feel, that in respect of many a lesson of meekness and obedience, I ought rather to be learning of him.

Thus, being kindly affectioned one to another, with
brotherly love, in honour we prefer one another; each
esteeming others better than himself.

Now, it is in this spirit of blended love and brotherly love;
love, pure and true as is the love that dwells in the heart of
God ; brotherly love, kind and meek as that home feeling
which makes an unselfish household one; that you are to
enter on the duties of your several callings in the Church
of Christ,—to prophesy, to minister, to teach, to exhort, to
rule, to give, to show mercy ; full of love to all, of
brotherly love among yourselves. These are the elements
or component parts of that living stream which is to set
in motion, and ever freshly keep in motion, all the acti-
vities of your Christian life ; the one element divine, the
other human ; together, by the electric spark of heavenly
grace, forming a pure river of the water of life, proceeding
from the throne of God, and of the Lamb. Whatever, as
members of the Church of Christ, you undertake and do,
it is thus that you are to undertake and do it; loving all
men, as God in Christ loves them, with a love that like

his condemns all sin, while it yearns to embrace every sinner ; loving one another, as Christ loved his own, for the Father's sake, who gave him them, and for their sympathy with him as the Father's Son ; loving one another, therefore, with a love, like his, of warmest fellow-feeling and of lowliest self-abasement. Animated by this double love, you will find every yoke easy, every burden light. It will be your meat to do the will of Him who sends you, to finish his work,—to go about doing good. It will be your joy to aid in every good work. It will be your special joy to aid in the good work of sending everywhere, and among all men, the glorious gospel of the grace of God, which proclaims the large and free benevolence of the Everlasting Father, and by means of which the Eternal Spirit is to gather into one brotherhood, in Christ the Son, the great multitude of all nations and kindreds, and peoples and tongues, who are to stand together before the throne of God and of the Lamb, clothed with white robes and palms in their hands, and to cry together, with loud voice, " Salvation to our God, which sitteth upon the throne, and unto the Lamb."

7

CHARACTERISTICS OF ACTIVE MEMBER-SHIP: DILIGENCE, FERVOR & SERVICE

"Not slothful in business: fervent in spirit; serving the Lord."
—*Romans 12:11*

THERE is no reference here to what men call the business of life. The verse is misinterpreted and misapplied when it is made, as it were, the priest or minister to celebrate a marriage-union between secular duty and spiritual devotion. Doubtless it is most desirable that such an alliance should be effected. In the case of a true Christian, there will be no divorce or separation between the ordinary every-day work of his worldly calling, and the worship of his closet and his heart. He may not, indeed, be willing to identify the two, or to speak as if he could fall in with the favourite formula of some, that work is worship. But he will not forbid the banns when it is proposed to join them in a holy and happy matrimony. He will have the twain to be one spirit. That diligence in the common business of life should be joined to fervency of spirit in religion, is a proposition, therefore, which he will admit and maintain. But if he is intelligent, he will look somewhere else than to this verse for his proof-text in support of it.

The word "business" here, is the same in the original

as the word "diligence" in the eighth verse of the chapter ;—" He that ruleth, with diligence." So here : "Not slothful as regards diligence." The term indicates, not the kind of work to be done, but simply the manner of doing it. It does not point to men's ordinary worldly callings and occupations, as in contradistinction to their spiritual exercises or spiritual frames. It is not the Apostle's present object to harmonize, and reconcile, and blend the two in one. The expression " business " characterizes, not the work, but the worker; not the action, but the agent. The real meaning is, that in respect of diligence, or activity, in the matter to which this whole passage refers, you are to be not slothful. It is very much the wise man's maxim : " Whatsoever thy hand findeth to do, do it with thy might" (Eccles. ix. 10).

The Apostle is still, let it be remembered, speaking of the different offices and functions which fall to be distributed among believers, as the many members of one body. He has in view, not what you have to do in your common character and capacity, as members of society in general, but what you have to do in your special calling, as members of the Christian society. No doubt, in a sense, the whole of your work, in the ordinary business of life, may be comprehended under that head. " Whether you eat or drink, or whatever you do, you are to do all to the glory of God." " Whatever you do, in word or deed, you are to do in the name of the Lord Jesus, giving thanks unto God, even the Father, by him." Every occupation of yours, like every creature of God, is to be " sanctified by the word of God and by prayer." You are not to separate what you

do as men from what you do as Christians. You cannot
thus divide yourself. It is the life which you live in the
flesh that you are to live by faith. All that is true.
But, on the other hand, it is no less true that your believing, your becoming members of Christ and of his Church,
not only invests old works and duties with a new character, but imposes new ones. It calls you to work for
yourselves and for society in a new spirit. It does more.
It calls you to work directly for Christ. You may say
that your working for yourselves and for society, in a new
spirit, is your working for Christ. It may be so. But
in any sense relevant to the Apostle's present appeal, it
can be so only when, in your so working for yourselves
and for society, you not merely cherish devout Christian
feelings in your own heart, but expressly aim at a
Christian object; the Christian object, namely, of commending Christ to others, and shutting them up into
him. It is in working with that aim, and for that
object, that you are to be,—I. Not slothful in business ;
II. Fervent in spirit ; III. Serving the Lord.

I. The word rendered " business," or " diligence,"—
denotes originally haste or speed. It conveys the idea of
eagerness, zeal, intense and earnest effort ; the doing of
what is to be done, as one would say, in a business-like
way,—with a will ; making a real business of it ; taking
it up in earnest, as a business that admits of no remissness, no slackness, no sloth.[1]

---

[1] Under the explanation already given, the practical idea involved in our
English word " business,"—that of real work as opposed to *dilettante* trifling—

You all know what this means in any worldly calling; and you know also how in every worldly calling, it is an indispensable condition of eminence and success. There must be industry; strenuous, unremitting, untiring industry; willing to forego the-luxury of ease, " to scorn delights, and live laborious days." For the most part, this is a faculty to be acquired ; a habit to be cultivated. It is a faculty which cannot be acquired too early ; a habit that cannot be cultivated too assiduously. It may cost you an effort ; nay, many an effort. Indolence is natural to you. Carelessness is natural to you. To fix and sustain the attention, to persevere in irksome toil, is a lesson which you must learn. You must learn it patiently and with much pains.

It is good advice, and advice which cannot be too often or too emphatically repeated, especially to the young ;—Learn this lesson soon, and learn it well. Accustom yourself, train yourself to this " diligence in business." Do this systematically in whatever you undertake.

---

may be turned to good account in enforcing the Apostle's maxim. In further confirmation of the view which I have adopted, it may be interesting to observe the harmony of our English versions. I subjoin, accordingly, the entire verse as it stands in the five translations preceding our present authorized one. Two of them, it will be seen, prefer the various reading in the last clause, of καίρῳ, time or season, for Κυρίῳ, the Lord. The others abide by the text as it stands :— " Not slowe in bisynesse, feruent in spirit, seruynge to the Lord."—*Wiclif*, 1388. " Let not the busynes which ye have in honde be tedious to you. Be feruent in the sprite. Applye youre selves to the tyme."—*Tyndale*, 1534. " Be not slouthfull in the busynes whych ye haue in hande. Be feruent in the sprite. Applye youre selues to the tyme."—*Cranmer*, 1539. " Not slothful to do seruice. Feruent in sprite. Seruing the Lord."—*Geneva*, 1557. " In carefulness not slothful. In spirit feruent. Seruing our Lord."—*Rheims*, 1582. " Not slothfull in busines : feruent in spirit. Seruing the Lord."—*Authorized*, 1611.

Act upon the principle, that whatever it is worth while to acquire, it is worth while to acquire thoroughly; whatever it is worth while to do at all, it is worth while to do well. Let it not be your object merely to get through your task or work with as little trouble to yourself as possible. Beware of a perfunctory, or a desultory, discharge of duty. Whatever you have on hand, give your mind to it as if it were the business of your life. It is so for the time. Let it be felt by you to be so. Sloth may raise difficulties ; " There is a lion in the way." Or there may be whispered in your ear that most dispiriting of all questions ;—*Cui bono?* What is the use ? . Resist that devil. Whatever you are about, trouble not yourself by asking what good may hereafter come of it. Give yourself to it wholly and heartily now. It is your calling now. As such, look it fairly in the face, and go up to it resolutely like a man. This way of doing business, and this alone, is worthy of your manhood. This is real work, earnest life. And it is this that the Apostle desires to see exemplified in the Church of Christ, and among you who are its members. It is thus that he would have you to undertake and prosecute the work of your Christian calling, to perform the functions of whatever you may find to be your office in the Church, the body of Christ, of which you are members.

Here, let it be observed, there is a peculiar difficulty, arising out of the nature of that work and these functions. They are essentially spiritual. They make a demand upon your spiritual tendencies and tastes. In any circumstances, the faculty or habit which is desiderated is of difficult acquisition. But the difficulty is less when the objects about which it is to be occupied are congenial to your temperament and inclinations. Nay, in such a case the difficulty is often scarcely felt at all.

Absorbed and wrapt in his favourite theme, the ripe scholar, the enthusiastic student, fastens on it, as if instinctively, the whole energy of his soul. The diligence, the earnestness, the systematic and persevering industry, which is such a forced effort to his less ardent comrade, is spontaneous and almost unconscious with him. He knows not what it is to grow weary of his work. In his way of doing business there is no sloth. So, also, any ruling passion, as the thirst of glory, or of riches, or of power, will keep the man whom it possesses always eager and on the stretch ; intent on what is his one great end in life. In the pursuit of that end he knows well what he is about. Nothing diverts his eye ; nothing slackens his speed. You need not preach attention and industry to him. No! nor need you preach it to that other man whom a higher motive sways, whom a more generous impulse prompts. To him, his patriotism, his philanthropy, or whatever noble sentiment inspires his breast, is business-habit enough, and business-talent too. There is no risk of slovenliness or supineness marring any enterprise of his. He is sure to do his work, like a true workman, in thorough business-like style and fashion ; for it is the work which his heart identifies with himself. His work is his life. Read the biographies of scholars, of ambitious generals, of statesmen, of philanthropists; and see their manner of doing the work of their several callings ! What untiring assiduity and perseverance,—what careful diligence,—is theirs! Truly there is no slothfulness in business with them!

It is apt to be otherwise when the work you have on hand is the Church's work ; the work of Christ, the Church's Head. That work is not according to the natural bent and bias of your minds. You do not take naturally to it. Even when you are renewed and quickened by the Spirit, and become spiritual men, it is not a work in which you can trust to the spontaneous working of your new affections, however warm, as if these were of themselves sufficient to secure its due performance.

This is a consideration of which you are all too apt to lose sight. And from not attending to it, you are liable to suffer loss and damage, as regards both the work of your own personal sanctification, on the one hand, and on the other, the work of whatever ministry may be yours in the Church of God.

1. Thus, as to the first of these great concerns, how often are you inclined, when serious impressions are made upon you, to imagine that your spiritual life is to go on, through all its stages of purification from evil and ripening for glory, very much as a life of feeling, and warm emotion, and strong affection! You are weary of routine. You have had enough of that. The very custom of bowing the knee at night and in the morning, familiar from your earliest childhood, is felt to be grievous, because it is so formal. You would now dispense with all forms and all formality. You are to be moved by an impulse from within, not regulated by

rules and restrictions from without. The new life in you will work itself out freely, spontaneously, if left to itself and its own natural development. To systematize or formalize it again, is simply, as you imagine, to kill it. To bring it at all under business rules, to turn it in any degree into a matter of business ;—thus to treat that new, free, fresh, living and loving faith, and living and loving fellowship, of which you have got some sense and taste ;—is to bind the old, servile chains of constraint and ceremony round your emancipated soul. You will not make a mere business of your religion any more. It is not to be a martinet's drill or a field-day's parade. It is to be all, at each successive moment, freshly and freely extemporized. So you think and feel, under the impulse of a spiritual awakening. You are impatient and intolerant of all that might give anything like a business air and aspect to your Christian life. You would have it to be not a practical, and perhaps painful, business-like realization,—but, as it were, an elevating ideal,—of good.

But if you are in earnest, you soon find that this will not do. You must, if you are to keep your ground and make progress, be methodistic. You must lay down a plan, you must adopt a method, and adhere to it. You must adjust your arrangements, and methodize your whole conduct, as you would do in a secular profession in which your worldly interests were embarked and your worldly all was at stake.

Do you at all know experimentally the power of that slothfulness which is so apt to creep over you in your religious experience ? How lifeless do you become, under its

influence, and how drowsy ! You cannot stir yourself up
to think or to feel. Neither sin's exceeding sinfulness,
nor the loving Saviour's exceeding beauty, moves you.
There is a strange insensibility creeping over you. And
it is the more distressing when you call to mind the
livelier emotions of your first love. You were not then
so dull and dead. You had gracious impulses and
heavenly inspirations then, in which you thought you
could place a life-long confidence. Your heart burned
within you. Oh ! but did you not make an idol of these
movements of the Spirit ? Did you not at all events
begin to reckon and rely on them ? You thought that they
would naturally, easily, spontaneously, without effort or
trouble on your part, work on till they worked out in
you the character that was to fit you for glory. It seemed
as if there was no occasion now for strict rules and severe
habits of application. Your new-born spiritual life would
unfold itself better untrammelled, untutored and un-
schooled. Alas! you forgot how slow and sluggish even
the renewed soul is in that new spiritual course on which
it enters, when it is awakened out of the sleep of death,
to receive the light of life ! You thought all would go
on well, when once you came under Christian impressions
and Christian influences. It seemed as if you were trans-
lated into a higher region, in which all must be left to
free, spontaneous impulse ; in which pains-taking, business-like, hard-working, and plodding industry is out of
place. Thus you start in the race, anticipating only
accelerated speed as you rush on impetuously. But it is
an up-hill race, as you soon discover. The old nature in

you, strained and thwarted, pleads for a little ease, a little rest. You flag and faint. You feel as if your first impressions were all effaced, and your first love all gone. It is a sad discovery. But count it not strange. Rather learn from it the lesson, that even in the spiritual life, free and fresh as it should ever be, you cannot dispense with discipline and rule. Your sanctification must be made a matter of business. It must be cared for and prosecuted in a business-like way ; not indolently and slothfully, as if it were a process that might be left to itself, but industriously, sedulously, diligently, with regularity and punctuality, as you would manage a worldly concern, on the common principles of worldly energy, and worldly care, and worldly zeal.

Oh ! that in this work of your soul's growth in grace and preparation for glory you were thus "not slothful in business !" Would that you brought to bear upon it the same systematic industry and attention that you would devote to the business of a secular calling on which your welfare in this world depended ! You would not then, as regards the best interests of your soul, live so loosely,— so much at random, and, as it were, by chance, as you are now but too apt to do. You would not be so ready as you are now to dispense with stated times and fixed rules and methods of devotion. You would task yourself, and have your self-imposed and self-enforced discipline of study, meditation and prayer. You would not disdain the help of means, and methods, and arrangements by which you might force yourself to take an interest in holy exercises and duties, which, without such strict rule, sloth might tempt you to evade. You would lay down the plan of your spiritual life, and suffer no interruptions to interfere with it. You would make conscience of your daily walk with God, in faith and love, being at least as systematically and strenuously attended to as your daily work in the world. You would methodize the one as you methodize the other. In the one, as in the other, you would be " not slothful in business."

2. In the work to which you are called, as it were officially, in the Church of Christ, as well as in the work of your personal growth in grace and in the knowledge of Christ, this faculty or habit of business-like energy and order is indispensable. Here, too, you are apt at first to fancy that mere feeling will carry you through. Under the impulse of your own fresh experience of the grace of Christ,—your first love,—you are moved to enlist under his banner. Yours is the fervour of new recruits, of ardent volunteers. What place will you not occupy, —what danger will you not face,—what will you not do and dare, in the ranks you have so eagerly joined, in the cause you have so warmly espoused? You spurn the drill and discipline of martinet routine. Your soul is all on fire for action. You will go forth at once on your work and office of "teaching transgressors the ways of the Lord, that sinners may be converted to him." You are impetuous and impatient. It is not stern duty with you, but strong excitement.

But, alas! may not all this be only, as it were, the undisciplined valour of enthusiasts, taking up arms hastily on the spur of the occasion? And is that to be preferred to the trained skill and hardihood of the regular soldiery, marshalled regularly for the battle ? Be sure that it is this last kind of force that in the long run will win the day. If you would fight for Christ, you must fight deliberately, with cool head as well as warm heart ; with fixed and resolute determination, upon principle rather than upon impulse. If you would work for Christ, you must work systematically, and you must work on with patient and persevering energy, with firm purpose not to give up or to give in.

There is the utmost danger of fitfulness and remissness here. You take up your position, you enter on your office, you begin your labour of love, whatever it may be, high in hope, sanguine and confident in your bright anticipations of success. There is even a sort of charm and halo of romance about your undertaking. How delightful to have something to do for Christ ; to be able, to be called, to make yourself useful in some way in his Church and for his cause ! Yes, you will be up and doing ; you will run to and fro on errands of divine love and affectionate brotherly kindness. You will instruct the ignorant ; you will warn the unruly ; you will reclaim the backslider ; you will train the young ; you will be a helper to the old ; you will visit the sick ; you will minister to the poor ; you will comfort the mourner ; you will speak a word in season to the weary. It will be no drudgery, no task. It will be your privilege, your pleasure, your chief happiness and joy.

Do I speak to any beloved brother or sister, any young Christian, whose bosom burns with such generous

sentiments, and such gracious feelings as these? Far be it
from me to damp the glowing ardour of your soul. It is
a right and good affection. Keep it, cherish it; let it
grow and increase more and more. But let me remind
you that "you have need of patience if you would so do
the will of God as to inherit the promise." For, alas!
who that has ever fairly tried the work;—to live for Christ,
to speak for Christ, to come to close quarters with men,
or women, or children, on Christ's behalf, to discharge a
Christian's duty, and do a Christian's office, among the
families around his dwelling, or among the members even
of his own family;—will not tell you that it is a work in
which pre-eminently you have need of patience?

Ah! my young friend, he will say, it looks all very easy
and pleasant beforehand ; it presents a fascinating picture
of days of usefulness, rewarded by nights of calm rejoicing
over much good done and many grateful thanks received.
But once get immersed and involved in it. You will
soon find that the picture has its dark side. The labour
even of love is not all light. You witness disagreeable
scenes. You come in contact with uncongenial manners.
Rough usage often awaits you. You have to encounter
stubbornness, stupidity, perverseness ; the opposition of
anger; or the still more provoking opposition of stolid
insensibility. And then your spirit flags ; your nerves
give way ; you get discouraged, disheartened, weak, and
weary; and it is often all you can do to drag your aching
limbs along the walk of customary duty ; the very walk
which, as the walk of joyous love, your feet once trod so
lightly.

Do I hear any advanced servant of the Lord complaining thus ? Ah, my brother ! you too I must remind that you have need of patience. You especially I must exhort to be " not slothful in business." Surely you laid your account with such annoyances as these when you consented to follow Christ. He who called you to follow him bade you count the cost. He told you what you had to expect when, as the Father sent him into the world, so he sent you into the world. Is the disciple above his Master ? Is the servant above his Lord ? Ye have not yet resisted unto blood, striving against sin. Consider Him who endured such contradiction of sinners against himself, lest ye be weary and faint in your mind. And that ye may not be weary, that ye may not faint in your mind, consider how he endured it; in what spirit, and after what manner. "Wot ye not that I must be about my Father's business?"—that was his motto throughout. Let it be yours. I must be about my Father's business. It is not my pleasure, but my Father's business. I must be about it as my Father's business, whatever my own frames and feelings may be. It is my Father's business, and it must be done, not for my gratification, but for his glory.

This then is the meaning of the Apostle's maxim, or precept, in both the practical applications of which it is susceptible.

In the first place, make a business of your personal Christianity ; the cultivation of your Christian character ; your progressive sanctification ; your walk with God ; your walk before God in the world. Make

this your business. Go about it; keep at it; in a
business-like way. Be diligent in it and about it as a
business; as the business of your lives. Make it your
business to be holy, to sanctify yourselves. Read, pray,
study, meditate, not as idlers obeying an impulse, but as
earnest men, diligently doing business. " Give diligence
to make your calling and election sure." " Giving all diligence, add to your faith, virtue; and to virtue, knowledge;
and to knowledge, temperance; and to temperance, patience;
and to patience, godliness; and to godliness, brotherly-kindness; and to brotherly-kindness, charity. For if these
things be in you, and abound, they make you that ye
shall neither be barren nor unfruitful in the knowledge of
our Lord Jesus Christ" (2 Peter i. 5–8).

And do all this as earnest men, diligently doing business. Force yourselves often, when you are not inclined,
to engage in religious exercises and duties, or to perform
acts of self-denial, even when it is, so to speak, against
the grain. Be regular, systematic, pains-taking, persevering; fixed in your adherence to some well-considered and
well-ordered plan of self-discipline and godly study. No
matter though it may be sometimes irksome. Hold on,
as earnest men, not slothful in business. Your diligence
will have its reward. The Lord will enlarge your hearts.
Your toil, even if it be a toil, will become a pleasure.
Your path being the path of the just, will be as the shining light, which shineth more and more unto the perfect
day. And oh, how blessed, to be secured by such a habit
against the self-indulgence and self-seeking, against the
fitfulnesses and inconsistencies, that are so apt to charac-

terize an indolent and uncertain Christianity; and so to be enabled to " adorn the doctrine of God our Saviour by a life and conversation in all things becoming the gospel ! "

And, secondly, as workers for Christ, having offices to fill and functions to discharge, in your capacity of members of his body, make a business of whatever your hand findeth to do, and be diligent in it and about it as a business. Put yourselves as it were in harness. Set about doing good, not upon impulse, but after a business-like fashion, diligently. Lay your account with meeting what will be but too likely to cool the ardour of your fitful enthusiasm, if that be your only or your chief motive. The business of doing good as you have opportunity may often weary you. It sometimes wearied Christ. Still he remembered, and do you remember, that it is his Father's business ; his Father's and your Father's. Regarding it in that light, you will not suffer yourselves to " grow weary in well-doing." You will resist all such tendencies. You will hold on ; and as you hold on, you will more and more find your growing insight into the character of him whose business it is, and your growing sympathy with him in his business, turning all into a labour of love indeed. You will become more and more engrossed in it, as a labour of love. It will be to you, this business of your Father, which is the doing of good and the saving of souls, as little of a drudgery, and as much of a delight, as ever the high toil of learning was to the most ardent student, or the sleepless care of empire to ambition's most aspiring votary. It will be your meat to do your Father's will.

II. As in respect of the diligence with which the Lord's work is to be done, you are to be not slothful; so in respect of the spirit in which it is to be done, you are to be " fervent."

The idea suggested by the word "fervent," is that of water heated to the boiling point. The figure is common in poetry and rhetoric. We speak of a man boiling with resentment; boiling over with rage. And the more generous and gentle affections, as well as the fiercer passions, are represented as working in this way. A patriot's soul boils over with indignation at his country's wrongs. A kind heart boils over with compassion when it sees a brother's woe. Warmth, enthusiasm, zeal; amounting even, if there be occasion, to passionate grief, or pity, or anger; such is the frame or temperament here commended or enjoined.

The fervency, however, is to be spiritual. It is not animal excitement. It is not the natural fire or fervency of a hot and heady temper; or of keen, nervous sensibility and susceptibility; or of vehement personal feeling, unaccustomed to self-control. Fervency of one or other of these, or the like kinds, has often taken possession of Christian men, in their devotions and their doings, with little credit or profit to the cause of Christianity. Many a season of revival has been thus marred; many scandals, and even crimes, have had a sacred halo shed in this way over the bad motives that prompted them. The wrath of man has thus sought to work the righteousness of God. Worship has got to be a frenzy, and work a riot or a fight, through nature's boilings and boilings over being mistaken for those of grace and of the Spirit.

For it is in the Spirit that you are to be fervent. So the clause may be understood: and probably so it ought to be understood. The expression indeed must be admitted to be ambiguous or doubtful. "Fervent in spirit," is a fair enough way of putting it. And the meaning may be, that you are to be fervent in your spirit; fervent in the spiritual part of your nature; fervent in that new spiritual life and being of yours into which, as members of Christ and of his body, you enter. You are spiritual men. It is as spiritual men, and not merely as business men, that you are called to undertake offices and functions in the Church,—to work in, and with, and for, Christ. See that in your spirituality you are fervent. Let yours be not a cold or lukewarm spirituality, but a spirituality that is hot and boiling. On the other hand, it may with at least equal propriety be maintained, that it is the Holy Spirit, as personally dwelling in you, that is meant. "Fervent in the Spirit" is an exact rendering of the original. But in fact the two renderings are at one: fervent in spirit; fervent in the Spirit. The fervency is, in every view of it, spiritual. It is so, inasmuch as it is fervency, not in the natural, but in the spiritual part of you: fervency working in you, not as carnal, but as spiritual. And it is so also because it is fervency wrought in you by the Holy Spirit. The last clause of this triune verse undoubtedly refers to Christ personally;—" serving the Lord." There is a congruity or suitableness in there being a reference also in the second clause to the Holy Spirit personally. And the three clauses thus hang well together. Do your work—or rather, be about your

Father's business—diligently; let there be no slackness or sloth in your diligence. Do it as those who are warmed by the Holy Ghost. Do it as those who serve the Lord Christ.

This fervency, then, is to be spiritual. It is to have its seat in the heart's core of your spiritual life; it is to be the direct fruit of the Spirit there.

1. Observe, in the first place, generally, that to be fervent in spirit is something more than mere earnestness. Doing the work simply as a matter of business, you may do it very earnestly; taking a real interest in it, throwing your whole soul into it. But the interest which you take in it may be such as you might take in any employment that stimulated your activity and gave scope for the exercise of your natural sensibility. You may throw your soul into it, as into some heroic enterprise or sentimental scheme, that had power to charm by its novelty or fascinate by its romance. But the essential element of real spirituality may be wanting; and with much bustling stir and much boiling enthusiasm in what you take to be religious work and duty, you may still need to be affectionately warned, that "to be carnally-minded is death, but to be spiritually-minded is life and peace."

For genuine spirituality is faith; intelligent and loving faith; not feeling, but faith; the faith which understands, embraces, loves the Saviour Jesus Christ. It reposes on a calm sense of the love of God in his Son. It is the peace of God which passeth understanding, keeping your hearts and minds through Christ Jesus.

2. Hence, let it be observed, in the second place, more particularly, as to what it is to be fervent in spirit,—that it is a frame or habit of mind opposed to that turbulence which invariably marks, more or less, the religious strivings of those whose consciences are uneasy and unsettled on the great question of their personal standing before God; their acceptance in his sight. Look at such a one as Paul, while he was yet a Pharisee. He was no tame, self-righteous formalist. He was no dull plodder, pacing with unflagging diligence the incessant round of pious observances, working hard as any dray-horse at his appointed task or self-imposed toil. There was fire in his eye, and boiling passion in his bosom. He was zealous, even to slaying. He would compass sea and land to make proselytes. Fervent he was : and one would say his fervency was surely spiritual. It all related to spiritual matters. It was all expended on spiritual movements and spiritual objects. But it bore the impress of an unquiet conscience and a mind ill at ease. The man was working, often in hot haste and with a sort of fierce energy; lacerating himself, persecuting others. But it was the haste and energy of one unhappy, and struggling almost with despair. Or if in another mood of mind, he came forth from his devotions in the temple exulting, and went abroad on his service of duty, even joyous, there might be seen in his conscious look and air of complacency and defiance, the working of a soul rather for the moment on good terms with itself, than permanently reconciled and habitually submissive to its God. Thus to vibrate or alternate between the desperate vehe-

mence of one who battles for his very life, and battles, alas! in the dark, and the heady impetuosity of one whom a fit of self-assurance has elated,—this is a state or habit of soul not allied, but opposed, to that genial, perennial glow of warm affection, which alone is worthy to be called fervency of spirit, such fervency as the Holy Spirit inspires. For that is a frame of mind peculiarly and pre-eminently unselfish ; free alike from the feverish agitation of selfish fear, and from the fitful excitement of selfish confidence.

3. Hence again, let it be observed, still more particularly, in the third place, that the very first condition of this spiritual fervency is that clear insight into the divine method of peace, or that belief of the truth as it is in Jesus, which casts out self-righteousness, self-seeking, and self-esteem. "It is a good thing that the heart be established with grace, not with meats, which have not profited them that have been exercised therein" (Heb. xiii. 9). It is so on many accounts and for many reasons; among others for this, that the grace which establishes the heart, while it quenches one fire there, kindles another and a better ;—brighter, purer, warmer by far.

The fire which it quenches is the fire of merely natural feeling in religion : the natural feeling of selfish anxiety and alarm on the one hand, or the natural feeling of selfish elation on the other. That fire may burn very strongly, causing the swelling tide in your agitated bosom to boil fiercely over. Your natural feelings, stirred and quickened by some spiritual movement,— some work of the Spirit in you,—may raise a violent tumult in your bosom. Remorse of conscience, an awful sense of sin, a terrible fear of wrath, the horror as of an open vision of heaven all but lost and hell already near, may possess you; and under that impulse you may apply yourselves hastily, and oh, how vehemently and warmly, to whatever your hand findeth to do that may "the tempest of your boiling blood becalm." Relieved perhaps by some desperate expedients of self-righteous zeal, with a rebound from that dark agony, you rush to the very opposite extreme. Your heated soul now swells with latent pride; the pride of conscious merit, disguising itself under the mask of fervent and even passionate devotion ; such devotion as might light the flame of a new crusade, or send another Jesuit Zavier to convert the Indies. These feelings, of either kind, are real and genuine. They often prevail, more or less, wherever religious earnestness is revived. But they are simply natural. They are occupied, no doubt, about spiritual things, conversant with spiritual thoughts and experiences, occasioned and caused by spiritual movements. It may even be a work of the Holy Spirit in the inner man that gives rise to them; a work of conviction and awakening. Still they are not the proper fruit of the Spirit. If His work is arrested when such feelings merely are produced; if from any cause it stops short there; it is not saving: nor is the fervour that may spring out of it spiritual fervour. It is, on the contrary, essentially carnal. It is of the flesh. And the works it does are works of the flesh. It is the fervour, not of the Spirit, but of nature : of nature put in agitation by contact with the Spirit's fire, but still of nature only. It is nature, or the natural feelings, worked upon by the things of the Spirit of God.

But now let grace prevail, the grace by which the heart is established; the free, rich, sovereign grace, which the glorious gospel proclaims; the grace, gratuitous, unconditional, unreserved, which the Father holds out to you in the Son, and which the Spirit moves you to accept. Be ye under grace; let grace reign in you, through righteousness, unto eternal life. Let the work of the Spirit in you be, not initial merely, but conclusive—not partial, but complete and thorough. Let Him thoroughly and completely unite you to Christ, and show you how thoroughly you are complete in Christ. Let there be no more attempts on your part to right yourselves with God, or even any wish to right yourselves with God, by any painful discipline of self-imposed penance, or any great doings, such as excited feelings of contrition and fear might prompt you to aim at. Nor let there be any more of the sort of high-wrought complacency which the idea of your righting yourselves with God is sure to foster. Let God put you right with himself. Believe that he does so, and trust him accordingly. Receive his love as his own gift, his present gift, absolutely and out and out his gift, his gift to you. Accept at his hands free pardon and peace; full pardon, perfect peace. Upon the credit of his own word, believe and be sure, that "he hath given to us eternal life, and that this life is in his Son," (1 John v. 11.)

Plainly now, in the first place, those old natural fires, which, when fanned by winds from the spiritual region, made the heart and bosom burn, are extin-

guished and die out. There is no room now for the feelings of keen self-torture, or hot and heady self-elation,
which once by turns inflamed the unsteadfast soul.
And then, secondly, new fires are kindled; feelings of
an entirely new kind come in to occupy the place of the
expelled. Ah! how far more gentle are they, and how
far more calm! and withal, how warm, how steadily and
uniformly warm! Not spasmodic bursts of flame, but a
quiet and constant glow, now keeps the heart aboil.
They fluctuate, it is true, these feelings. Their new fire
too often flickers. Alas! the more the pity. There is
nothing in them or about them that should make them
fluctuate or flicker; nothing like the exciting and ex-
hausting fury of those passions which may rend the
untamed and unsubdued spirit of a proud and guilty man
in pieces. The feelings which are to warm you for work,
and to keep you warm in working, are of a character to
continue with you;—and to continue with you substantially always the same. For the source of them continues
always the same. That source is Christ; Christ living
in you; Christ in you, the hope of glory. Let his word
dwell in you richly. Let the love of God in Christ be shed
abroad in your hearts by the Holy Ghost, which is given
to you. Go to work now; keep at work now; under the
influence of that love, known, believed, felt by you to be
all freely yours. Will not this make you not only diligent in business, but fervent in spirit, at your work?

Oh, with what fervour should your bosom glow, ye who
are thus debtors to grace, when you go about your Father's
business, counting it your meat to do the will of Him that

sends you, and to finish his work! You go about it all as his children, accepted in the Beloved. Of every one of you, as of him, the Father says, "This is my beloved son, in whom I am well pleased." On every one of you, as on him, the Holy Ghost descends like a dove. In every one of you, as in him, the Spirit, crying "Abba, Father," dwells. How can you work coldly, hardly ;—as if it were upon mere compulsion ; as if you were driven to it by dire necessity, by the lash ; as if you could only make a toil and drudgery of it? How can you work thus at the business of such a Father, of one who deals with you so graciously, receives you so fondly, loves you so freely? Surely, if at any time you find his business, any business of his that he would have you to go about, hanging heavy on your hearts; if ever, when he says, "Son, go work in my vineyard," you are tempted to say, "I will not;" or if you go, to go with a grudge and as to a task ;—surely it is a sign that your faith is failing. Surely, when you love little, you forget how much you are forgiven.

Is it so? Is it because you feel sin less than you once did,—that you feel the love shown in its forgiveness less than you once did also? Is that the reason why, in your religious duties, in working the work of Him that sends you, you are less fervent in spirit than you would desire to be,—perhaps than you were wont to be?

Then read and ponder that wondrous passage in which the prophet Isaiah records the manner of his preparation for the office he was to fill, and the work he was to accomplish.[1]

---

[1] "In the year that king Uzziah died I saw also the Lord sitting upon a throne, high and lifted up, and his train filled the temple. Above it stood the

Let the Spirit carry you where he carried the prophet of old. Let Him place you where he placed him; within the veil. Let Him show you what he showed him; the Lord sitting upon a throne, high and lifted up, his train filling the temple;—seraphim standing above; one crying to another, "Holy, holy, holy is the Lord of hosts: the whole earth is full of his glory." Then, in that awful presence, let the Spirit smite you, as he smote the prophet, and lay you flat upon your face before the Holy One. Let him bring your own sin, that you have been ceasing to feel, and the world's sin, that you have been beginning to tolerate, vividly before your startled eye. Let him move you as he moved the prophet, under a new discovery of the Lord's holiness and sin's exceeding sinfulness, to exclaim, "Woe is me! for I am undone; because I am a man of unclean lips, and I dwell among a people of unclean lips: for mine eyes have seen the King, the Lord of hosts." Then let the Spirit minister to you, as he ministered to the prophet's prostrate, stricken soul. Let a live coal from off the altar touch your mouth. Hark! what words are these? "Lo, this hath touched thy lips; and thine iniquity is taken away, and thy sin purged." Yes, if you

---

seraphims: each one had six wings; with twain he covered his face, and with twain he covered his feet, and with twain he did fly. And one cried unto another, and said, Holy, holy, holy is the Lord of hosts: the whole earth is full of his glory. And the posts of the door moved at the voice of him that cried, and the house was filled with smoke. Then said I, Woe is me! for I am undone; because I am a man of unclean lips, and I dwell in the midst of a people of unclean lips; for mine eyes have seen the King, the Lord of hosts. Then flew one of the seraphims unto me, having a live coal in his hand, which he had taken with the tongs from off the altar: and he laid it upon my mouth, and said, Lo, this hath touched thy lips; and thine iniquity is taken away, and thy sin purged. Also I heard the voice of the Lord, saying, Whom shall I send, and who will go for us? Then said I, Here am I; send me" (Isa. vi. 1–8).

are forgetting your first love, repent and do the first works. Get anew much forgiveness for your much sin. Then, when you hear, as the prophet heard, the voice of the Lord, saying, "Whom shall I send, and who will go for us?"—it will be with no cold sense of irksome duty, but with much love, springing out of much forgiveness, that, fervent in spirit, you will join the prophet in his prompt and eager reply, "Then said I, Here am I; send me."

III. As in any and in every work you have to do, you are to be diligent in business and fervent in spirit, so you are to do it always as "serving the Lord." You are to do it, not as a work voluntarily undertaken, but as a service imposed and required by a master.

It is true that, as in Isaiah's case, the Lord may seem to put it to yourselves to come forward for his service of your own accord. In great kindness and condescension, he allows you the satisfaction of offering yourselves as volunteers. Your engagement with him is to have the grace, or graceful aspect, of being not so much a stern command on his part, leaving you no alternative but to enlist; but rather, in the first instance, a spontaneous act on your part, hastening to place yourselves and your services at his disposal.

Let it be observed, however, in the first place, that to one exercised as the prophet has been exercised, to one dealt with as he has been dealt with, the very hearing, or as it were overhearing by accident, that voice of the Lord, "Whom shall I send, and who will go for us?" has all the force of a command. He must feel that the very

idea of that Holy One, by whom he has been so wonderfully humbled first, and then lifted up, having work to
be done, errands to be executed, lays him under an obligation to say, " Here am I." He has absolutely no alternative here, any more than if the most peremptory order had
been issued. He is very thankful for the generous consideration which allows him to have the pleasure of volun-
teering ; but he cannot on that account for a moment
imagine that he has really any discretion in the matter,
or any right to hesitate or hang back.

And then, secondly, at all events, when he is enlisted
and engaged; when his offer is accepted, and he is taken
at his word ; he is clearly now a servant under the yoke.
He is not at liberty to decline any work that may be
assigned to him, however difficult and laborious; however
perilous and painful to flesh and blood. It may be different from what he anticipated; not so pleasant, not so
honourable. But what of that? When he offered himself, he asked no questions; he had no right to ask any.
He stipulated for no conditions; it would have been
unbelief to do so. Unreservedly he said, " Whatever be
the errand, here am I; send me." And he cannot qualify
his offer, or attempt to make terms, now. Nor is this all.
Not only must he undertake, as a servant, whatever work
the Lord appoints; but he must go through with it as a
servant. He must feel himself to be a servant, bound to
do the work, be it what it may. He must feel himself
to be a servant, from first to last, in the doing of it.

This is a most important point, a most material element, as regards the manner in which the Lord's work

is to be done. It is essential to harmonize and temper the other two qualities: diligence in business, and fervency in spirit. The three agree in one. You may do the Lord's work with untiring business-like industry and attention. You may do it with lively interest, with warm, affectionate enthusiasm. You may be busy about it, and fervent about it; throwing into it your whole heart, as well as your whole mind and soul. And yet there is a risk of it being ill done after all, if you forget that you are to do it as the Lord's servants, and as all throughout apprehending and realizing yourselves, in the doing of it, to be the Lord's servants.

But is not this, you may ask, a lowering of the whole tone and style of my intercourse with the Lord, and my engagement for his work? After all seemed to be placed on the footing of a large and free commerce of love and confidence;—when the adjustment of the whole question of my standing with God, and my relation to him, had been taken out of the hands of law, and out of the category of legal bargaining, and transferred to a higher region, in which grace and honour reign;—am I again to come down to the level of a menial condition, and own myself to be a servant? Yes, brother; and if you please, a hired servant too. And why should this offend you? It did not offend Christ when he was doing his Father's work on earth. He did it as a servant; yes, even as a hired servant; when, "for the joy that was set before him, he endured the cross, despising the shame." Would you be better or higher than he? Nay, for that matter, would you choose to be like the ungodly? They are impatient of the position of a servant. " Our lips are our own ; who is lord over us ?" " Who is the Almighty, that we should serve him ?"—that is the language of their hearts. Let us be our own masters. By all means let us show our respect and do our duty to our Maker. But let it be at our own discretion. We shall take our own time and our own way of doing it. That such should be their feelings need not appear surprising ; but that any of you who believe, and believing, are the Lord's children, should in any measure sympathize with them in such feelings, is surely passing strange and sad.

And yet you are sometimes tempted almost to wish that you were left more to yourselves in your religion. It seems a poor way of manifesting the fervency of love, to be merely obedient servants, keeping the command- ments of a master. You would do some greater thing. You would devise some more excellent way. You would work unbidden; you would run unsent. Trust us, you are tempted inwardly to say to your Lord and Saviour ; let us be put upon our honour. Instead of always reminding us that we are thy servants, and thou our Lord, confide in our good faith, and see if the generous impulse of warm affection, seizing spontaneously on the best means and methods of pleasing him who is its object, will not go further than the most scrupulous sense of duty, executing, as a servant, the orders even of the very best of masters.

So you may be apt to feel, when your soul boils over with love to Him who first loved you, and your heart burns within you. But beware lest in all this there be something like a lurking inclination to evade the idea of obligation and responsibility. That idea is not naturally a welcome one ;—no, not even always to you who are no more servants merely, but friends and sons as well. But why should it not be welcome? Obligation and responsibility are not badges of degradation. On the contrary, for intelligent creatures, on a right footing with their Creator, they are elements and conditions of highest glory and purest joy. Angels in heaven now work as servants; nay, as hired servants; for He whom they serve will never accept service unrequited. They work as servants, under obligation; upon their responsibility. It is in that character and capacity that they are summoned to join in the universal song of praise ;—" Bless the Lord, ye his angels, that excel in strength, that do his commandments, hearkening unto the voice of his word. Bless ye the Lord, all ye his hosts; ye ministers of his, that do his pleasure" (Ps. ciii. 20, 21). Saints in heaven hereafter will work in like manner; in fact, one chief element of heaven's blessedness and glory is this, that there " His servants shall serve him" (Rev. xxii. 3). And be sure that as to all your work here on earth, you will do it all the better if you do it, not as at your own hand, but as " serving the Lord." It is thus only that your diligence in business will be conscientious, and your fervency in spirit constant and consistent. Your whole religion, personal and official ;—personal, as bearing on your own sanctification and salvation; and official, as it relates to the doing of the Lord's will in the world, and the executing of your mission from the Lord into the world ;—your whole religion will possess a strong and stable character; it will have all the stability and strength of a threefold cord that is not quickly broken. It will be your life-business, to which, as your life-business, you will not slothfully, but sedulously and systematically, devote your energy. It will be your life-joy, your labour of love, in which your fervent soul delights to give scope and vent to the grateful and gracious feelings that the Spirit causes to rise up and boil over in your bosom. And it will be your life-business and your life-joy, because it is your life-service;—your life-service, of which you calmly and steadily at all times make conscience. For you work and watch as servants, looking for the coming of Him who is to call you to account; who is bountifully, liberally, generously to recompense the very giving of a cup of cold water in his name; and from whose gracious hands they who are faithful unto death are to receive the crown of life.

8

CHARACTERISTICS OF ACTIVE MEMBER-SHIP: HOPE, PATIENCE & PRAYER

"Rejoicing in hope; patient in tribulation; continuing instant in prayer."
—*Romans 12:12*

THESE three features of character, or habits of the inner life, are intimately connected. They are qualities most important to all who work in the Church and in the cause of Christ, as members of the one body of Christ; having different gifts and offices; animated by a love that is genuine and discriminating, true and pure, and a brotherly love that is affectionate and humble; diligent in the work as a matter of business; fervent and zealous about it as a spiritual concern; and conscientious in it as the service of the Lord.

Believing in Jesus, and called as believers to be fellow-labourers with him, you have need of a temper or frame of mind equal to either fortune; not insensible to the joy of hope, yet capable of endurance when trouble comes; and finding at once the outlet of its joy, and the stay and strength of its endurance, in that prayer of faith in which it continues instant evermore. For it is this last habit of the inner life that firmly binds and knits together the other two; and imparts to the feeblest member of

Christ's body, working with fear and trembling the Lord's work, a character of serene inward equanimity, whatever the outward aspect of affairs may be ; such a character of equanimity as, in philosophic schools, is wont to be considered the highest and rarest attainment of human wisdom. To rise above the influence of things without,—things over which the mind has no control ; to steel the heart, in stern insensibility, as in a panoply of triple brass, against feelings of pleasure or pain, of weal or woe ; is the idle boast of stoical virtue or stoical pride. To be praying always; holding on and continuing instant and incessant in prayer ; is your far better specific for preserving an equal mind, whatever may befall you ; preserving it, not at the cost of a warm, loving, feeling heart, that may be moved to tears and gladness ; but by means of that heart's communion, in its gladness and in its tears, with its God. Your joy in hope, and your patience in tribulation, are sustained and sanctified by your continuing instant in prayer.

I. You are to be found at your appointed post, and in your allotted labour, " rejoicing in hope." This is not your privilege merely, but your duty. It is the way in which the Lord would have you to go about his work, whatever your department of that work may be. He would have you to go about it hopefully, and therefore joyfully ;—in a hopeful, and therefore a joyful, spirit ;— 1. In hope ; and, 2. Rejoicing in hope.

1. You work in hope. You ought to see, and feel, and acknowledge that you do so.

The word "hope," as here used, refers, it must be admitted, not so much to the inward sentiment as to the outward occasion of it. The idea is that of your rejoicing when there is ground of hope—when matters look hopeful; just as the corresponding idea is that of your being patient when there is cause of trouble. But you all know how much the state of things around you,—the crowd of circumstances in the midst of which you are placed,—takes its colour from the mood of the mind within. A sanguine temperament will see brightest promise of dawning day where, to one apt to despond, there is nothing but the gloom of night. You are to rejoice in hope, in whatever is hopeful, in connection with the work given you to do. Plainly, if that is your duty, you must note what is hopeful. You must look out for it and recognise it. To let any hopeful sign or symptom escape your observation, is not only folly, but ingratitude and sin.

Almost all things on this side of the grave have their fair side as well as their foul. The blackest cloud has some lining of silvery white. "In everything give thanks," says the Apostle; "for this is the will of God in Christ Jesus concerning you." If that be the will of God, he must be understood as undertaking for it, that in everything you shall have some cause of thanksgiving. Let it be yours to seize thankfully some germ of hope, in every work and in every way of the Lord.

For yourselves, never despair. While there is life there is hope. In the worst straits of temporal distress; steeped in poverty; worn with sickness; heartbroken under the pressure of family sorrow, or family

sin; threatened with the loss of all earthly goods; ready
to say with Jacob, " All these things are against me ;"—
still search, be ever searching, for some gleam of hope.
Let your heart be cheered by the twilight of better
days that may be coming.   And in spiritual trials;
when you see not your signs; and there is none to tell
you how long; when your sin finds you out, and you
feel as if you could not find out your Saviour; still
never despair.   Watch and wait for something hopeful.
Lay hold of what is hopeful in your most desperate plight.
For there is always something hopeful in your most
desperate plight here below.   There is some word of God
borne in upon your mind.   There is some stirring of soul
within you; some moving of the Spirit upon its dark
and troubled waters.   There is some memory of Christ,
the sinner's Friend.   Lay hold of that.   Be sure that
there is hope for you still.   Catch, as a drowning man
would catch, at any straw.   If you are in earnest; if it
is really with you an affair of eternity, and of your soul's
salvation in eternity; what you catch at, in trembling
faith, will prove no straw, no shadow, but "a hope that
maketh not ashamed."

And in serving the Lord, as well as in seeking the
Lord, never despair.   It may be little that you can do for
him; and what little you can do, may seem to bear little
fruit.   What means have you, in your humble sphere, of
either glorifying God or doing good to men ?   Situated as
you are, destitute of advantages which others have,—
wealth, leisure, talent, influence—what opportunities of
usefulness can you find ?   Of what avail would it be for

you to offer yourself for any ministry in the Lord's cause,
or to take up any marked position on the Lord's side?
What hope could you have of being listened to, and attended to, in anything you might say? What hope of
anything you could do making any impression on Satan's
kingdom, or winning any trophy or triumph for the King
in Zion? Think not thus; feel not thus. It is a temptation. It is the suggestion of sloth, of selfishness, of unbelief. It is not true humility, but false pride. Rather
learn to take a hopeful view of your position, and of the
facilities which it affords for labours of love, as well as for
growth in grace. Think of what many, not so well off
by far as you, with tenfold more discouragements than you
have to contend with, have been enabled to become, and
have been honoured to accomplish ; children far younger
than you ; men far poorer than you ; women far weaker
than you ; merchants, artisans, lawyers, physicians, far
busier than any of you ; plain, simple Christians, of far
meaner capacity, and more slender endowments, than the
least gifted among you, in your most self-depreciating
mood, can pretend to be. Take courage then. Be decided.
Set about the work of living, testifying, acting for the
Lord, in all that you say and do. It is a hopeful work,
even for you. Set about it hopefully. Nor let the first
or second difficulty or disappointment you may meet
with—no, nor the hundredth, disconcert you, or drive
you to despair. Look out still always for hopeful
symptoms, hopeful signs. Do you stumble or fall?
Ask the Lord to raise you up again. Do you fail once,
or twice, or ten times? Ask the Lord to give you

grace that you may try again. Let the subject you
would operate upon be ever so impracticable, and let the
case you have to deal with be apparently ever so unmanageable, do not give him up, do not give it up as desperate. Continue to operate upon the impracticable subject,
and to deal with the unmanageable case, "against hope,
believing in hope" (Rom. iv. 18).

Christian father, Christian mother, despair not of thy
poor prodigal child ! Thou hast laid hold of the covenant
for him ; thou hast dedicated him to the Lord when he
was but a babe. Thou hast sown good seed in his soul,
and sought a blessing from the Lord on thy sowing of it.
Hold on hopefully in faith. All is not lost. There are
promises on which thy faith may fasten. There is ground
of hope in the faithfulness and pity of Him whose promises
thy faith grasps. Plead, then, with the child of thy love ;
pray for him. Plead with him and pray for him, continuing still hopeful. Child of God, little child, forced in
that dreary home of thine to recognise, in sister, brother,
father, mother, one whom Satan is leading captive ; when
thy tender heart is all but breaking ; pierced with many
a bitter pang ; as all thy earnest, plaintive entreaties, re-
monstrances and tears, are met only with rude and sinful
scoffing; be not altogether cast down. The wretched victim
and slave of vice,—whom still thou lovest so dearly,—
for the welfare of whose soul and body thou art so affec
tionately anxious,—for whose salvation thou wouldest lay
down thy life,—sees thee bending thy knee to God: hears
thee singing thy simple, holy hymn, or pouring out thy
heart in cries and supplications for mercy to the lost.

Be hopeful still. The meekness and gentleness of Christ shown in thee may,—shall I say, must?—by his own gracious blessing, prevail at last. Thy prayers and pains, thou mayest hope, will in the end win the day.

In every walk of common life, as well as in every enterprise of piety or philanthropy, the believer does well to cultivate a hopeful spirit, in serving the Lord. Accustom yourself, in all circumstances, to discover and dwell upon what is fitted, not to dishearten, but to cheer and encourage you, in fighting the good fight, and persevering in the right way. If it is the Lord's work that you are engaged in,—and whatever work you do, doing it unto the Lord, and for the Lord, becomes his,—it must be more or less hopeful. The Lord must see to it that in one way or another good shall come out of it. To think otherwise, would be ungrateful and ungracious. Learn, therefore, more and more, the lesson of anticipating good rather than evil, when you are doing good. Remember that true charity, genuine love, " hopeth all things."

2. Working thus in hope, you rejoice in the hope in which you work. It is a hope in which you may rejoice. For it is a hope " that maketh not ashamed."

It is of Christian hope alone that this can be said. All other hope is proverbially fallacious, and puts to shame those whom it misleads.

> " Condemned to hope's delusive mine,
> We onward toil from day to day ; "

—and still, as we toil on, thinking at every moment that we have the precious ore of happiness and full contentment in our grasp ; succeeding, and disappointed in our very success ; the mine of hope in which we are condemned to toil is felt, the longer we toil in it, to be more and more delusive. The joy of such a hope as that is like the " laughter of fools, which is as the crackling of thorns under a pot." It is like the joy of the belated wanderer in the dark and dreary wilderness, when his eye catches the dazzling meteor that is shining only to plunge him in the fatal bog.

But your hope, believers, is one in which you may confidently rejoice.

For, in the first place, its object is sure and satisfying; —sure of being attained ; satisfying when attained. For yourselves personally, it is the glory of God ; the approving smile and gracious reward of your reconciled Father, who is " not unrighteous to forget your work and labour of love." And beyond yourselves, apart from your own personal interest and concern, which is your complete salvation, you have a great and certain object of hope, in the final, glorious, and everlasting triumph of Christ and his righteous kingdom of peace. It is upon nothing doubtful, either as regards its being fulfilled at all, or as regards its giving contentment when fulfilled, that your expectation is set. Yours is a hope, sure of its object being got,—and sure also of its object, when got, being found to yield full and lasting bliss. For it is a hope bound up with the hope held out to your Redeemer and Lord himself, in that promise of the Father to him: " He shall see of the travail of his soul, and shall be satisfied."

Then, secondly, the ground or warrant of your hope is sure; it is the divine faithfulness; the faithfulness of the divine word. You set your hope in God. Your hope is in the Lord your God.

And, in the third place, the source of this hope in you may give you assurance of it. It is a hope wrought in you by the Lord himself. It is the fruit of the Spirit. You may appeal, therefore, to God and say, "Remember thy word unto thy servant, upon which thou hast caused me to hope" (Ps. cxix. 49). He will not make void the word which is his own. The hope which his own Spirit has caused you to place upon that word will not make you ashamed.

You may well, therefore, in every view of it, rejoice in hope, as you wait for the salvation of the Lord. And not only with reference to what is the end of your faith, as regards yourselves, which is the salvation of your souls; and with reference to what is the end of your desire and expectation, as regards the kingdom of God, which is the final overthrow of evil and the eternal victory of good;— not only with reference to these ultimate results, may you rejoice in hope ; but with reference also to whatever is promising and encouraging, in the meanwhile, in your present experience ;—as, on the one hand, you work out in detail your own salvation ; and as, on the other hand, you are busy in the particular labour which the Lord, from time to time, is giving you to do.

Whatever hopeful feature you discover in your own character, as by the Spirit's help you are seeking to mould and fashion it more and more according to the image of Christ; or in the character of any sinner with

whom, relying on the Spirit's help, you are dealing to
convert him; or in the character of any brother in the
Lord whom you would fain lead further away from sin
and further on in holiness;—whatever favourable indication,—whatever hopeful appearance,—you discern in
yourselves or in others, of a change for the better,—of
progress,—of advancement;—rejoice in it. Whatever
hopeful circumstance shows itself in any department of
the Lord's service in which you are engaged; in any mis-
sion-field, home or foreign, which has had enlisted on its
behalf your sympathies, your prayers, your abundant
liberalities, your scanty alms, or your personal ministra-
tions of any kind;—if anything hopeful meets your eye,
or reaches your ear, concerning the Sabbath class you
are teaching, or the families you are visiting, or the
society you are managing, or the tracts and Bibles you
are circulating, or whatever your labour of love may be;—
should there be any really hopeful promise of good,
among the hungry, the naked, the sick, the prisoners, to
whom in the Lord's name and for the Lord's sake you
minister;—rejoice in it. Be sure that it is a legitimate
and trustworthy occasion of joy. Wherever, and in whatever, there is good hope through grace,—there, and in
that, there is cause of joy. It may be a fearful joy that
you snatch. There may be too good reason why you
should rejoice with trembling. Experience may have made
you cautious. Your sadly acquired knowledge of human
nature, alike in the young and in the old whom you have
been trying to guard or to reclaim; and the memory of
too many instances in which you have been mistaken or

deceived,—when those who seemed to run well have broken down, or turned aside ; may cause you to be suspicious and incredulous when new cases of good done, or of good got, come before you. Beware of such a temper ; beware of such a tendency growing upon you. It fits too well and too easily into your natural love of ease, and your inclination to excuse yourself from self-denying toil and trouble, by the plea of its being all in vain. Do not hesitate,—be not afraid,—freely and heartily to rejoice in hope. It is a miserable thing to have the warm and living spirit of love chilled and deadened by that sort of universal scepticism, which will believe neither God nor man; which will give credit to no promise of God, and no profession of man. Better far to be the dupe of a whole host of hypocrites and impostors; to trust and trust again ; and again and again to have my trust belied and betrayed ; to be a very proverb and byword for facility in believing all things, and thinking evil of no man; than to settle down into a universal questioner and doubter ; labouring to do good, perhaps, out of a constraining sense of duty; but in utter hopelessness of almost any good being done ; taking always the worst view of things ; refusing to be cheered by any tokens or any tidings of success. The service of the Lord, the loving service of the God of love, is not thus joyless and heartless. It is the service of the heart; of a heart that is hopeful ; of a heart that rejoices in hope.

II. But while thus you work in hope, and rejoice

in the hope in which you work, you have need of patience; you are required and commanded to be "patient in tribulation."

"You are saved by hope; but hope that is seen is not hope; for what a man seeth, why doth he yet hope for? But if you hope for that you see not, then do you with patience wait for it" (Rom. viii. 24, 25). And you wait, prepared to be "patient in tribulation."

For however quick you are to discern, and sanguine to grasp, whatever is hopeful in the Lord's dealings with yourself, or with those whose good you seek, you are not blind or insensible to what is of an opposite character. Your rejoicing in hope is not the fond conceit and fool's paradise of one who shuts his eyes to the annoyances of his real position, and laps himself in some dream of ideal conquest, and rest, and glory. It is a sober habit of mind. It is the habit of a mind accustoming itself to make the best of everything; to put the best construction possible on every promise of good in any one's character and conduct; to see every object and every event in the best light. But still, it is the habit of a mind sensible and sensitive; all the more apt to be vexed and troubled by adverse circumstances and influences, the more simple and confident it is in its belief and anticipation of good; and therefore all the more having need of patience.

Yes. Your sanguine man is often apt to be impatient. He seizes eagerly on whatever is hopeful. He is intolerant of what hurts or hinders the cause to which he is committed, or the enterprise on which his heart is set.

Tribulation, therefore, is to him hard to bear; harder to him than to those who are less inclined, or less accustomed, to rejoice in hope.

Is the tribulation a personal one? Are you personally disabled for the work in which it has been your joy hopefully to abound? Is it your sad lot to lie wounded and helpless on your weary couch, while the battle in which you love to have a part is raging at your very door? It is indeed a trial of your patience; a trial severe and sore, in proportion to the joyous hope with which, were it possible, you would cast yourself into the thickest of the fight. Paul, in his Roman dungeon, had that trial to endure. Bonds and imprisonment laid an arrest on his indefatigable activity in preaching the gospel of Christ. To his ardent spirit, it was a trial more severe than, to a colder soul, sickness, loss of fortune, death of friends, or any other earthly calamity, can well be. For him to be patient in such a tribulation is indeed a triumph of faith; and a proof that his sanguine zeal, his joyous hope, in serving the Lord, is of the right sort. It is not the "rejoicing in hope," of successful ambition, or gratified vanity; of self-glorification or self-aggrandizement. If it were, he could but ill endure the evil chance that cuts his career short in the hour of its brightest promise. But his "rejoicing in hope," while he is free to labour, is of a godly sort. It is rejoicing in hope, not of his own glory, but of the Lord's. And therefore he is patient in the tribulation that interrupts his labour, however prematurely and however painfully. He is willing that " Christ should be magnified in his body, whether it be by life, or by death" (Phil. i. 20).

To be patient in tribulation!—it is a great attainment! Many are the afflictions of the righteous. He is in trouble, not only like other men, but more than other men. As members of Christ's body; having to bear your part, according to the grace that is given to you, in the offices and functions of the body ; you are liable to be troubled on every side. The ordinary evils of life beset you; and other evils besides, to which your Christian calling and profession lay you open. Tribulation comes to you ; not only in the form of personal suffering and domestic distress, but in the form also of persecution for righteousness' sake. You share the common lot of man. You sicken, or are hurt. Your family is smitten. You are bereaved of your beloved. And you share also, moreover, the lot of Christ; for you are members of his body. You are treated as he was treated. It should be so ; it must be so, if you are his. And all this may come upon you in the midst of most hopeful and well-grounded anticipations of good. It may look as if the wettest of all blankets were thrown over your burning zeal ; as if the cruelest of all arrests were put, —and that too in the very crisis of their success,—upon your best and most benevolent undertakings. Truly, in such circumstances, you have need of patience. The tribulation in which you have to be patient, is not merely sad and sorrowful in itself; as all tribulation must be whether to a selfish or to a sympathizing sufferer ; to "the tender groaning for another's pain," or "to the unfeeling

groaning for his own." It is aggravated, in your case, by
the interruption which it causes in your joy; the joy of
your hopeful industry in the service of the Lord.
Physical, bodily, pain is hard to bear. Pain in the
affections,—the lacerating, not of material ligaments, but
of the tissues of the heart,—is harder still to bear. But
hardest to be borne of all, to a soul that in serving the
Lord rejoices in hope, is the pain of being laid aside, or
cut off, from that most loved and hopeful and joyous
service; laid aside by God; cut off by man; doomed to
pine in helpless inactivity, when all within is on fire
for the Lord's glory and the salvation of souls. To be
patient in tribulation, thus viewed; to combine patience
in tribulation with rejoicing in hope; patient endurance
of what in agony hinders work, with the joyous buoyancy
of hope in work, when work is possible;—this is the test
of godliness; this is the function and the fruit of prayer.

III. For it is the habit of prayer which harmonizes
these two other habits of mind; the cheerful joy of
hope in serving the Lord, and patience, meekness, submission, in enduring tribulation.

It may not be the same sort of prayer in both instances;
when you have reason to rejoice in hope, and when you
are called to be patient in tribulation. Your prayer will
naturally and fitly assume different characters, according
to the varying circumstances of your outward position,
and the varying moods of your spirit within you. "Is
any merry? Let him sing psalms. Is any afflicted?
Let him pray." In a bright day of hope, when the heart

is merry, your prayer may be very much thanksgiving; the offering of praise; the singing of psalms. In the hour of sorrow, when the heart is sad, it will be "supplications, with strong crying and tears" (Heb. v. 7). It will be "groanings which cannot be uttered" (Rom. viii. 26). Still prayer of some sort will be always seasonable; and you, serving the Lord equally in sunshine and in gloom,—whether rejoicing in hope, or patient in tribulation,—will be found always praying;—continuing instant, unwearied, without intermission, in prayer. So will your joy in hope be chastened. So will your patience in tribulation be sustained.

Jesus, on one occasion, rejoiced. It was when the seventy returned from their evangelistic mission with joy, saying, "Lord, even the devils are subject unto us through thy name." Yes! the Lord replies; and you may hail that as a sign of the serpent's overthrow;—"I beheld Satan as lightning fall from heaven." And therefore you may expect triumphs more illustrious than the one in which now you rejoice;—"Behold, I give unto you power to tread on serpents and scorpions, and over all the power of the enemy; and nothing shall by any means hurt you." Does this give you new and additional joy: this prospect of a safe and sure victory over the powers of darkness? It is well. "Notwithstanding, in this rejoice not;" in this alone, in this chiefly, "that the spirits are subject unto you; but rather rejoice, because your names are written in heaven" (Luke x. 17-20).

"In that hour Jesus" himself "rejoiced in spirit!" The Man of Sorrows for once appears rejoicing. He is rejoicing in hope. In the fall of Satan ; in the salvation of these little ones; a salvation secured by the recorded decree of Heaven ; he sees by anticipation " of the travail of his soul, and is satisfied." Yes ! in spite of all delays, and disappointments, and discouragements ; in spite of all the contradiction of sinners against himself that he has to endure; in spite of all the unbelief of earth, and all the rage and wrath of hell ; it is a hopeful enterprise in which he is embarked. And he may rejoice in the hopefulness of it. For his joy is not self-glorifying ; it is not self-seeking. It is the joy of filial gratitude to the Father, and filial submission to the Father ;—of filial acknowledgment of the Father's sovereignty, and filial acquiescence in the Father's will. And accordingly, when he is seen " rejoicing in hope," he is seen at the same time " continuing instant in prayer." He gives utterance to his hopeful joy in prayer,—in a psalm of praise ;—" In that hour Jesus rejoiced in spirit, and said, I thank thee, O Father, Lord of heaven and earth, that thou hast hid these things from the wise and prudent, and hast revealed them unto babes: even so, Father; for so it seemed good in thy sight" (Luke x. 21).

So let it be with you. When you rejoice in hope, let it be the instinct, the impulse, the instant and urgent passion of your soul, to give vent to your joy in thankful prayer. Carry your feelings to the bosom of the Eternal " Father, Lord of heaven and earth." Link on any success, or any prospect of success, that cheers you, to the throne of his sovereignty; his sovereign will ; his sovereign grace. Enter, as prayer alone can enable you to enter, into the wide and vast sweep of his eternal counsels. Recognise the tie that binds your little hope, in your limited sphere, to the great hope of the Everlasting Father, that ranges over heaven and earth, and embraces the interests of his universal and everlasting empire. Such prayer, unflagging and unwearied, will raise you above all the poor and low self-congratulations of that self-complacency which might tempt you to feel as if your small measure of good got, or of good gained, were worthy of a world's gaze ; or as if "your own sword got the land, and your own right hand wrought out the salvation." Your prayer, your instant and unwearied prayer, will be your giving to God all the glory; owning your dependence on him for all, your submission to him in all. It will merge also past and present satisfaction in new aspirings for the future. It carries you on to new efforts ; new labours ; new successes. Thus prayer, your continuing instant and unwearied in prayer, will chasten, elevate, and hallow, your "rejoicing in hope."

Nor is it less effectual to sustain your "patience in tribulation." It was through his "continuing instant in prayer" that Jesus was able to be patient in his tribulation. Prayer was his refuge amid the trials and troubles of his active and working life, when he was about his Father's business; not slothful in it ; fervent in spirit ; serving the Lord. Ever in the midst of his laborious ministry, beset as it was with tribulation of every sort, he continued instant in prayer. He spent whole nights in prayer to God. He went often into a mountain apart to pray. He was ever appealing to his

Father, calling upon his Father, confiding in his Father, in all the experiences and exigencies of the troubled course through which he had to pass, as he was doing his Father's will and finishing his Father's work. And when the time came for suffering, and not for doing; when the tribulation appointed for him was not that incident to his active service of the Father, but that connected with his endurance of the chastisement of our peace; the judgment of our sins, laid upon him by the Father's hand ; oh ! how did he turn, in his distress, to that very Father who was smiting him ; continuing still instant in prayer ; in prayer under the agony of the garden ; "Father, if it be possible, let the cup pass;"——in the threefold prayer, the threefold cry, of desolation, of compassion, and of faith upon the cross: " My God, my God, why hast thou forsaken me?" " Father, forgive them ; for they know not what they do;" " Father, into thy hands I commend my spirit."

Be ye, like Christ, unwearied and persevering, always " continuing instant in prayer;" that so, like him, you may rejoice in spirit, in the assured hope of the things which are hidden from the wise and prudent, being revealed unto babes ; and that so, like him also, amid whatever tribulation you have to meet, in your active service of the Lord, or in your suffering under his hand, you may possess your souls in patience, waiting for his salvation. In all things, whether as regards your own personal welfare here and hereafter, or as regards your work and warfare in the Church and cause of Christ, let prayer, your continuing instant in prayer, sustain you in cheerful hope, as you seize upon every hopeful sign, and make the most of it. And let it sustain you in cheerful submission also, as you accept every seemingly adverse token and make the best of it. In a word, act always upon the maxim, " Be careful for nothing ; but in everything by prayer and supplication, with thanksgiving, let your requests be made known unto God;" and appropriate the promise that is annexed to that maxim, and associated with it : "And the peace of God, which passeth all understanding, shall keep your hearts and minds through Christ Jesus" (Phil. iv. 6, 7). This peace of God, thus keeping your hearts and minds, is the source and perennial spring of that joyous hope with which you throw yourselves, heart and soul, into "whatever your hand findeth to do," for the saving of your own soul and the advancement of the good cause. The same inward peace imparts calmness and serenity amid whatever tribulation tries and taxes your power of patient endurance, your principle of patient obedience. And it is a peace which only prayer can preserve and perpetuate,—your continuing instant in the prayer and supplication by which, without carefulness and with thankfulness, you make known your requests unto God.

9

CHARACTERISTICS OF ACTIVE MEMBERSHIP: MUTUAL BENEFICENCE & HOSPITALITY

"Distributing to the necessity of saints; given to hospitality."

—*Romans 12:13*

THE two duties here enjoined are obviously of the same nature. The members of Christ's Church, self-devoted to the Lord; separated from the world; united in one body, but having different offices and different functions; full of true and holy love, inspiring a brotherly love kind and lowly; working in their several spheres of Christian duty and activity, with business-like diligence, with spiritual fervour, with conscience towards the Lord whom they serve; working also hopefully, patiently, prayerfully; are called to consider the case of those among themselves who may stand in need of special sympathy and help. These may be either permanent residenters in any place,—tarriers at home; or they may be casual and occasional visitors, —travellers abroad. Both classes have claims on their brethren, and each its own claim. Hence the double precept : I. " Distributing to the necessity of saints; II. given to hospitality."

I. The case of suffering brethren generally is to be first

met. Apart from the peculiar title to assistance which
those of them have who journey—especially when they
journey in the Lord's cause,—the wants of all who love
the Lord anywhere, everywhere, demand relief. The
general duty, accordingly, of " distributing to the necessity
of saints," takes precedence of what is a particular instance of it,—the exercise of hospitality.

The "necessity" here meant is plainly of an outward
and temporal, not an inward and spiritual sort. It is
not the necessity of an awakened conscience, or an in-
quiring spirit, or an anxious soul. With that necessity
also,—with that necessity pre-eminently,—you are bound,
as members of Christ's body, discharging offices of trust
and love in his Church, to be ever making common
cause. But it is another kind of necessity that is now
in view; the necessity of distressed or straitened circumstances ; the hard necessity of poverty, of pain, of persecution.

And how is such "necessity" of saints to be treated ?
You are to make common cause with it ; to be joint partakers of it ; to have the communion of it with them ; to
be communicants in it with them. Such is the real import of the word used by the Apostle, and somewhat
feebly and inadequately rendered in our translation. It
is not a mere distribution of alms from your purse, or
crumbs from your table. It is not a mere conveyance of
charitable gifts and offerings, on however large a scale.
It is that, no doubt ; it is that at the very least. But
it is something more than that, and something better.
It is communion; fellowship; joint participation.

The same expression is used elsewhere to denote substantially the same idea.

Thus, writing to the Romans (xv. 25-27), and referring to the commission which he had received from certain Gentile churches, "to go to Jerusalem, to minister unto the saints," the Apostle first speaks approvingly of their liberality,—"It hath pleased them of Macedonia and Achaia to make a certain contribution for the poor saints which are at Jerusalem;" and then he goes on at once to indicate the reasonableness, and to explain the nature, of this liberality on the part of these Gentile churches: "It hath pleased them verily; and their debtors they are. For if the Gentiles have been made partakers of their spiritual things, their duty is also to minister unto them in carnal things." The ministry in carnal things must undoubtedly be of the same sort with the communion in spiritual things which it reciprocates and requites. It implies, not the mere transference of a benefit from one party to another, but the mutual association of one with the other in the benefit. The Gentiles are associated with the Jews in the spiritual benefit; and in a corresponding manner, the Jews are to be associated with the Gentiles in the temporal benefit. So also, writing to the Philippians (iv. 15-18), Paul gratefully acknowledges their care of himself and mindfulness of his wants; theirs being the only church which, when he left Macedonia, "communicated with him as concerning giving and receiving." And he intimates that he values their gift, not for itself, but chiefly as a proof and instance of their making common cause with him, or having communion and joint participation with him, in his necessity.

The practice of the early Christians, associated in the Pentecostal church, realized the ideal of this communion. Among them the stream of love and liberality flowed so copiously, so freshly and so freely, from the warm source and fountain of sympathizing hearts, that it was not merely a distribution of needful things, on the part of those who had them, among those who had them not, but such an identification of the whole in one, as amounted virtually and practically to a community of goods (Acts ii. 44 ; iv. 32-34). The brethren made common cause with one another, as regarded the real use and usufruct of all their possessions.

The grace enjoined in the passage now before us is the converse and the complement of that described as characterizing the Pentecostal church. It is, in fact, the same grace, only viewed, as it were, from the opposite side. There, it is a communion, or community, of goods, between him who has and him who has not. Here, it is a communion, or community, of necessity, between him who needs and him who does not need. In either view, the principle is the same. The saints,— "all that believe, being together,"—one in Christ, have all things in common. Their possessions and goods are common. Their necessity is common. My possessions and goods are common to my necessitous brother and myself. His necessity is common to me and him. Thus, really and effectively, though not by express or formal compact, he and I have all things in common. My means, and his needs, are common to both. This is, so far as the things of this world are concerned, the practical expression, the substantial proof, of our oneness in Christ. It is our making common cause with one another; holding our resources to be available for one another, as if they were a common stock; entering into one another's necessities, as if they were a common calamity. The Christian brotherhood, the fellowship of the saints, is thus practically exemplified and proved.

In the department of the inner spiritual life, that communion is very close; and the closeness of it is declared and sealed in the sacrament of communion;—"The cup of blessing which we bless, is it not the communion of the blood of Christ? The bread which we break, is it not the communion of the body of Christ? For we, being many, are one bread, and one body : for we are all partakers of that one bread" (1 Cor. x. 16, 17). We are joint partakers of the one bread of life; of the life of which He is the bread. We are jointly incorporated into him; being "members of his body, of his flesh, and of his bones" (Eph. v. 30). As his mystical body, we, jointly as well as severally, are consecrated by his sacrifice of atonement, and consecrate ourselves, to be a sacrifice of praise to "his Father and our Father, his God and our God." As being "many members in one body, yet all members not having the same office," we have communion, or joint participation, each according to the grace held to be given to him, upon a sober estimate of himself, in the offices and works which the Church, as Christ's body, has to discharge and do ;— as well as also in the spirit or frame of mind in which they are to be discharged and done. And now it is intimated that we are to have communion, or joint participation, in the varieties of outward fortune to which the body, or its several members, may be exposed. The living body is organized for originating action from within, and for receiving impressions and meeting influences from without; it works, and it is worked upon. And as in the life, so also in both these forms or phases of the life—the active and the receptive—the members have communion, or joint participation. All among them is in common.

It is, therefore, upon a very high and holy footing that the duty of "distributing to the necessity of saints" may be seen to rest. The claim which the very least of Christ's little ones has on all the members of his body, and on each one in particular, is peculiarly sacred. You, my brother, as a member of Christ's body, are bound to see to it, so far as in you lies, that no necessitous member of the same body, within the reach of your means of discovery and of deliverance, remains for a single hour unhelped and unrelieved. It is your part to visit him without delay; or if that may not be, to make sure that he is visited, in your name, and on your behalf. Nor let any light hinderance interfere with your visit being paid in person. Communion by proxy, or at second hand, is a cold affair at the best. The obligation lies upon you personally. Let it, if there be no insuperable obstacle, physical or moral, be personally fulfilled. And that it may be fulfilled faithfully, be not content to sit at home and wait till tidings of needy cases happen to reach your ears. Go forth in search of poor or suffering saints of God, where-

ever there is, I say not a likelihood, but a chance or possibility, of any, of a single one, being found. Search, as
with a candle, the dark places near your dwelling. Cause
the dark places further off to be searched for you. Then,
when you are brought into contact with a child of God,
—born of the Spirit long ago, or it may be now, through
God's blessing on your very search for him,—make his
case your own. Lay yourself out to ascertain and to
understand his necessity. Your own insight often, if it
be the insight of genuine Christian and human sympathy,
will help you to see it, without your questioning him, or
his telling you. What makes his lot hard and heavy to
bear, and his Christian profession very difficult to maintain, you will be quick-sighted to discern. And you will
be prompt to succour him ; and in doing so, to make him
feel that he is not to consider himself a pensioner dependent on your bounty, or a mendicant accepting your
alms ; but that he and you, being one in Christ, have but
one common interest,—you in his necessity, and he in your
means of meeting it. Thus, while "as you have opportunity, you do good unto all men," you do good "especially to them who are of the household of faith" (Gal.
vi. 10). You recognise their special claim upon you, as
being fellow-members with you of the body of Christ. In
ministering to them you minister to Christ's body—nay,
rather, you minister to Christ himself. And you humbly
hope for his gracious acknowledgment of your ministry
in the day when he shall utter these wonderful words :
"Inasmuch as ye did it to the least of these my brethren,
ye did it unto me." For you thus most truly and fully

carry out the idea of his own parable: "When thou makest a dinner or a supper, call not thy friends, nor thy brethren, neither thy kinsmen, nor thy rich neighbours; lest they also bid thee again, and a recompence be made thee. But when thou makest a feast, call the poor, the maimed, the lame, the blind: and thou shalt be blessed; for they cannot recompense thee: for thou shalt be recompensed at the resurrection of the just" (Luke xiv. 12–14).

II. Under the general head of "distributing to the necessity of saints," the Apostle specifies one particular branch of that virtue ;—"given to hospitality."

Now, the hospitality here commended is not that of promiscuous benevolence and general good-will, as if one should throw open his house, and spread his table, and prepare the couch of rest, for all and sundry to enter in, and eat and sleep. Nor is it the hospitality of private acquaintanceship, as when one entertains a single friend, or a party of friends, on the ground of ties or relations in ordinary life connecting them together and suggesting social intercourse. Both of these kinds of hospitality are lawful, and, within due bounds, commendable. To receive strangers and travellers, who are in need of accommodation—to treat them kindly and minister to their wants, whoever they may be, and whatever their creed or calling or condition,—is an obvious duty of humanity. To share with those whom we esteem and love the temperate repast and genial fireside fellowship of home, is a welcome solace amid the carking cares of this working world. But the hospitality which Paul is now speaking of is something different from both of these. It is hospitality to the children of God. It is a particular branch or department of the general obligation to distribute to the necessity of saints. It contemplates the case of believers away from their ordinary abodes; specially of believers in exile, or on a journey. In this view, the grace or virtue in question was more largely and constantly called into exercise in the early Church than it ordinarily is now. The circumstances then were peculiar. Christians were to a large extent literally "strangers scattered throughout Pontus, Galatia, Cappadocia, Asia, and Bithynia,"—in fact throughout all provinces and countries of the world. As preachers of the truth, or as persecuted for the truth's sake, they went abroad everywhere; and wherever they went they were dependent mainly on the hospitality of their brethren in the common faith.

It was much the same in the patriarchal times. The remnant of the godly, in the unsettled state of society which then prevailed, were often wanderers on the face of the earth; going hither and thither, bearing witness on behalf of the primeval and traditionary religion amid the growing degeneracy of mankind; or seeking refuge, as fugitives, from the rage and wrath which their testimony provoked. Hence the pious practice was seasonable which righteous men like Abraham and Lot adopted, of sitting at the door of their tents, at noonday or at eventide, to arrest any passers-by who might seem to need their kind offices, and bid them welcome to bed and board (Gen. xviii. 1; xix. 1).

The circumstances of the early Christians were such as

to recall the memory of these old days, and give point to the allusion which Paul makes to them when he says, "Be not forgetful to entertain strangers : for thereby some have entertained angels unawares " (Heb. xiii. 2). A still higher motive is suggested in anticipation by our Lord ;—" He that receiveth you, receiveth me ; and he that receiveth me, receiveth him that sent me. He that receiveth a prophet in the name of a prophet, shall receive a prophet's reward ; and he that receiveth a righteous man in the name of a righteous man, shall receive a righteous man's reward. And whosoever shall give to drink unto one of these little ones a cup of cold water only in the name of a disciple, verily I say unto you, he shall in no wise lose his reward " (Matt. x. 40-42).

Hence the practice in the early Church of sending letters of introduction, or of commendation, by the hands of persons moving from one place to another. To this practice Paul refers when he boasts, as it were, of his own independence of such letters;—" Do we begin again to commend ourselves ? or need we, as some others, epistles of commendation to you, or letters of commendation from you ? " (2 Cor. iii. 1). And we have instances of the practice among the salutations with which the epistles usually close ; as in this Epistle to the Romans (xvi. 1, 2), —" I commend unto you Phebe our sister, which is a servant of the church which is at Cenchrea ; that ye receive her in the Lord, as becometh saints, and that ye assist her in whatsoever business she hath need of you : for she hath been a, succourer of many, and of myself also;" and in the First Epistle to the Corinthians (xvi. 17, 18),—" I am glad of the coming of Stephanas, and Fortunatus, and Achaicus: for that which was lacking on your part they have supplied. For they have refreshed my spirit and yours: therefore acknowledge ye them that are such." The Second and Third Epistles of the beloved Apostle John seem to be such letters of introduction. At all events they treat of the subject of these letters. And, by contrast with one another, they bring out the duty in its twofold aspect; as requiring true believers on the one hand to abstain from exercising brotherly hospitality towards false teachers; and as requiring them on the other hand to exercise such hospitality towards all true members of the body of Christ.

For the principle might be violated in two ways; either by hospitably entertaining, as a true brother, one who was heretical, in doctrine or in practice; or by refusing to entertain hospitably, as a brother, one who was sound in faith,—in that faith which worketh by love. And these two epistles of John have respect to these two ways of violating the principle. The second contains a strong exhortation against receiving false professors;—the third, again, contains an equally strong approval of the receiving of such as are true.

1. Thus in the former of these epistles (2 John), "the elder," writing to "the elect lady and her children,"—after warmly commending her own and her household's steadfast adherence to the truth, and enforcing the new, and yet old, commandment, that "we love one another,"— lays down the test or criterion of the genuineness of that

holy affection;—"And this is love, that we walk after his commandments. This is the commandment, That, as ye have heard from the beginning, ye should walk in it" (ver. 6). For, as is here manifestly implied, that is not real love, which, in its eagerness to enlarge the circle of the Christian brotherhood, would relax the authority of Christ, the head, over his body, the Church; or wander from the old paths in which the footsteps of the flock are to be traced. All the rather is it needful to beware of that plausible snare, because, as the Apostle testifies, "many deceivers are entered into the world, who confess not that Jesus Christ is come in the flesh. This is a deceiver and an antichrist" (ver. 7). For your own sakes, therefore, and for the truth's sake, be on your guard against countenancing "transgressors who abide not in the doctrine of Christ" (ver. 9). And especially, in the exercise of hospitality towards those who roam over the world in the character of the Lord's servants and witnesses,—persecuted, perhaps, and persecuted apparently on account of their Christian profession,—use a careful discrimination. "He," and he only, "that abideth in the doctrine of Christ, he hath both the Father and the Son" (ver. 9). Therefore, "if there come any unto you, and bring not this doctrine, receive him not into your house, neither bid him God speed: for he that biddeth him God speed is partaker of his evil deeds" (ver. 10, 11).

Such is the rule laid down by the Apostle of love to regulate our treatment of all whose testimony, or whose teaching, is away from the truth. Hospitality to them, as brethren, is expressly and very peremptorily forbidden.

I say, hospitality towards them as brethren. For it need scarcely be remarked that the Apostle cannot be understood as condemning the benevolence which would open its house as a house of refuge for the weary wanderer, without question as to creed, or character, or colour, or country, and provide shelter, food, and comfort for all alike and indiscriminately who are in want. Nay, he does not and cannot mean to prohibit the extension of such sort of hospitality even to those whom he denounces so strongly as deceivers. To entertain them kindly when they appeal to your generosity and pity, simply as your fellowmen, in destitution and distress, is unquestionably lawful and right. But let them not be owned by you as disciples or apostles of the Lord. Let them not be welcomed and embraced as your brethren in Christ. Let it not be in that character that you receive them into your house and speed them on their way. Let it never be forgotten that, as Christian love is always based on Christian truth, so every manifestation of mutual love, in the body of Christ, must proceed avowedly and unequivocally upon the mutual recognition of "the truth as it is in Jesus." Those whom I love, after the model and example of John the beloved, "I love in the truth: and not I only, but also all they that have known the truth ; for the truth's sake, which dwelleth in us, and shall be with us for ever" (ver. 1).

2. In the other epistle (3 John) "the elder" manifests the same anxiety that all love among Christians should be grounded on the truth. He salutes Gaius, "whom," he adds, "I love in the truth" (ver. 1). He expresses the

joy he felt when he found the brethren who came from
Gaius all testifying, as he writes to his friend, " of the
truth that is in thee, even as thou walkest in the truth"
(ver. 3). His cordial delight in those who hold by the
truth is quite equal to his holy dread and dislike of such
as wander themselves, and lead others to wander, into
error. " I have no greater joy," he exclaims with trans-
port, "than to hear that my children walk in truth ! "
(ver. 4). And having no occasion, as it would seem, to
put his present correspondent on his guard against that
ultra-liberal stretch of Christian hospitality of which it
had been necessary to bid the " elect lady" beware,—he
makes it very plain that it is no mere cold and cautious
negative concern to avoid the risk of countenancing evil
that will content his loving soul. For it is with no ordinary fervour that he pronounces his commendation of
the open house and open heart of Gaius ;—" Beloved, thou
doest faithfully whatsoever thou doest to the brethren,
and to strangers ; which have borne witness of thy charity
before the church : whom if thou bring forward on their
journey after a godly sort, thou shalt do well : because
that for his name's sake they went forth, taking nothing
of the Gentiles. We therefore ought to receive such, that
we might be fellow-helpers to the truth " (ver. 5-8).

Thus the beloved Apostle, full of his own favourite theme
of love in the truth, enforces in both aspects of it, the prohibitive and the enactive, the virtue of which Paul speaks
when he describes the members of Christ's body as " distributing to the necessity of saints ; given to hospitality."

It is a virtue, as I have already observed, specially called into exercise in such times as cause exile or flight among the professed followers of Christ; and in such times, I would now add, it is peculiarly tried and tested. Two instances occur for illustration here.

When the first French Revolution began to convulse society, multitudes of priests, and other members of the Church of Rome, sought and found refuge on our country's hospitable shores. Their coming amongst us kindled an enthusiasm of religious resentment against the cruel oppression of which they were the victims. Everywhere, and by all classes, they were welcomed;—not merely as men suffering wrongfully, and in that character entitled to sympathy and help to the very uttermost;—but as confessors, and all but martyrs, in the cause of Christianity, and on that account having a claim to be entertained on the footing of a common brotherhood with us in our common Lord. Now it might be so far true that they were persecuted for their Christianity, such as it was. It was their religion that made them odious in revolutionary eyes, and obnoxious to revolutionary fury; although, making due allowance for the sincerity and piety of not a few, it should never have been forgotten that it was that very religion of theirs that had sowed the seeds of the very anarchy and crime from which they were now constrained to flee,—in the dissolution of manners among the great, the oppression of the masses, the universal corruption of morals, and the spread of both a lettered and a vulgar infidelity among all classes of the community. Still it was not unnatural, nor, to some extent, unwarrantable, to regard with somewhat more than ordinary interest these fugitives from the violence of lawless atheism. It cannot be denied, however, that this interest led to a fraternization far too close with themselves, and an estimation far too indulgent of their creed and their confession. The antichristian character of their principles and their practices was lost sight of, in admiration of the Christian meekness and magnanimity with which so many of them bore their sufferings; the hospitality even of sound Protestants towards their Popish visitors ceased to be the hospitality of Christian humanity, and became the hospitality of Christian brotherhood; and hence, at least in part, may have arisen that latitudinarian indifference to the distinction between Christ and Antichrist, between truth and error, between a pure and an idolatrous worship of the living God, which has since prevailed so largely and so disastrously in the councils of statesmen and the opinions of society. Certainly the caution addressed by "the elder" to the "elect lady" would have been seasonable at that crisis, if the men of that generation had had ears to hear.

Long before, in the history of the same great nation, events of which the reign of terror may fairly be regarded as the avenger, had sent the best of her children, by hundreds, beyond her borders. The massacre of St. Bartholomew, in one century, and still more, the revocation of the Edict of Nantes in that which followed,—fatal blunders as well as crimes of Popery,—emptied France of many of the Lord's faithful people. The Protestant states, and conspicuously among them our own free country, welcomed the refugees. There could be no hesitation, in that instance, as to the sort of hospitality that was due. These persecuted saints were to be entertained as brethren, in the Lord's name and for the Lord's sake. That they were largely so entertained is matter of history; and in so far as they were so entertained, our Christian hospitality was, even in a temporal point of view, richly blessed and amply rewarded. But perhaps a richer blessing still, and an ampler reward, might have been ours, had the spirit which John commends in Gaius been then, and always, more uniformly and unequivocally characteristic of that ready protection which our country extends to exiles of all sorts and from all quarters. It is our just boast that the homeless and houseless wanderer finds a safe asylum within our borders; no questions asked; no condition imposed, beyond that of living peaceably. But while all are thus free to seek shelter under the shade of our constitutional liberty and independence, let it never be lost sight of that the Lord's own people, when driven to our shores, have a sacred right to far more than toleration and charitable help, at the hands of all who love the Lord himself, and are, in his behalf, "given to hospitality."

And now, in fine, whether we view these virtues of brotherly communion and hospitality as more particularly called into exercise in troublous times, such as often already have made, and may yet again make,—sooner, perhaps, than we think,—many preachers and professors of the pure gospel of Christ impoverished sufferers and

persecuted wanderers on the face of the earth; or consider them as virtues which are ever more or less in
demand;—let us make conscience of feeling and apprehending fully our common brotherhood with all who are
fellow-members with us of the one body of Christ. Let
this gracious bond of union ever be considered paramount
over all other distinctions, of whatever nature. Let us be
of one mind and of one heart, in our consecration of ourselves to God and our separation of ourselves from the
world; in our earnest working for the Lord, according
to our different gifts and graces, and in our different
spheres and offices; and in our generous and unselfish
willingness to make common cause with one another, alike
in weal and in woe. Let the exhortation of another
inspired Apostle be ever faithfully carried out in practice;—"Above all things, have fervent charity among
yourselves: for charity shall cover the multitude of sins.
Use hospitality one to another without grudging. As
every man hath received the gift, even so minister the
same one to another, as good stewards of the manifold
grace of God" (1 Pet. iv. 8–10).

PART THREE

THE CHRISTIAN'S RELATIONSHIP
TO A HOSTILE WORLD
(12:14-21)

10

THE ALTERNATIVE OF
BLESSING OR CURSING

"Bless them which persecute you: bless, and curse not."
—*Romans 12:14*

THIS verse evidently has respect,—as indeed the entire remainder of the chapter has respect,—to the position which Christians occupy in the midst of an evil world. Their position is one of liability and exposure to persecution. So the Lord himself taught them beforehand to regard it. The law of his kingdom,—the normal state of his Church,—according to his own faithful warning, is that it is apt to be persecuted, nay, that it is sure to be persecuted. It must be so. His followers, making common cause with him, must lay their account with having a common lot with him. "If the world hate you, ye know that it hated me before it hated you. If ye were of the world, the world would love his own : but because ye are not of the world, but I have chosen you out of the world, therefore the world hateth you. Remember the word that I said unto you, The servant is not greater than his lord.　If they have persecuted me, they will also persecute you ; if they have kept my saying, they will keep yours also " (John xv. 18-20). The mode and measure of the persecution may vary. There are different ways of persecuting, with different degrees of intensity, in different ages of the world and different conditions of society.　But the ordinary principle and rule of the Christian profession, and the invariable experience of those who truly adopt it is, that, in one way or another, " all who will live godly in Christ Jesus shall suffer persecution" (2 Tim. iii. 12).

Hence the precept, " Bless them which persecute you," is always applicable ; and the practical illustration and enforcement of it must be always seasonable.

Generally, the precept is identical with that of our Lord in the sermon on the mount ;—" Ye have heard that it hath been said, Thou shalt love thy neighbour, and hate thine enemy : but I say unto you, Love your enemies, bless them that curse you, do good to them that hate you, and pray for them which despitefully use you, and persecute you."　Thus the great Lawgiver interprets his own law.　And he enforces the command by an appeal to the highest of all examples, that of God himself ;— " That ye may be the children of your Father which is in heaven : for he maketh his sun to rise on the evil and on the good, and sendeth rain on the just and on the unjust. . . . . Be ye therefore perfect, even as your Father which is in heaven is perfect" (Matt. v. 43-45, 48).

This is a high and animating motive. Cherishing and manifesting the spirit that is enjoined, you prove yourselves, by your family likeness, to be the children of your Father in heaven. To yourselves, in your own happy consciousness ; to others, through your gracious conduct and demeanour ; your claim of filial relationship to God is verified, attested, and made good. You feel yourselves, and others see, that you are, in this matter, of the same mind and character with your Father in heaven ; partakers of his divine nature ; perfect as he is perfect, in the divine accomplishment of loving your enemies, and doing them good ;—his children, therefore, in nature as well as in name ; not in word only, but in deed and in truth.

This motive is not expressly urged by the Apostle in the verse now before us,—although doubtless he had it in his mind. The command or exhortation, he may be understood to say, is not mine, but the Lord's. In the spirit which he recommends, and after the pattern to which he points, "Bless them which persecute you."

"Bless, and curse not," the Apostle adds. Why? To what effect ? Is not the addition rather a weakening of the sense and import of the precept? What need of telling you, who are bound to bless your persecutors, that you are to take care not to curse them ? Is not that something like an anticlimax, a figure of the bathos ;—a coming down from the enjoining of what is a noble positive attainment of divine perfection, to a mere and poor negative prohibition of what one animated by the ambition of being thus godlike could never be supposed to dream of? First you are exhorted to bless them that persecute you ; and then not to curse them.

That is not the manner of Paul. He does not think or write so inconsequentially and so loosely as such a tame construction of his language would imply. There is a special force and point in his words, "Bless, and curse not." A vitally important principle of morality is in them. Bless, that you may not curse. Bless, if you would not curse. As you would keep yourselves safe and free from the risk of committing the great sin of cursing, see to it that you are always blessing. Bless, be ever blessing, lest you should curse. For you must be either blessing or cursing. One or other of these attitudes you must be adopting ; one or other of these frames of mind you must be cherishing, at every moment. There is no intermediate position or posture. "Bless, and curse not."

I. And here, let it be observed, in the first place, the risk and danger of your being tempted to curse them that persecute you is strong ; stronger than you might at first be prepared to allow. It is the tendency of human nature. And it is a tendency which continues to exist, and is apt to prevail, even when nature is sanctified by grace. Nay, there is in that case a new and peculiar temptation.

You identify yourselves, and rightly, with Christ and his cause. The persecution which you have to encounter is not merely a personal affront and injury to you. It is opposition to the Lord and his Anointed. Your selfish resentment of the wrong done to yourselves is, as it might seem, merged in the generous indignation with which your bosom burns against the outrage offered to your Master. It is the zeal of his house that hath eaten you up. Ah! what room is there here for self-deception; for the wrath of man, which worketh not the righteousness of God, putting on the guise of a holy and disinterested concern for the kingdom of God and his righteousness!

And the danger is the greater in proportion as your Christianity is of a decided sort, and of an impulsive and aggressive character, and is on that account calculated to provoke and stimulate, among those with whom you come in contact, the principle of hostility to the truth as it is in Jesus,—the enmity of the carnal mind against God and against his holy law.

There is, indeed, a kind of Christianity which leaves those who profess and practise it sufficiently secure, in all conscience, as regards the danger now in question. There is the quiescent piety, not insincere, in its way, so far as it goes; nay, deeply spiritual perhaps, after a fashion; which almost makes a merit of not obtruding itself, or thrusting itself forward, so as materially to interfere with the customary ungodliness of the world lying in wickedness. And, what is far more common, there is the nominal and formal piety, which comes to a virtual understanding that, if it is itself let alone, it will let the world alone. If your religion is of such a nature as either of these; if you keep it, as you say, to yourselves, as a matter entirely private, between you and your God; if you keep it exclusively for the closet and the church— for the hour of secret devotion and the day of social

worship ; if, when you go among your fellow-men, you
go to be very much what they are, and to live very much
as they live,—not troubling them with any very high
testimony, any very holy example, any very close dealing
with their consciences and hearts ;—you can have little or
no experience, either of the personal irritation which the
truth, when faithfully urged home by faithful witnesses,
causes in the minds of men who will not embrace it ; or
of the trial to which the witnesses of the truth are subjected, when they have to overcome their proneness to
be personally irritated in their turn.   Your Christianity
the world will tolerate, and not persecute.   You have no
need to be warned against cherishing vindictive feelings
towards any persecutors.   Yours is a very mild and
bland protest on the subject of the world's alienation
from God.   The world's temper is not seriously ruffled
by it against you ; nor is there anything in the treatment you meet with at its hands to ruffle very seriously
your temper against the world.

   It will be otherwise if you are more in earnest and
more decided in your separation from the world, and
your self-consecration to God ; more unsparing and
uncompromising in your condemnation of all unrighteousness ; more thoroughly under the influence of zeal
for the glory of God, love to Jesus Christ, and desire of
saving souls.   You will not, indeed, even when such high
motives animate you, omit or neglect any fair method of
conciliation.   You will not needlessly, by any peculiarity
or any infirmity of yours, give offence, or cause vexation
and annoyance.   You will be " wise as serpents and harm-

less as doves." You will not court reproach, or obloquy, or ill-usage, as if that were to be the seal of your fidelity,—the proof and evidence of pre-eminent sanctity or of surpassing consistency. You will not be in haste to ascribe to hatred of the gospel manifestations of feeling that, your humble esteem of yourselves may suggest, are occasioned possibly by your imperfect or unworthy manner of commending it. You will do all that in you lies to disarm suspicion, and distrust, and jealous fear. You will make all possible allowance for the natural disposition of men to assert independence, and to dislike any intermeddling with their notions and ways. You will watch for, and be ready to welcome kindly, such relentings, such tender softenings of heart, as your affectionate and friendly dealings may be expected to call forth among not a few, even of the most obdurate, on whom you bring the appliances of your Christian influence to bear. Still, with all that, you must lay your account, as Christ's witnesses and Christ's workers, discharging offices of love in his Church, with having persecution, real persecution, to bear. You will meet with not a little that will be real persecution to you; persecution of the nature that fell to the lot of Him who "endured such contradiction of sinners against himself." You may not have to "resist unto blood, striving against sin." You may not be stoned, or imprisoned, or scourged. You may not suffer loss of goods, or loss of standing. But there may be those among the objects of your most earnest solicitude who but ill requite your care and kindness. You come in contact with coarse and hard minds, suspicious souls, obdurate hearts. In proportion to the decision of your protest and testimony, and the aggressiveness of your Christian zeal and love, you meet with opposition in quarters in which to meet with it is very trying. And the kind of opposition may be hard to bear. Your good is evil spoken of; your frailties are exposed and magnified; your motives are misconstrued; your manners ridiculed or criticised. Or, all credit being given you for good intentions, your well-meant efforts are received with the cold smile of politeness, or the suppressed sneer of contempt. Your most faithful and affectionate advances are repelled. And those for whose salvation your very bowels are yearning are among the first to hint that you are troublesome, or that you are mad.

Is there no temptation besetting you, in circumstances like these, to let angry passions rise? Is the old nature not stirred within you? Do you not find that it costs you an effort, often difficult and painful, to keep down the deep feelings of disappointment and vexation that are swelling your bosom to suffocation, and dimming your eye with bitter tears; yes! and to suppress the indignant remonstrance of self-defence, or the keen retort of justly-merited defiance, that is already trembling upon your lips?

Ah! there is a struggle in your hearts. You take yourselves to task. You search and try your ways; your ways of witnessing for God and seeking to win souls to Christ. Alas! you discover that the ill success which distresses you, and the opposition which vexes you, may be partly owing to yourselves, to your own fault; your faulty manner of testifying and working ; your want of tact, or of temper, or of patience, or of prudence, or of forbearance, or of kindness. Be it so. The discovery, or the suspicion, humbles you ; but it does not allay the fever or still the tempest of your bosom. You feel as if, notwithstanding such shortcoming on your part, you were still harshly judged and hardly used ; that allowances might be made for you, in consideration of your good faith and good will ; and that, after all, it is too bad that you should, on such slight grounds as these, be so cruelly misunderstood, and "persecuted without a cause."

Yes ; and it may be that you fix upon some one or two among your circle of acquaintance, or within the range and round of your walks of Christian philanthropy, of whom you might have expected, and did once expect, and had a good right and good reason to expect, better things. That they too should turn against you, and, on some frivolous pretence, or for some petty provocation, begin to thwart you in your work of faith and labour of love; taking part with those who reproach and suspect you ; fomenting whatever hostility there may be in men's minds toward you ;—that surely is intolerable. Can flesh and blood stand it ? Can you abstain, in your hearts, from venting what is but too near akin to a malediction or a curse ? Can you help yourselves from partly giving way to what may seem fully justifiable emotions of personal resentment, and a personal sense of unprovoked and undeserved wrong ?

No ! not unless you make conscience of blessing those whom you are thus tempted to curse. It is not a merely negative exercise of moral principle, the putting of an enforced restraint upon such natural tendencies, that will suffice. They are not to be curbed, or checked, or kept in, " by bit and bridle." The outward expression of them, by word or sign, may be thus suppressed. But inwardly they chafe and fret the more for being stifled and pent up. The house will not long remain " empty, swept, and garnished." A seven-fold worse possession than the first may befall it. A vexed and soured temper,—a certain dark brooding over inevitable evil,—a sort of universal scepticism, that will do its duty doggedly, but always in despair of any other return than ingratitude and misrepresentation,—these and such like brooding harpies prey upon your spirits. " Woe is me that I dwell among such people;" " Woe is unto them that I dwell among them in vain ;"—is apt to become the secret burden of your prophesying and your ministering. If it is not a malignant wishing of evil, it is at least a gloomy acquiescence in evil. It lies in the direction of cursing, if it does not actually reach so far. If I am to be safe from so sad a frame of mind, I must have something more than a " curse not" for my motto. My watchword,—or rather my Master's word of command,—must ring true with an element, not of passive suppression, but of active power. " Bless, and curse not," is my rallying cry. Let me bless ; let me be always blessing, wherever there is the slightest risk of my being tempted,—almost, if not altogether,—to curse. Let me single out the parties whose ill-reception and ill-requital of my kind Christian advances I find to be most irritating and trying. Let me make them especially and by name

the objects of my special good-will. Let me be in heart
and soul blessing them ; blessing, and not cursing.

II. For now, in the second place, let it be noted, this
blending of the positive and negative in one command,
—"Bless, and curse not,"—involves a principle of wide
application in the department of morals and religion,—
in the ethical and spiritual sphere of human sensibility and
activity. The principle is this, that neutrality is impossible. When any object is presented soliciting regard, the
heart cannot remain in equipoise or *in equilibrio*. One
way or other it must be affected, and must decide. It
must either approve or disapprove, like or dislike, love or
hate. It cannot occupy a position of indifference.

It is upon this principle that our Lord's two correlative
and corresponding maxims are based ;—" He that is not
against us is for us " (Luke ix. 50); and, " He that is not
with me is against me " (Matt. xii. 30). Every man
who comes in contact with Christ and his gospel,—every
man to whom Christ, in his gospel and by his Spirit, is
brought near,—must of necessity take a side, and, in point
of fact, does take a side. There can be no evasion or
compromise. Either Christ is precious to him, as " to
them that believe ; " or else he is a stumbling-block and
an offence, and is disesteemed and disliked. When at any
moment Christ is presented to me, I must, at that moment, be either accepting or rejecting him ; I must in my
heart's affections be either a friend or a foe ; no intermediate frame of mind is, if I may so say, realizeable; that
is the only alternative. And upon that, as the only possible

alternative, I am to proceed, in my judgment of charity, as regards my neighbour; and in my judgment of faithfulness, as regards myself.

On the one hand, as regards my neighbour, do I see in his character and conduct something that is plainly irreconcilable with his being against Christ? Is there enough, in the temper he manifests and the works he does, to satisfy me, upon a fair view of it, that he cannot be an enemy? Does he show a spirit, and follow a course, that clearly cannot be explained in consistency with any such supposition as that? Then let me unhesitatingly recognise him as one who not merely is not against us, but is for us. He cannot, I am sure, be the one; and therefore he must be the other. Difficulties may present themselves to me in the way of coming to such a conclusion. From my stand-point, or point of view, I may be at a loss to account for sundry differences of opinion, and even of practice, between him and me. " He follows not with us." He has ways of his own. Still, if he is casting out devils in the name of Christ; if even in some one single unequivocal instance he is found feeling and acting in a manner that is incompatible with the very notion of his being against Christ; let me give him the full benefit of that evidence. And on the strength of the principle, that neutrality with regard to Christ and his cause is impossible, let me cheerfully acquiesce in the judgment of charity, that since I cannot but be satisfied that he is not against us, he must be, and must be held to be, virtually and truly on our side.

But on the other hand, as regards myself always,—and

sometimes, when necessary, as regards my neighbour also, —let me wield in another and opposite direction this two-edged sword. Let me not indulge, either a free and easy laxity in judging of myself, or a mawkish, exaggerated, and sentimental affectation of liberality in judging of my neighbour. Let me be faithful as well as charitable. And when I discover or detect a line of action, or habit of thought, that no sophistry or casuistry can harmonize with real attachment to my Lord and Saviour,—when I see another doing, or find myself doing, or desiring to do, anything palpably at variance with the essential character of a disciple,—let me not for an instant entangle myself in the meshes of special pleading. Let me at once boldly face the actual state of the case. One who does such a thing, or has pleasure in those who do it, cannot, by any stretch of charitable construction, be believed to be on the Lord's side. It is not possible that such a one can be for Christ. He must therefore be against Christ. Let me open my eyes to the truth. Let me hear the faithful word of Peter to Simon Magus, and faithfully obey it;-– " Repent therefore of this thy wickedness, and pray God, if perhaps the thought of thine heart may be forgiven thee. For I perceive that thou art in the gall of bitterness, and in the bond of iniquity" (Acts viii. 22, 23).

The same principle is to be applied as a rule of conduct as well as a rule of judgment. You are to remember that, since neutrality is impossible, your only security against the risk of an evil affection prevailing over you, is the strenuous cultivation and exercise of its opposite.

If you would make sure of not wishing or not doing evil to any one, you must make conscience of wishing him well and doing him good.

So the Apostle teaches, in this epistle, with reference to the general duty of benevolence ;—" Love worketh no ill to his neighbour : therefore love is the fulfilling of the law" (Rom. xiii. 10). It may seem a poor commendation of charity, or love, to say of it merely negatively that " it worketh no ill to his neighbour ;" and to make that the ground of the high place assigned to it, as " fulfilling the law," may at first sight be felt to be somewhat strange. Is it really so,—that the working of no ill to my neighbour is the fulfilling of the law ? Is my simply abstaining from inflicting injury, and doing actual harm, all that is required to meet and satisfy the second of the two great commandments,—which is like unto the first,—" Thou shalt love thy neighbour as thyself ?" No. But the Apostle would enforce the lesson that there is no intermediate state of mind or of heart between working ill to your neighbour and loving him. The positive affection of love is the source and the only safeguard of the negative virtue of harmlessness. If love, active love, is absent from your bosom, there must be present in it that " hating of one another" which is characteristic of the natural man ;—and which, though in the absence of provocation it may seem to lie dormant, is sure to manifest itself at any moment when your path is crossed or your wish is thwarted.

Now if this be so when it is your neighbour generally —any one of your fellow-men—with whom you have to do, how much more must it be so when it is one who "persecutes" you ! In that case, the alternative is to be very stringently insisted upon. Either you must be blessing or you must be cursing. Bless, therefore, that you may not curse. Smarting under the sting of some petty annoyance, some poor sarcasm against your faith, some senseless taunt, or some cruel perversion of your Christian offices of kindness,—pause and think, what are the two states of feeling between which, and between which alone, you have to choose.

The persecution, whatever it may be, and of whatever sort, may be viewed in one or other of two lights. You may fix your thoughts on those features of the persecutor's conduct which make it peculiarly offensive. You may dwell on all the aggravating circumstances connected with it;—how entirely and absolutely it is without cause on your part, and therefore inexcusable on his part ; how sadly it disappoints your hopes and damps your zeal ; what insensibility and hard-hearted unthankfulness it indicates ; how seriously it is fitted to mar your usefulness in the sphere of influence in which you move. These and other elements of all but intolerable bitterness you may so brood over as to nurse into increasing strength your sense of ill-usage, and make you feel as if you did well to be angry. You may put a restraint on yourself, and abstain from showing how deeply you are wounded. You may even secretly take credit for continuing to treat the offender as if nothing painful had occurred. But in heart, alas ! may you not be in danger of cursing him?—giving him up, and giving him over, almost contentedly and with complacency, as one upon whom your most dutiful efforts are lost,—who must be, and you are almost tempted to add —who deserves to be, a castaway?

Yield not to this temptation. Rather when you suffer wrong, call to mind the considerations which should bring the wrong-doer before you in a very different light. Look at his case rather than your own. Ah! if you put yourself in his place, you will see much, very much, that should charm all your resentment away, and turn it into tenderest pity and concern. A thousand pleas will occur to you, which, if they do not excuse, at least explain, his aversion to the truth and his dislike of its witness. You picture to yourself his whole history, with its scanty means of good and its myriad influences of evil; you ask yourself what, if his history had been yours, you would have been;—how you, if his lot were yours,—his training, his habits, his companions,—would be inclined to think, and feel, and act. You cease to wonder at his obtuseness and his opposition. You are drawn, and not repelled, by that too easily accounted for infatuation of his, which really hurts not you, but, alas! is ruining his own benighted soul. No thought of self can find harbour within you. All your thought is of him. Your bowels yearn over him the more for the very blindness and madness which make him a persecutor. And so you bless, and do not curse.

11

THE CHARM OF THE
BLESSING: SYMPATHY

"Rejoice with them that do rejoice, and weep with them that weep."
—*Romans 12:15*

THIS precept I hold to be closely connected with the
preceding. Whatever wider application it may have, it
very specially includes "them which persecute you." It
refers to your manner of dealing with the world, and
with those in the world whom you are apt, it may be
with too good reason, to regard as antagonistic and
hostile to your Lord and his cause ;—and to yourselves as
your Lord's witnesses, and the advocates and promoters
of his cause. What is enjoined is a certain genial "milk
of human kindness," such as will move you to feel for,
and feel with, your fellow-men, simply as your fellow-
men, altogether apart from any more special or particular
relation in which they may stand to you, or you may
stand to them. The generous, wide, and unrestricted
tide of genuine human sympathy is to have its full and
free course, amid whatever lines of distinction and
demarcation other considerations may render necessary.
Christianity itself is not to supersede humanity. I am a
Christian ; and nothing that touches Christ and Christi-

anity can be matter of indifference in my esteem. But I am also a man, and nothing that touches man is of foreign concern to me.

As a Christian, I must discriminate and divide men into classes. I cannot look with equal eye on the friends and foes of Him " whom having not seen I love ; and in whom, though now I see him not, yet believing, I rejoice with joy unspeakable and full of glory." I love both ;— but it is with a difference. Those who love Christ and his cause and his people, I love with a brotherly affection true and tender, kind and meek ; embracing them and clasping them to my heart ; giving them all honour above myself, for the Lord's sake. Those that are still opposing themselves to my Lord, and to me his servant on his account, I also love ; with a love that restrains every bitter feeling which their opposition might awaken, and moves me to bless them, to wish them well, to do them good.

But just as that former particular affection of brotherly love would be apt to become narrow, selfish, sectarian; the love merely of those who agree with me, because they agree with me ; unless it were allied to the higher, wider, universal and divine principle of love ; the love which is of God ;— so, the particular modification of love called into exercise when I contemplate them that persecute me as the enemies of my Lord, and therefore mine ; prompting, as it does, forbearance, forgiveness, the returning of good for evil, blessing for cursing ; would be apt to assume the character of a sort of supercilious, patronizing pity,—to give itself the air of a superior condescending to be

benevolent to one beneath him,—were it not tempered by
the infusion of that natural human sympathy and fellow-
feeling, which inclines me, irrespectively of all other
thoughts, whenever I see a fellow-creature rejoicing, to
rejoice with him ; or weeping, to weep with him.

The precept, then, in this view, may be considered,—
I., generally ; and II., in its more particular connection
with your " blessing them which persecute you."

I. The general import of the precept is plain enough.
You are to make your neighbour's case your own, and
suffer what befalls him to affect you, as it affects him.
Nor is it difficult to see how this special duty of sympathy
comes under, and forms part of, the great and broad law
of charity ;—" Thou shalt love thy neighbour as thyself."
As this law is originally given in the Old Testament
(Lev. xix. 18), it stands conspicuous among commandments enforcing such mutual good offices as imply this
putting of yourself in your neighbour's place and realizing
his joy or sorrow as your own ; while in the New Testament that same law is illustrated both by the teaching
and the example of the Lord ;—by his teaching, in such
parables as that of the good Samaritan ; and by his
example, in such scenes as those of Cana and of Bethany;
—and always in such a manner as to enforce the obligation, not of fellow-helping only, if one may use such a
phrase, but of fellow-feeling also.

There is a foundation for this virtue in the constitution
of our nature. There is a natural instinct or principle of
sympathy, which moves us, by an irresistible impulse, to

enter into the pathos or the passion of any scene that is presented to us, or any tale that we are told. It is, in the main, a genuine instinct and trustworthy principle, fitted to be of much practical use, both as a motive to right conduct, and as a help, at any rate, towards the forming of right moral judgments.

But if it is to be a safe guide, it must itself be guided; it must be trained and educated. If it is left undisciplined, and more especially if it is allowed to choose its own objects, and set them in whatever light it pleases, —it becomes a dazzling and bewildering earthly meteor, rather than a fixed heavenly star. For in that case this natural sympathy is apt to create or to seek a world for itself;—a world, whose incidents of varied interest may be moulded and fashioned to suit its own fastidiousness or its own caprice.

Hence the zest with which it revels in story and romance, and finds congenial food, delicious but dangerous, in works of fancy and of fiction. Such works make their appeal to your social and sympathetic sensibility; they stir the deep fountains of emotion within you ; they cast you by turns into all those moods of mind which, in their almost infinitely varied compass, only smiles and tears can express. The excessive study of them,—and any study of them, unless very carefully guarded, tends to become excessive,—may cause such a strain on this sensitive part of your nature as shall render it either impotent or morbid. The faculty of self-control is lost, and a sickly, soft, and sentimental tenderness relaxes and unnerves the soul. It must be so. For the sphere in

which you are accustoming yourselves sympathizingly
to rejoice and to weep, is purely ideal ; its scenes and
incidents are altogether imaginary. They carry you
away from the stern realities of life, which call for sober
action as well as strong passion, into regions of fairyland
in which, with nothing practical to chasten or subdue
your spirits, the thrilling pathos of pity and fierce power
of terror may be intensified to any pitch to which
inventive genius can aspire ; and the burning tear and
the wild laugh may alternate with each other, as the
vivid page presents the picture, by turns, of unheard of
woe and unnatural mirth, with which the heated and
fantastic brain is expected to throb in unison.

This may look like exaggeration ; or it may be
thought that I am putting an extreme case. Be that as
it may, the root and real source of the evil is in every
human bosom. It is that inveterate egotistic leaning
which is ever apt to turn sympathy from being a social,
into becoming a selfish, affection. I go forth into the
world, whether of fiction or of fact, in which I feel
myself most at home. Let it be a world of the latter sort;
let it be real life, and not ideal. I mingle with my
fellow-men, and have my circle of interest and influence
among them. I come in contact with people of different
classes and different characters. I have my friendships
and companionships, my intimacies and familiarities,
among the households of my acquaintance. I take my
part in the incidents and ongoings of the caste to which
I belong, and the department of society in the midst of
which I move, as well as in the comments and conversa-

tions to which these give rise. I enter into the pursuits and pleasures of the passing day. I am open to the impression of its changes and chances. And in addition, perhaps I have, outside of my own proper social sphere, my chosen or appointed walk of duty among my fellow-men of another grade. I have my round of visits among the poor, or at least I am accessible to applications on their behalf. My ear is open to the complaints of want and misery. I take an interest in what I see and hear, and give the tribute of a sincere look, or word, or grasp of sensibility when a suffering brother, or one exulting in sudden relief from suffering, is before me.

Yes; but all the while it may be a merely natural sensibility that I am indulging; and I may be indulging it after a merely natural and selfish fashion. It may still be in a world of its own that my sympathy is really exercising itself; selecting its own congenial materials, or investing with its own colour the materials presented to it; so as to suit them to its refinement and delicacy of taste, and insure that nothing too coarse shall come " betwixt the wind and its nobility." My " rejoicing with them that rejoice, and weeping with them that weep," may thus, after all, be little better than the sort of senti-mental susceptibility that is called forth by romantic re-presentations of interesting scenes and attractive objects of regard;—and therefore as unfit as that is, for standing the wear and tear of actual contact and collision with the stern realities which present themselves in the un-varnished experience of common life.

But now let the merely natural instinct of sympathy

become, through grace, a Christian virtue ; let it be the
discharge of a Christian duty; and what a change is
wrought ! Now, all is real. I deal with a real world,
and with real men and women in it. I have to do with
things as they are, and take people as I find them.

Ah ! how much am I sure to meet with, that, so far
from attracting my fellow-feeling, is fitted to disgust and
to repel ! The persons to whom that fellow-feeling is to
be extended are often those with whom I can have little
or nothing in common; their characters being uncongenial ;
their manners distasteful ; their very air and appearance
perhaps intolerably offensive.   And then, the places where
I have to seek them ; the circumstances with which they
are surrounded ; the companions with whom they are associated,—all about them, in short, may be such as to
make a delicately nurtured mental and moral frame shrink
back in pain or horror.

To overcome obstacles like these, or rather to cease
from regarding them as obstacles at all ; to get through
the barrier which a coarse, forbidding derangement or
deformity may interpose ; to open the door which gives
vent only to sounds that shock the ear and odours loath-
some and stifling to the breath ; to enter the sordid
hovel where, not the elegant refinement of reduced gen-
tility, but the rudest, barest, and most squalid degradation
of poverty reigns ; to face disorder and disease, quarrel-
ling and strife ; and in the midst of all that, to sit down
beside the bed on which some poor sufferer is groaning,
or listen to the news which some gladdened soul is burning to tell ; and, losing all thought of the disagreeable

features of the scene, and the distastefulness of the things and persons belonging to it,—simply and naturally to weep with the weeping, and rejoice with the rejoicing,—that is an attainment, a habit, which nature never owned, —which only grace can reach and sustain. Nor is it only when you sound the lowest depths of the social fabric that your sympathy, if it is of the right sort, will be tried. Wherever you go on your errands of kindness and good will,—in whatever circles you move and mingle,—you will have to encounter influences most unfavourable to the genial flow of feeling. The very forms and usages of common-place routine and conventional etiquette are chilling. You inhale an atmosphere of indifference and frivolity ; or you are all but stifled by the vapour of mean jealousies and angry passions. The gladness and the grief which appeal to your sensibility exhibit themselves in a strange, uncouth guise, to which you cannot get reconciled. The scene, in spite of all its truth and reality, its actual power or pathos, has become so beclouded with the mists of exaggeration and false sentiment,—the din and clamour grow so confusing,—and the parties most concerned seem so unamiable and uninviting,—that you are fain to make your escape, as best you may, from a circle in which you are so little at home, and seek for more congenial fellowship elsewhere.

But no ! Your Christian faith and love forbid. You call to mind that it is not left to your own discretion to say when and where,—in what circumstances and towards what persons,—you shall exercise your sympathy. It is not a matter of taste or of sentiment, but of conscience. The command is universal and unconditional; laying you under an obligation to get the better of all obstacles and embarrassments, all annoyances and dislikes; and requiring you, not for your own pleasure or relief, but for your divine Master's sake, and after his example, always and everywhere to be ready to "rejoice with them that do rejoice, and weep with them that weep."

II. This conscientious and Christian exercise of sympathy is called for very specially towards "them which persecute you." Here, in addition to all the other general difficulties with which the grace or virtue in question may have to contend, there is the one particular consideration, that they who are to be its objects are your enemies, because they are the enemies of your Lord. That consideration, however, is to be lost sight of; all thought of it is to be extinguished. The very point of the precept, indeed, is this;—I must altogether cease to regard these persons as my persecutors; I must come to regard them exclusively as my neighbours and my fellow-men. The precept bids me recognise the essential manhood, or humanity, of every individual with whom I have anything to do,—his possession of a common nature with myself; it bids me recognise that alone; it bids me ignore, and mentally annihilate, everything else about him. He is to me simply a man; a human being; nothing more, nothing less, nothing else. I must strip off from him all adventitious trappings. I must pull down his dwelling, whether it be a palace or a filthy hut. I must disperse his companions, whether I like them or

not. Nay more. I must divest him of his habits, his
manners, his works and ways,—no matter what these are
or have been. I must extricate him out of the entanglements of events and circumstances. To me, he has no
history ; no character, I would almost say. He is before
me bare and naked as a man, that I may feel for him as
a man,—that I may feel with him as a man. In particular, if he is known to me as my persecutor, I know
him in that character no more. I know him only as
a man. And knowing him only in the character of a
man, I, being myself a man, rejoice in his joy and mingle
my tears with his.

Hence the propriety and admirable grace of this commandment respecting sympathy being made immediately
to follow the injunction, "Bless them which persecute
you." In obeying that injunction, you recognise the
persons in view as persecutors. The fact of their being
persecutors is before you ; and is, in truth, expressly and
consciously the ground of your treatment of them. It is
as persecutors that you refuse to curse them. It is as
persecutors that you resolve to bless them. But now
that fact is to be out of sight and out of mind. Now
they are not persecutors, but simply men ; men of like
passions and sensibilities with yourselves. You have
now no thought of the different positions which they and
you occupy with reference to one another. The nature
you have in common is all that is in your mind. As
man to man you draw near to visit every one of them ;
as man with man you commune with him in his joy and
in his sorrow; as fellow-men you laugh and weep together.

This genuine, equal, human sympathy, is indispensable, if you would so bless them who persecute you as not to vex them but to win them. For there is a style and manner of blessing " them which persecute you,"—there is a way of dealing with those who oppose themselves,—which, while it looks like, and may pass for, a strict compliance with the precept, is wholly at variance with its spirit ;—as when one stands aloof and apart, and from some eminence of serene and unruffled equanimity,—some height of transcendental spirituality and heavenly-mindedness,— seems to be ever saying, by look and gesture,—or to be ever thinking in his heart,—Lo ! you there who, out of the depths of your ungodliness and unbelief, try to shoot at me for my attachment to my Lord, see how impotent are all your shafts ; they touch me not ; I stand unscathed. And looking down upon your miserable infatuation, I can afford to dismiss from my mind every feeling of resentment; nay, I cannot find it in my heart to curse you. Rather, as you see, I lift up my hands and bless you. I pardon you, and pity you, and wish you well. And if you will allow me, I will come among you to give my benediction in the form of good offices and good advices ; for, unmoved by your ingratitude, and having patience with your perverseness, I am still ready to be your benefactor and your friend.

Is it any wonder that even an honest desire to do good, if it be clothed in the garb, and affect the airs, of such supercilious condescension, should find doors and hearts shut against it when it goes round among the families of the working men of this working world? The

deep craving, the earnest yearning, for the equal inter-
change of sympathy, that lies, as a sealed spring, in every
human bosom, however sunken, is not thus to be reached
and opened.   But go, O child of God, among your neighbours round your dwelling.   Show them, quite naturally,
that you care not what else they may be, knowing them
only as your fellow-men.   Ah! there is a charm, as you
will find, altogether resistless in its power to cause genial
streams to flow from flinty rocks, in your knowing how,
with artless and guileless fellow-feeling, to " rejoice
with them that do rejoice, and to weep with them that
weep."

12

THE CHARM OF SYMPATHY: MIND ACCOMMODATING ITSELF TO MIND

"Be of the same mind one toward another. Mind not high things, but condescend to men of low estate. Be not wise in your own conceits."
—*Romans 12:16*

THE three clauses of this verse are more closely connected, in point of phraseology, in the original than in our translation. In them all, some form or modification of the word rendered " mind " occurs. And the word must be understood as used in its old sense, to denote purpose or inclination ; the bent and bias of one's character, temperament, or will ;—as when it is said of him that he is so and so minded ; thus minded and not otherwise. In this view, three different faults, or faulty tendencies, of the mind are here pointed out and condemned ; and yet the three are so intimately associated that they may almost be said to be really one. A perverse mind, prone to differ ; a partial mind, preferring what is high, and passing by the lowly ; a proud mind, self-confident and self-conceited ;—these three characteristics ; first, wrong-headedness or pertinacity; secondly, sycophancy or respect of persons ; thirdly, vanity or self-complacency ; mark, or make up, a spirit or habit of mind fatal to the genial flow of natural human sympathy, and such as must

impart an air of stiffness, and artificial patronizing condescension, to that grace in the exercise of which you
study, like your Lord, amid whatever contradiction of
sinners against yourself you may have to endure, to
" rejoice with them that do rejoice, and weep with
them that weep." Thus the precepts in this sixteenth
verse fit into and supplement those of the fourteenth
and fifteenth.

For surely this is the connection in which the verse is
to be taken. The entire passage in the midst of which
it occurs refers, not to the sentiments and affections which
Christians are to cherish among themselves, or towards
one another as Christians, but to the way in which they
are to feel and act towards them that are without. We
cannot imagine that the Apostle means abruptly to return
to the former topic, which has been occupying the preceding part of the chapter ; and that he does so merely
to thrust in for the use of believers an additional exhortation to brotherly unanimity and humility, not certainly
in harmony or in keeping either with what goes before
or with what comes after. This is scarcely doing justice
to the Apostle's line of thought. And it is the less likely
that he should intend thus awkwardly to resume that
subject, because he has already sufficiently handled it, in
the verse in which he has been exhorting the members of
Christ's body to be " kindly affectioned one to another
with brotherly love ; in honour preferring one another ;"
and especially in that earnest appeal, " I say, through the
grace given unto me, to every man that is among you,
not to think of himself more highly than he ought to

think ; but to think soberly, according as God hath dealt to every man the measure of faith." There the very term upon which the precept in the text turns is used ;—not to be high-minded ; to be soberly-minded.

Among yourselves, the Apostle has been saying, in your church arrangements, in your Christian fellowship, be not minded to exalt yourselves ; be not minded to cause rivalry or jealousy among yourselves ; be minded rather to form a sober estimate of your own gifts and claims, and to do full justice to your brother's. And now he widens and extends the range of the exhortation. He applies it to the relation in which you stand to the world; even to the world at whose hands you may expect persecution. With reference to that world he has been laying down the law of charity and fellow-feeling ;—" Bless them which persecute you : bless, and curse not. Rejoice with them that do rejoice, and weep with them that weep." And now, still with reference to these apparently unworthy objects of your blessing and your sympathy, he exhorts you to be minded rather to agree than to differ ; —" Be of the same mind one toward another. Mind not high things, but condescend to men of low estate. Be not wise in your own conceits."

It is not easy, in any translation, to bring out the verbal link of connection running through the three clauses of this verse ; but a sort of expository comment or paraphrase may be attempted.

" Be ye minding the same thing among one another ; let there be a disposition, on your part, when you come in contact with your fellow-men, in their gladness and in their grief, so to identify yourselves with them, that there shall be, between you and them, a common mind, or a community of mind or sentiment, as regards the matter which is agitating them. In order to this, see to it, on the one hand, that you do not so exclusively mind, or regard, high things,—even the things of highest moment to you as Christians,—but that you may suffer yourselves to be led along the more humble walk of ordinary human experience, so as to take an interest in those lower matters about which your fellow-men, simply as men, are occupied.[1] And on the other hand, see to it also that you are not selfishly-minded,—apt to hug yourselves in your own opinion of your superior wisdom, intelligence, and spirituality,—as if you alone, or you especially, were right-minded, and those around you were to be looked down upon as mindless and aimless triflers."

By some such explanatory rendering as this, the meaning which, so far as I can judge, ought to be attached to this verse, may be in some measure indicated. And so the way may be prepared for considering,—I. What that community of mind is which is recommended in the first clause ;—and, II. What are those two other habits of mind which are condemned in the other two clauses as being incompatible with what is recommended in the first.

---

[1] The clause, " Condescend to men of low degree," is of doubtful interpretation. The word "men" is not in the original ; " things" may be equally well supplied. And "condescend" is perhaps too strong a rendering. The idea seems to be that which I have endeavoured to express in the paraphrase. Or it may be put thus : " Mind not high things, but accommodate yourselves to the lowly. Be not in your mind self-conceited, or self-sufficient."

I. "Be of the same mind one toward another." This cannot mean, if the precept is of as wide an application as I take it to be, agreement of opinion. Those with reference to whom you are to cultivate the spirit here enjoined, may be persons with whom you have little in common ; from whom, indeed, you are wide as the poles asunder, as regards the views which you and they respectively hold on questions of most vital interest. It must be so, if you are of God, as his little children, and they are still of the world which lieth in wickedness. The rule, in that case, is clear;—" Be ye not unequally yoked together with unbelievers : for what fellowship hath righteousness with unrighteousness? and what communion hath light with darkness? and what concord hath Christ with Belial? or what part hath he that believeth with an infidel? and what agreement hath the temple of God with idols? for ye are the temple of the living God ; as God hath said, I will dwell in them, and walk in them : and I will be their God, and they shall be my people. Wherefore come out from among them, and be ye separate, saith the Lord, and touch not the unclean thing ; and I will receive you, and will be a Father unto you, and ye shall be my sons and daughters, saith the Lord Almighty " (2 Cor. vi. 14–18).

But while you come out from among them, and are separate from their worldly ways, touching not the unclean thing ; you go among them, sent by your Lord into the world, as he was sent by the Father into the world,—-on the same errand and mission of self-denying, self-sacrificing love. You are not taken out of the world, though you are kept from the evil. You mix with your fellow-men, on lawful occasions, simply as your fellow-men. You visit them, and seek them out, and converse and deal with them; going about to do them good. You come in contact with them. You see what the things are about which they are engaged and interested. You learn what causes their rejoicing, what occasions their weeping. Their cause of joy may not be such as you think would win a smile from you. The occasion of their grief may seem to you unworthy of a tear. But what then? Do you check the flow of your genial fellow-feeling? No. You try to put yourselves in their place. You look at the things which so affect them from their standpoint, or point of view, and not from your own. And so you come to be, and they come to see that you are, of the same mind with them; minding these things as they mind them; noticing and appreciating them as they are noticed and appreciated by them.

This is the heart of genuine human sympathy, its heart of hearts. It is something more than "rejoicing with them that do rejoice, and weeping with them that weep." That may be, after all, as we have seen, a mere instinct of sensibility; scarcely anything else than an affection of the nerves. Laughter is contagious, and so is weeping. The simple sight of the outward manifestations or signs of joy and grief, especially when strongly indulged and unrestrainedly and vehemently expressed, moves you who are spectators beyond control. What may be the matter, you do not know. Before you can hear the tale that is to be told to account for what you see, your countenance catches the look of his on whose face you gaze, and your eyes are as full as his.

So far the man is pleased or soothed. But he wishes to explain, to open up his mind. He would have you to understand what it is that is agitating him so much. You listen. But he perceives that you listen impatiently. He becomes painfully sensible that things do not strike you as they strike him. Your mind does not go along with what he opens up to you of his mind. Embarrassment ensues, on both sides ; and disappointment. There is an interruption, or an end, of sympathy. He is mortified when he discovers that you can so little enter into the grounds of that emotion on his part of which the outward sign, whether cheerful or sad, seemed to find so prompt an echo in your bosom. And you are vexed, ready to be angry with yourself as well as with him, because you cannot see the matter in question in the same light in which it presents itself to him.

What is it that is here wanting ? The very essence and reality of sympathy. For sympathy is not merely the irresistible impulse to laugh when you see laughter, and to weep when you see tears. It is the communion of mind with mind, alike in laughter and in tears.

I speak of mind, not in any high, transcendental and spiritual sense of the word,—as if it were only in the region of pure reason and divine intuition that sympathy could exist. No doubt it is there only that it can exist in full perfection ; when enlightened and holy souls thoroughly comprehend and approve of one another. I speak of mind in the ordinary and common-place use of the phrase,—the mind which, as regards the things that touch you as sentient and social beings, you can have in common with the whole, or with any one, of the human family. Only this community of mind must be genuine. It cannot be either forced or feigned.

A good test or illustration may be found in your intercourse with children. We may experiment with them, because they are so natural. A laughing child, a crying child, who can withstand? The clear, bright ring of the laugh; the sad, wailing cry; go straight to your heart. You are irresistibly attracted. You draw near. The little one notices your radiant face, or your clouded brow. He too is irresistibly attracted. He welcomes your advances. He runs to meet you. He seats himself on your knee and nestles in your bosom. He is ready and eager to tell you all his story. He has a budget of news to open up to you. The triumph he has won; or the dire mishap and grievance he has met with; you must hear it all. On he goes fluently and freely. But he watches your eye. He feels your embrace. And soon, in your listless or averted look; in your slackened hold of him; in your drowsy apathy, or ill-concealed weariness and disgust; he catches evidence enough that your mind is not with his mind. The charm is speedily broken; the spell is dissolved. You and he are soon strangers again; strangers even more than you ever were before. In vain you try to put a constraint upon yourself, and compel yourself to feel or show an interest in the little fellow's recital of his successes or his wrongs. He is a quick observer of the countenance and shrewd reader of the heart; too shrewd to be easily imposed upon. Anything artificial he soon detects. If you would keep him after you have won him, you must be natural. Spontaneously, in genuine fellow-feeling, you must be moved to lay your mind alongside of his mind.

Be it so. You enter into his childhood and are a child with him. You enter with him into childhood's way of viewing things, and feeling things, and talking about things. In and with him, you speak as a child, you understand as a child, you think as a child. And you do so without an effort. It is your disposition and your delight to do so. And doing so thus, you make your prattling friend your own; you get him to trust and love you. Nay more, you get him to sympathize with you, as you sympathize with him. You draw him up to look at things from your stand-point, or point of view, through your being so willing and able to look at them from his. And if he has had any grudge or suspicion against you when you first began to deal with him, your unaffected cordiality in overlooking his petty offences, and provocations, and outbreaks of mischief; your kindness to him in spite of them; your ready smile and tear when he is glad or sorry; and above all, your cheerful patience in listening to what he has to say, and your prompt intelligence in taking up and taking in details and experiences which he cannot always get his seniors to comprehend,—these manifestations of real good-will and a hearty good understanding may go far to make a conquest of him for the only purpose you care to have in view,—his learning to be of the same mind with you, and being brought to sit as a meek and quiet disciple at your feet and at your Master's.

That is the object, and the sole object, which you really contemplate in all your intercourse with "them which persecute you." Your heart's desire and prayer is, that they should be of the same mind with you, like-minded with you as regards all that concerns the glory of God and the salvation of souls ; the divine honour and their own true interests in time and for eternity. That is the way in which you would have your "being of the same mind," you and they together, "one toward another," ultimately brought about. With an eye to that you seek them and their fellows, in the intercourse of ordinary life, or in special endeavours to do them good.

But they thwart and oppose you. And their opposition often takes a form and character peculiarly fitted to irritate and annoy. You have some difficulty in curbing your sorely-tried temper, and suppressing your rising indignation. There is a swelling of righteous anger in your bosom, if not even something almost approaching to a half-smothered malediction on your lips. But you curse not ; no, not in your bed-chamber, not in your inmost soul. And that you may be sure not to curse,—safe against the risk of the slightest approach to cursing, even in a passing thought, you make a point, you make conscience, of blessing. You select and single out the very individual toward whom, for his sore and ceaseless troublesomeness and pertinacity of opposition, you might be most tempted to indulge a slight feeling of vindictiveness. He is to be the special object of your good wishes and good offices, your fervent prayers and pious assiduities. Nor is it as if you were a superior and isolated being, dropping a compliment or an alms down from above to one far beneath and away from you. Not thus supercilious and arrogantly condescending, or cold and distant, is your benediction to be. He is to you a man and a brother. Though not yet a fellow-Christian, he is a fellow-man ; one who, like yourself, when tickled must laugh, and when smitten is fain to cry. As a fellow-man, you feel for him and with him. His rejoicing and his weeping may not be altogether such as yours now are. Your rejoicing in God, your weeping for sin, he cannot understand or appreciate. And his joy for some worldly success, his grief for some worldly loss, may not be altogether such as your chastened spirit in the like circumstances would feel. But they are human and natural, at all events ; and as human and natural, they make an appeal to that human and natural sensibility in you, which your new Christian principle of godlike philanthropy, so far from quenching, only quickens and refines and intensifies tenfold.

For you will not, you cannot, so separate yourself from your worst enemy, or the worst enemy of your Lord, as to be able to school your mind into the habit of looking on unmoved while his whole frame is quivering with rapture or with agony. The agents and servile ministers of a cold and bloody superstition may be somehow trained to some such custom of insensibility. When the opposers of her proud Antichristian pretensions are helplessly in her hands, as the victims of her lawless power, Rome can get her priests and satellites to bless those whom she teaches them to regard as offenders and persecutors. Yes! It is with a blessing pronounced over their heads; it is as their well-wishers, consulting for their good; that Rome's inquisitors consign her enemies to the devouring fire ;—not certainly rejoicing with them when they rejoice, or weeping with them when they weep ; but heartlessly mocking their song of praise, and exulting with fiendish delight over the cries and groans which intolerable torture wrings reluctantly from flesh and blood.

It is not so, however, that you have learned Christ. It is not thus that you bless them which persecute you. Nor is it stiffly and half contemptuously, as if from a distance or from an eminence, standing upon a pinnacle where you may exult in your independence of all their assaults. No. You are among them as men of like passions, like susceptibilities and sensibilities, with themselves. They see that you can smile, and laugh, and weep, as they do ; that you joy in their joy, and mix your tears with theirs. Nor is this a mere transient, superficial emotion on your part ; all traces of it passing away when their grief or gladness is out of sight, or when they try to draw you into their confidence, and open to you their minds. No. They find that you can readily enter into their views and wishes ; sit beside them and listen to all that they have to say, not only without weariness, but with a quick apprehension of their meaning and a warm interest in their tale.

Meet your fellow-men thus ; simply, unostentatiously,

naturally. Watch for opportunities of access to their homes and hearts in seasons when these hearts are opened by some mercy, or softened by some sore stroke of Providence. They may have been accustomed to conceive of you as censors and monitors, frowning on their pleasures, fatiguing them with common-place discourse. Let them see, in some hour of deep movement of soul, that, not as if you were making an effort, or had a purpose to serve, but spontaneously, on the impulse of genuine human feeling, you are with them on the first tidings of their weal or woe; to congratulate, to condole, to be one of themselves;—not thrusting upon them some high-flown spiritual view of your own, which, you think, they ought to be taking of their case; but unaffectedly ready to take simply their natural view of it, and for the time to make it yours.

They thought, if you visited them at all, it would be to lecture them; to reprove and scold them; to find fault with their way of looking at the matter, as nature bids them look at it, in its aspect of natural joy or grief; and to insist upon their looking at it through your eyes; eyes so rapt in the contemplation of the supernatural and the heavenly as to leave no room for the sight and sense of homely household cares. But now they find that you are really one of themselves; thinking, feeling, joying, sorrowing, like them.

May not their hearts be thus touched? Ah! they begin to be ashamed of the injustice they have been doing you. The roughest and hardest begin to understand and know you. They relent towards you. As they see how you enter, intelligently as well as sympathizingly, into their joys and sorrows, they come to have some idea of yours, and to think on their part of entering into yours. They now can imagine how you feel, and how you are minded, amid the opposition, the suspicion, the reproach, which they have been inflicting on you. They are seriously inclined to be of the same mind now with you, and to sympathize with you. In spite of themselves, almost, they are led to do so. For thus simply meeting them, as men meeting men, you throw yourselves upon them, when you throw yourselves among them. Freely, frankly, unreservedly, you let them know your case, as you show them that you know their case. They learn to understand you, as they see that you can understand them. Suspicion of you gradually gives place to sympathy with you. They were jealous of you as intruders ; they perceive that you are friends,—that you not only feel for them and with them, but are desirous that they should feel for you and with you. Win them thus, in matters of common humanity, to apprehend how much you and they have in common ; and you open up a way for still further winning them, by divine grace, to understand those higher matters of God and of eternity, in respect of which ultimately your aim is that they and you should be of the same mind, in the Lord.

II. Such being the import of the positive command, "Be of the same mind one toward another," the propriety of the two negative or prohibitive injunctions which follow will readily appear.

1. " Mind not high things, but condescend to men" or things "of low estate." That obviously is a necessary condition of your cultivating the sort of genial and natural community of mind which is required. You have undoubtedly high things to mind ; but you are not so to mind them as to be above accommodating yourselves to men and things that may seem to you to be of inferior moment. For there is a temptation here. You may be apt to regard, if not your fellow-men themselves, at least many of the matters about which they are occupied, and about which, for the most part, they rejoice and are sad, as frivolous or mean ; unworthy of the serious regard of one whose "conversation is in heaven." The importance which they attach to such things, the work they make about them, and the keenness of their feelings, too often neither very amiable nor very respectable, in connection with them, all tend to awaken in you a certain impatient and intolerant sentiment of disgust. You see trifles exaggerated, mountains made of molehills,—extravagant excitement for the most flimsy cause, or no cause at all ;—your sensitive soul revolts and recoils; you cannot force yourselves to descend into scenes so far beneath the usual height of the spiritual atmosphere in which you live ; you cannot really bring your mind to be on a level with what passes there.

But see ! while you are hesitating, yonder follower of Jesus,—certainly, as you must own, as well entitled and as much accustomed to mind high things as you can be. No scruples trouble him; no awkward reserve or false shame embarrasses him. Away he goes, and down he plunges, among the lowest concerns of the lowest class of his neighbours. Without affectation, without an effort, without seeming to condescend or to stoop;—naturally; simply, spontaneously, he puts himself alongside of that rejoicing or weeping household; he sets his mind alongside of theirs. He is one of them. Their interests are his. No matter how much there may be of what is poor and base about the people he is among, and about the things they care for. He is at home with them; he makes them perceive that he is so; he is with them on equal terms; and he can so understand and feel how they are minded, and how in their circumstances they cannot but be minded, as to become similarly minded himself. Thus, not artificially, or to serve a purpose, but out of the genuine simplicity of an honest and good heart, he literally, and in a good sense, stoops to conquer. He thus, while your fastidious minding of high things may be keeping you aloof, wins access into many a house and many a heart,—first for his words of simple fellow-feeling, and then for words of heavenly wisdom; following the example of the Apostle, who was willing to " become all things to all men that he might win some ;" walking in the steps of the Saviour, who did not " break the bruised reed or quench the smoking flax ;" and earning for himself a share in that blessed promise, of which you may be in danger of coming short; —"They that be wise shall shine as the brightness of the firmament ; and they that turn many to righteousness as the stars for ever and ever" (Dan. xii. 3).

2. " Be not wise in your own conceits," is the other warning given in connection with the precept, "Be of the same mind one toward another." It is the fitting sup-

plement or counterpart of that previous warning, "Mind
not high things." Beware lest there be at the root of
your inability to unbend, something of the noxious element of spiritual pride or spiritual conceit. May it not
be the "high things" of self that you are minding, and
not the "high things" of God? And while you seem to
be repelled by the contrast between the low and trivial
affairs of earth with which your neighbours are taken up,
and the heavenly pursuits in which you are engaged,—
may not the repelling cause be in truth a contrast far
more personal? In the judgment of your superior spiritual wisdom they may be fools; and their works and
ways may be foolish. Self-esteem, after all,—or an undue
opinion or conceit of yourself in your own mind,—may
be the real hinderance to your having that genial and
frank community of mind which otherwise you might be
delighted to have with your fellow-men, simply as your
fellow-men, whatever may be their character, whatever
their relation to you, and whatever the difference between your ways and theirs. Therefore take this second
warning as a necessary addition to the former one. And
let neither the minding of high things, nor the minding
of self, come in the way of your accommodating your
mind to theirs, in the matters that interest them,—
always in the hope that you may thus, by God's blessing,
bring them in time to accommodate their minds to yours
in respect of the things which belong alike to their peace
and to yours.

And now, in fine, let it be ever borne in mind, that

the sovereign remedy for all such tendencies as those against which the Apostle warns you, is a right appreciation of the worth and value of every human being,— every member of the family of man. Be he who he may, and what he may,—be he ever so degraded and vile in your eyes and the eyes of others,—be he ever so unamiable, ever so uncongenial, ever so unfriendly,—still let him be to you what he is to God, and Christ, and the Holy Spirit—and holy angels too. Look at him, not in the light of earth's partial distinctions, but in the light of heaven's common and universal estimate ;—the estimate of Him who is "no respecter of persons "—before whom all alike are "concluded under sin" (Gal. iii. 22), and who "will have all men to be saved and to come unto the knowledge of the truth" (1 Tim. ii. 4). Recognise the dignity of every man ; let man, simply as man, be sacred in your eyes. Count no man beneath your regard ; nor anything about which any man may be naturally and honestly interested. Let him on whom Pharisees in the church, and the vulgar proud in society, affect to look down, see that you respect him, and that you would have him to respect himself. Be followers, in this way, of Him who was reproached as the "friend of publicans and sinners," and of whom it is testified that "the common people heard him gladly."

13

THE ESSENTIAL CONDITIONS: GENEROSITY AND HONOR

"Recompense to no man evil for evil. Provide things honest in the sight of all men." —*Romans 12:17*

THESE two precepts are to be viewed in the light of those that go before (ver. 14–16). The Apostle is laying down rules for your guidance as Christians, not in your special brotherly intercourse with one another, but in your general charitable intercourse with mankind.

You come in contact with the world; and you meet with persecution in the world. Instead of cursing them which persecute you, it is your duty to bless them. That you may be safe from the risk of cursing them, wishing them ill, or cherishing a grudge against them, as you might be tempted to do, when they thwart and hinder you in your Master's work, you are to make them very particularly the objects of your solicitude, in your prayers and pious efforts. Bless them. And see that you do so, and let them see that you do so, not with that air of superiority, that sort of supercilious, patronizing condescension, which is sure to irritate rather than win them; as if, separating yourself from them, and looking at their impotent rage or malice, or their still more provoking callousness and indifference, from a distance or from an eminence, you graciously vouchsafed, not to curse, but to bless. Show them that you have a real, hearty, human fellow-feeling with them as your fellow-men ; that they have your honest sympathy in their concerns (ver. 15). Let this sympathy, moreover, be intelligent and patient. Let it not be the mere fleeting tribute of a sentimental smile or sigh ; the evanescent emotion of one who is so far touched by the outward signs of grief or of gladness as to have a kindly word, or look, or gift, to bestow in passing, but who cares not to be troubled further about the case. There are few things so disappointing and chilling to a warm heart ; so likely to widen the breach between you and those to whom, in spite of their opposition to you and to Christianity, you would fain extend your good offices and good will ; as when they perceive, on their beginning to open their mind to you about the joy or sorrow with which you have seemed to be sympathizing, that you cannot spare the time, or take the pains, or open your mind, to let their story in. Let not this be the manner of your sympathy. Show them, not artificially and stiffly, but naturally, that you can lay your mind alongside of theirs, and can be at the trouble to understand what they think and feel ; that you do not "mock their useful toil, their homely joys and destiny obscure," or "hear with a disdainful smile the short and simple annals of the poor ;" that you are not so raised and elevated into a transcendental region of high and heavenly musing as to be above taking a human interest in "those trifles which make the sum of human bliss and woe ;" and more than all, that

you are not so wrapt up in the notion of your own
spiritual superiority as to count it a degradation or an
effort to condescend to them and their affairs (ver. 16).
Be ye thus "gentle unto all, apt to teach, patient; in
meekness instructing those that oppose themselves."

It is at this stage, and in this connection, that the two
precepts enjoining,—the one, forbearance or abstaining
from retaliation towards any man, and the other, honesty
or being upon honour with all men,—are introduced;
and as thus introduced, they will be found to harmonize
well with the general lesson the Apostle is enforcing;—
the lesson of what I would call—Christianized humanity.

I. As to the first of these precepts,—one might be
inclined to ask,—is it needful, after all that has been
already said, to add the warning,—"Recompense to no
man evil for evil?" What risk is there of your doing
so, if you go among your fellow-men in the spirit and
manner already described? Is it not, at any rate, a kind
of work of supererogation, if it be not even like casting
doubt on the simplicity and sincerity of that Christian
and human habit of sympathy which you may be supposed now to be cultivating, to bid you, who are thus
minded among yourselves and towards all men, beware
of so obvious a fault, and one so manifestly and flagrantly
incompatible with your being thus minded, as that of
retaliation? To the inspired Apostle, to the inspiring
Spirit, it does not appear to be so.

Let it be remembered that the principle of retaliation
has in it a certain element of righteousness. To a large

extent it commends itself to our natural sense of justice. " With what measure ye mete, it shall be measured to you again," is a sort of treatment which men feel to be fair.. The law of Moses expressly recognised and sanctioned the principle of retaliation as the rule of punishment in public criminal procedure ;—although it gave no countenance to the Pharisaic gloss, condemned by our Lord, which extended the application of the principle to the intercourse of private life. Even there, however, in a modified form, the principle may be apt to solicit occasional approval, and to solicit too the approval of men who are far from being destitute of Christian charity and Christian sympathy.

For the question may be raised in some such way as this : How am I to treat one who injures me ; and not merely injures myself personally, but in and through me, injures my Lord and his cause ? It may be put upon grounds and considerations altogether apart from any personal feeling of mine. And it may be put very plausibly in an extreme case.

Thus, personally, and so far as my own feelings are concerned, I am conscious of no ill-will. I can truly say that there is not in my bosom the slightest inclination to curse. On the contrary, I am certain that I wish the man well. It is in my heart to bless him, to pray for him,—to do him all the good in my power. But is it right to let his injurious conduct pass as if I did not notice it, or did not disapprove of it ? For the sake of the great interests involved, for the sake of the offender himself, should he not be made to feel to what he has justly exposed himself? It is not that I care for the wrong done to me, however ill he may be using me. All that I could bear; I could consent to lose all that I have,—fortune, and character, and life itself, if I alone and mine were the sufferers. But the cruel shaft strikes deeper and higher. Christ himself is wounded. The reproach falls on Him. And the assailant is very pertinacious. He will listen to no reason. All the resources of friendly and kindly dealing with him have been tried, and tried in vain. The case is really desperate. What is to be done? Of course, I would not for a moment dream of retaliating, in the way of inflicting upon him the very same kind of injury that he is inflicting upon me. But does not justice require that he should be made to suffer somehow? Is it not right that he should be visited with some recompense or requital for the evil he is doing? If it is in my power to expose him in certain quarters in which he is rendering me and my religion no good service; to show what sort of person he is, and how he is acting towards me and others like me; to vindicate and right myself, though at the expense of letting some of the legitimate consequences of his behaviour come down upon him;—am I not warranted in doing so? May it not be my duty to do so? Do I not owe it to myself and to him, to Christianity, to common honesty and justice, to do so? I may be instrumental in doing him some evil. But what of that? Can I help it? Is it not deserved?

Is there not room here for self-deception? Is there no danger of your gliding thus unconsciously into the false position of those of old time who said, "An eye for an eye, and a tooth for a tooth?" Insensibly you bring a judicial maxim, which may be right and good when punishment or retribution is to be awarded judicially, in terms of public law, to bear upon the regulation of your personal and private conduct as an individual. You make yourself a judge, and a judge in your own case.

This is the very subtlety of the snare. The evil done to you, as you dwell upon it with a natural tendency to exaggeration, so swells, and gradually grows in your estimate of it, that it comes to be lifted out of the class or category of personal and private wrongs, and assumes the aspect and character of a public offence, such as requires to be dealt with according to the principles of equity, and truth, and right. This is your danger. You quit the floor and usurp the bench. You forget that you are a party ; you assume to be the judge. Meeting the evil-doer, as man meeting man, on the common arena of ordinary life, you overlook the injury ; you have not a word to say about it ; you treat him as if it had never had an existence. But it has other than merely personal bearings. These bulk in your eye. They seem to you to demand consideration. How, in the view of these other bearings, the matter is to be disposed of, is a question that falls to be determined. Are you to determine that question? Do you set yourself to determine it ? Are you the fittest person to determine it ? May it be safely left to you to say, in what so nearly concerns yourself, how far reasons of a general nature, irrespective of what is personal to you, may require that the evil should be noticed, even at the risk or to the effect of its being recompensed with evil? Is not that really a judicial question? And are you a competent, or an impartial judge? Safer for you is the maxim of the text, " Recompense to no man evil for evil."

Or, as I may now put it, safer for you is the maxim of the Lord ;—" Judge not." For in part, at least, that maxim corresponds with the maxim of the Apostle, as I have been trying to explain it. And in that view the whole force of the motive which the Lord suggests may be brought to bear on the enforcing of it ;—" Judge not, that ye be not judged." Consider the manner in which you are now warranted to hope and believe that God deals with you, as regards the evil which you do to Him ; and deal ye in like manner with your fellow-men, in regard to the evil which they do to you.

How does God deal with you now for the evil which you have done to Him ? Does he recompense evil for evil ? Does he judge ?

Assuredly, if he does judge, it must be to the effect of recompensing evil for evil. That is the fixed, unchangeable law of his moral administration. And it is a law founded, not on any consideration of the evil as affecting himself personally, but on a view of it infinitely broader, deeper, higher. Your evil, O sinner, extendeth not to him personally, any more than does the goodness of the holiest of his saints. But it tarnishes the glory of his eternal name; it touches the foundation of his everlasting throne ; it puts to hazard the well-being of his whole intelligent creation ; it saps the pillars of law and justice which uphold the universe. On grounds like these must he proceed when, as a judge, he deals with you for the evil you have done ; and, proceeding upon such grounds, he must needs, in a terrible sense and to a terrible effect, recompense evil for evil.

Is it so that you now, O believing brethren, conceive of God as dealing with you? Why is it not so? Has God abdicated his functions as judge? Has he abandoned the seat of judgment? Ah ! you well know that he has not. But one has been found,—the Judge himself has found him, the very God against whom and in whose sight your evil has been done ; one has been found, able and willing to stand for you, and to answer for you in the judgment. With him God has dealt for your evil; judicially he has dealt with him ; in the fullest measure of justice, to the utmost extent of the requirements of law, recompensing evil for evil. And you, led by the Spirit, have been brought into such a relation of oneness and identity with this chosen one, that, virtually and truly, God's judicial dealing with him for your evil has become a judicial dealing personally with you. For you are crucified with Christ. With Christ for you, with you in Christ, God has dealt, as judge ; recompensing evil for evil. This you have believed, realized and felt, in your being ingrafted into Christ ; and so ingrafted into him as to be partakers of his death ; the death which he died when the recompense, or retribution, of your evil came upon him. And now, as there is no more recompensing of evil for evil,—evil deserved for evil done,—in his case, as your represen-

tative; so neither is there any more of that mode of
dealing on the part of God in your case, as represented
by Christ. The footing on which you now are with God
is such as to preclude,—as to any judicial application of
it,—the *lex talionis*, or principle of retaliation. There is
no more any judicial recompensing of evil for evil. That
is over and done, in Christ for you, and therefore to you
in Christ. It is not in that way, nor by that rule, that
God now deals with you. No. He does not in that sense
judge; recompensing evil for evil. His treatment of you
now is altogether gracious; good, and only good.

When you consider this; and when you consider at
what a cost, and by what a sacrifice, your God and Father
has, if we may dare so to speak, freed himself from the
necessity of dealing with you judicially, and recompensing
to you personally evil for evil,—even at the cost, and by
the sacrifice, of his laying upon his own beloved Son the
inflicted evil, in recompense for your committed evil,
which otherwise must have come upon you, and crushed
you everlastingly;—how can you ever think of introducing
again into your treatment of your fellow-men anything
like that element of judicial retaliation which your God
has thus, so marvellously and graciously, provided for
and disposed of, in his treatment of you? Ah! will you
not rather lean to the side of being willing almost,
yourself, like Christ, to be the victim in a case like this?
He consented to suffer, the just for the unjust, that he
might bring you to God. When your evil, the evil of
your sin against his Father and himself, was upon him,
he had no thought of recompensing evil for evil to you.

Are you called to suffer in this respect with him ? Be
content to suffer as he did. Be willing to bear all the
scath. Let him who does you the evil escape ; and be
you, in a sense, the victim and the scapegoat, bearing the
evil, and not resenting it. So you manifest your oneness
of spirit with Christ, as he manifested his oneness of
spirit with the Father. And so you go forth into a
hostile world, as he did, meek and lowly in heart, never
allowing any sense of wrong or apprehension of ill-usage
to interfere with the full flow of your warm and generous
humanity. The man who needs your blessing, whose joy
or sorrow calls for your sympathy, you learn to regard
simply as a man. You refuse to look at him in any
other light. You cast out of view all considerations of
his position, or his associations, or his habits and ways.
And if he has done, or is doing you, evil, you cast out of
view that consideration also. He is human and you are
human. The sole bond between him and you is your
common human fellow-feeling ;—intensified and hallowed,
on your part, by your longing desire to have him as a
fellow-partaker with yourself in the divine fellow-feeling
of " the man Christ Jesus."

II. The positive command, " Provide things honest in
the sight of all men," is a fitting sequel or supplement of
the preceding prohibition, " Recompense to no man evil
for evil."

The meaning of the expression, "Provide things honest,"
is not at first sight very clear. It might seem to point
to the duty of Christians making an honest and honour-

able provision for themselves and their households, by such habits of industry and economy as men generally approve of. No doubt that is a duty; and it is urged as such upon Christians elsewhere. But the introduction of it here would not be to the purpose. Nor does the language in the original require,—some would say, it does not even suggest,—that meaning. The phrase is wide and general. "Keep an honourable look-out;" or, "Be honourably on your guard;" or simply, "Be upon honour," before all men, as to the matter on hand;—that may fairly be said to be the import of the Apostle's recommendation.

But perhaps the meaning of the phrase generally, and as it is used here, may be best gathered from a passage in the Second Epistle to the Corinthians.[1]

Paul is there speaking of the collection which was in course of being made by the Gentile churches on behalf of the poor and persecuted saints in Jerusalem and throughout Judea. Among other arguments which he urges to encourage the liberality of the Corinthians, he adverts to the security which they had for the right and faithful management and administration of the fund to which they were asked to contribute. And in doing so, he lets them see, in a remarkable manner, his practical good sense, his

---

[1] Having spoken of Titus as being forward to visit Corinth, on the business of the collection, Paul adds;—"And we have sent with him the brother, whose praise is in the gospel throughout all the churches; and not that only, but who was also chosen of the churches to travel with us with this grace, which is administered by us to the glory of the same Lord, and declaration of your ready mind: avoiding this, that no man should blame us in this abundance which is administered by us: providing for honest things, not only in the sight of the Lord, but also in the sight of men"—(2 Cor. viii. 17-21).

business-like wisdom and sagacity. Surely, in so far as
the gathering in, and safe custody, and ultimate disposal of
this money were concerned, he might have asked a vote of
implicit confidence; he might have stood upon his character
and credit. What need, with such a man as Paul, of
witnesses, and checks, and auditors? Is not his word as
good as his bond? Are not his hands as trustworthy as
the Imperial Treasury? But no. See how careful he is
to guard against the risk of his good being evil spoken
of. He will have associated with himself in this business
persons whose concurrence and co-operation shall prevent
the possibility of suspicion. He is not content with one,
however unexceptionable. He must have two witnesses
at least. There must be joined to himself and Titus,
another accredited agent of undoubted and well-known
reputation for trustworthiness. And the reason which
the Apostle gives for such precaution is, that, on the
one hand, he may not be liable to even a whisper
that might be prejudicial to his good name;—" Avoiding this, that no man should blame us in this abundance
which is administered by us;"—but that, on the contrary,
and on the other hand, his scrupulous integrity and cor-
rectness may be clear before all eyes;—" Providing for
honest things, not only in the sight of the Lord, but also
in the sight of men."

Thus even in a pecuniary transaction, in the keeping
of an account, Paul's sense of honour was keen. He was
sensitively alive to the maintenance of his character as a
man of honour in the opinion of his fellow-men. It was
not enough for him to have the testimony of his own

conscience before God. He desires to stand well, as an honourable man, with his fellow-men. He takes pains to secure that he shall.

No doubt, with him, this regard for his own honour was subservient to a higher end. He sought to turn it to account for the greater glory of Him whose servant he was, and for the higher good of those with whom he desired to stand well. Still the material fact is, that he attaches value and importance to the opinion which men may form of him and of his conduct. He will see to it that, in any trust he may undertake, his honour shall not be open to question.

Now it is the same phraseology that the same Apostle uses, in his exhortation here addressed to the Romans, as in his protestation there to the Corinthians. He exhorts the Romans,—he exhorts you, believers, to be as sensitive on the point of honour as he tells you, in his Epistle to the Church at Corinth, that he was himself.

There is a difference as regards the matter at issue; but it is a difference which makes the exhortation all the stronger. Paul himself was sensitive as to his own honour, in a matter of mere pecuniary adjustment, in which he might have defied all assailants, and scorned to lead proof, or refer to any witnesses as associated for that purpose with himself. He would have you to be as sensitive as he was; but in a higher region or department of duty. For it is here not a special, and as one might say, financial, question; the auditing and settling of the accounts connected with a collection of alms. It is a question of far higher Christian duty.

It is virtually the question, as put by all men ; Are you in good faith ; are you upon honour, in your intercourse with us ?—with the world in which you and we meet ? Do you mean what you profess ? what you say ? Do you really "recompense to no man evil for evil ?"

It is a very searching question; and a question of very wide reach,—not to be restricted to one single particular, but of general application. It is nothing short of this question, addressed to Christians, as consecrated to God, bound in a holy fellowship among themselves, and called to exercise towards the world in which they live, the forbearance, the toleration, the unresisting and uncomplaining meekness of Christ himself ; Are you in earnest?—in good faith?—upon honour? And are you so in earnest that you may appeal, not only as men of piety to God, but as men of honour to the world itself? Can you stand confidently upon your honour, before the world, as you stand confidently upon your consciousness and your conscience before God?

That is the appeal. And it is a right and relevant appeal, when the matter to which it relates is not your intercourse with your God,—you alone with him alone, —but your intercourse with your fellow-men.

Nor is the appeal, alas ! by any means, unnecessary. For there certainly is an impression, even in quarters entitled to some respect, that a high profession of Christianity, —of Christian holiness or Christian meekness,—is sometimes regarded by those who make it as somehow setting them above, or setting them free from, some of the rules and considerations of truth and courtesy upon which honourable and high-minded men of the world consider themselves bound to act. No doubt the impression is often erroneous, the result of ignorance or prejudice. " The natural man" cannot fully understand " the spiritual" man. The spiritual man, being himself one of " the things of the Spirit of God," can be only "spiritually discerned" (1 Cor. ii. 14, 15). There may, therefore, be not a little in his demeanour and walk fitted to perplex onlookers, who have no insight into the character of his inner life of faith, and no sympathy with its motives. There may be anomalies of conduct, apparent deviations from the line that approves itself to their eyes as the straightest, which they may be at a loss to account for, in such a one as he is ; and which he himself, if called upon, would be at a loss to explain intelligibly to them. Still, admitting all that, it is to be feared that the blame is not always on one side. Beyond all question, your decided Christian and evangelical profession may so far, in this particular, be a snare to you. You may be apt to feel as if the higher and more heavenly principles upon which you are called to act, did to some extent supersede the ordinary and trite common-places of a lower and more earthly code of morals. It is human nature ; the nature of the human heart, which " is deceitful above all things, and desperately wicked."

You may not be conscious of this lurking antinomian tendency. But beware of it. Much scandal to religion may come of it ; and that in many ways.

Take, for instance, the case of a man of high religious profession, on whose Christian integrity in all his business

transactions, business men have been accustomed implicitly
to rely.   Suddenly it is discovered that he has been pursuing a course which common, vulgar, worldly honesty
condemns.   Perhaps the man is not a wilful hypocrite ;
deliberately trading on his Christian character, and making a gain of godliness.   Very probably his decline and
fall may be traced, as to their source or commencement, to
some sort of idea like this getting secret entrance into his
mind ;—' I am a Christian.   I must, as a Christian, conduct my business upon high Christian principles.   I mean
to do so.   My establishment is to be one that is sanctified by the word of God and by prayer.   So far as in me
lies, its atmosphere is to be pure and pious, spiritual
and heavenly.   I do not intend to be contented with the
mere conforming of my practice to the letter of the law,
and such a routine of plain dealing as may satisfy those
who know no higher standard than that of the world's
conventional morality.   I, for my part, aim at something
more.   I draw my rules and motives from above.'

So far well.   But as things move on, he comes into
contact with parties willing to be his instruments and
agents ; themselves not over-scrupulous as regards adherence to the rules of fair trading and fair play, and
ready enough to cover their laxity under the cloak of an
appeal to a sort of transcendental spirituality.   He gets
into difficulties.   He needs and accepts the help of such
allies.   Insensibly he sullies his bright shield, and lets
mists gather on " the eye " which, " even turned on empty
space," should " beam keen with honour."   His notions of
right and wrong are warped.   He becomes a practical

Jesuit,—a subtile schoolman,—a sophist,—a casuist. Nice
points about the lawful and the expedient perplex him.
Vague purposes of restitution, dreamy prospects of extri-
cation, lead him, like a meteor, deeper and deeper into
the bog. All the while, shedding a general halo and
odour of sanctity over his whole proceedings, and merging
questions of detail in the one grand end contemplated,
there is his Christian desire and intention of making
all ultimately subservient to the glory of God, the cause
of Christ, and the good of souls. So he bewilders himself in a spiritual ideal, while his real business life is becoming one practically of not only most unspiritual, but
most unrighteous management, and most unscrupulous
manœuvring,—on which all people of probity cry shame.

Oh ! to save himself from the yawning pit of fraud,
and from a bankruptcy worse than that of fortune ! And
what is needed to save him ? What, by God's help, will
save him ? Let him borrow for a moment the world's
eyes : yes ; the eyes of the unconverted, but yet unsophisticated world. Let him look upright men in the face,
and judge after their upright judgment. Let him "provide things honest in the sight of all men."

As it stands in the passage now before us, this precept,
or warning, is given in connection with the course of conduct which you are called to pursue, and the demeanour you
have to observe, as members of Christ's body, in your intercourse with the world, considered as a system of things and
state of society sure to be adverse, and apt to be persecuting. Here, too, there is room for the operating of the
temptation now in question. There is a risk,—those of

you who best know yourselves, and have been most tried
by being brought into close personal contact with scenes
and persons uncongenial to you as spiritual men, will be
the first to acknowledge that there is a serious risk,—of
your becoming, if not spiritually proud, yet, at all events,
spiritually sensitive, and spiritually selfish. You practise
meekness, no doubt, and exercise forbearance ; you bless,
and curse not ; you do good, moreover, as you have opportunity; you are not unkind ; you do not retaliate.
But somehow you draw off, and separate, and isolate
yourself. On the faith of that very patience and gentleness under evil treatment which you are enabled to exhibit,
you feel almost as if you were entitled to take your own
way, and pursue your own path, apart. Your fellows, with
whom you are associated, feel as if, while you bore with
them, you shunned them. You let them perceive how
much it costs you to bear with them, and how little you
and they have in common. They perceive that you are
determined to do your duty to them. But they perceive
also that it is to a large extent without the eye of honour,
and without the heart of sympathy and love.

To guard against so unhappy a result or tendency, the
Apostle would have you to recognise, not only your
fellow-men generally, but even those among them from
whom, on account of their opposition to you, or their
personal qualities, or any other cause, you may be most
inclined to keep your distance, as entitled nevertheless,
or rather all the more on that account, to your respect
and deference. It is an old maxim, that " the greatest
reverence is due to children,"—(*maxima debetur pueris*

reverentia). If you would win them and have influence over them, you must respect them, and be upon honour with them; they must be made, moreover, to feel that you do respect them, and really are upon honour with them. To treat them, however kindly, as if you were not in any sense or to any extent amenable to their judgment,—as if you could set at nought their criticism,— as if it mattered not to you what they thought of you,— as if they were incompetent to form any opinion of you or of your proceedings at all deserving of regard,— is to commit a fatal error, and to forfeit your moral hold over them. There is, there must be, some measure of awe in your conduct towards them. You must practically show them that you wish them to understand you,—that you value their approval, and desire to stand well with them,—that you do justice to them, and would have them to do justice to you,—if you would have them to take in good part the advances which you make to them in good faith, and to give to these advances a frank and cordial response.

In the same way you must deal with those in the world around you whose suspicious hostility you would disarm, and whose confidence you desire to conciliate. They must not be to you, or imagine that they are to you, a separate caste,—or a set of outcasts,—to whom you may extend, as over a gulf, the hand of benevolence, and some sign also of a common sympathy,—while between them and you there are no relations of equal and mutual responsibility recognised. Let them not suppose that you undervalue either themselves or their

thoughts of you,—that, contented with the verdict of
your conscience and your God, you care little for what
their impression or their feeling may be, as to your actions
and dispositions towards them.   Let it be in their sight,
as in the sight of all men, that you " provide things
honest,"—that you desire to be honourably approved.
Then they will apprehend that they are treated by you
really as your fellow-men.   Their just and reasonable
self-esteem will not be wounded, but satisfied and gratified.   All painful sense of inferiority will be extinguished.   The scowling brow will unbend ; the closed
hand will relax and open ; the jealous spirit will relent ;
the cold heart will warm ;—and the man who may have
been accustomed to shut his door against the visitor who
came only to act the part of a benefactor, a well-wisher,
a sympathizer, a patron, will welcome you who come to
him as man to man.   Instinctively perceiving that you
respect his manhood and desire him to respect yours, he
will with open arms receive you as his own and his
children's friend, and lend a ready ear,—the Spirit
making him willing,—to all that you have to say as
to that higher platform of divine as well as human
fellowship, on which you would fain find yourself in a
position honourably to respect his Christianity, as you
ask him honourably to respect yours.

14

THE END SOUGHT: PEACE

"If it be possible, as much as lieth in you, live peaceably with all men."
                                                       —*Romans 12:18*

THE qualifications or conditions attached to the precept, " Live peaceably with all men," instead of weakening its force, render it all the more emphatic. They are moreover, at all events, demanded by the nature of the case. They are not deemed necessary when the precept occurs, as it does occur, elsewhere in the New Testament, and in a different connection from that of our present text ;— as when the Lord says, " Salt is good; but if the salt have lost his saltness, wherewith will ye season it ? Have salt in yourselves, and have peace one with another" (Mark ix. 50);—or the Apostle Paul, " Finally, brethren, farewell. Be perfect, be of good comfort, be of one mind, live in peace; and the God of love and peace shall be with you" (2 Cor. xiii. 11);—or again, " We beseech you, brethren, to know them which labour among you, and are over you in the Lord, and admonish you ; and to esteem them very highly in love for their work's sake. And be at peace among yourselves" (1 Thess. v. 12, 13). In these passages the command refers to your intercourse and fellowship with one another as believers. The command, in that case, is absolute.

It must be so. To assume, or admit, that the maintenance of peace within the Church may be impossible, is out of the question. The Church is Christ's body. Its constituents, however many and diverse in office and function, are one body in Christ, and every one members one of another. To provide beforehand for a breach of the peace, as if it could be at any time, or in any circumstances, inevitable, would plainly be a suicidal and self-contradictory arrangement. It would be a surrender of the very principle on which the doctrine of your union and communion in Christ is based. The ideal of the one body with many members, or of the many members making up one body, implies that there always ought to be, and that there always may be, peace among themselves. Provision, indeed, is made for offences coming even into the Church, or body of Christ. In an alternative way this is done. Provision is made for the case in which I am in fault ;—" If thou bring thy gift to the altar, and there rememberest that thy brother hath ought against thee; leave there thy gift before the altar, and go thy way; first be reconciled to thy brother, and then come and offer thy gift " (Matt. v. 23, 24). Provision is also made for the case of my brother being in fault, walking disorderly, or giving just cause of offence to a fellow-disciple. But in the very law laid down for the treating of this, as of the other case, the principle, or ideal, of the Church's corporate unity is assumed. A Church member gratuitously and wilfully breaks the peace,

and will not suffer himself to be amenable either to private remonstrance or to more formal dealing. In these
circumstances, his conduct is to be viewed as so incompatible with his Christian character and standing, that to
the party offended, at least,—to me, if I am the party
offended,—he is to be "as an heathen man and a publican."
Henceforth my duty towards him, so far as his breach of
the peace is concerned, comes under the category of what
I owe, not to a Christian brother, but to one of the unbelieving ;—with whom, as with all men, I am commanded
indeed to live peaceably,—with the proviso, however,
" if it be possible."

Clearly, then, on every ground of consistency and
common sense, when the rule is given for the internal
pacification of the Church, and the guidance of its
members in their mutual relations among themselves, it
must be given unconditionally. The notion of its being
ever impossible to comply with the rule to live peaceably must be scouted as wholly inadmissible.

It is otherwise, however, when the precept is announced
universally, or with a more immediate and special reference to your connection with them that are without, and
your conduct towards them. Now, that is the case here.
It is your way of feeling and acting as regards the world,
or mankind generally,—the very world in which you are
to lay your account with being persecuted and evil-en-
treated,—that is to be regulated and ruled. The command, as applicable here, and in such a case, must obviously
be qualified. They with whom you have now to do are
not, or at least may not be, your brethren in the Lord.

You and they are not at one, and may have little or nothing in common. The principles and maxims which you hold sacred they do not acknowledge; and, indeed, cannot understand. Of the Spirit which worketh in you "the peaceable fruit of righteousness," they have no experience. Peace, which is, or ought to be, the element in which your soul moves and dwells, is a strange dream to them; for "there is no peace, saith my God, to the wicked." "The peace of God" does not "keep their hearts and minds." They are "like the troubled sea, when it cannot rest." With such unquiet neighbours you cannot always, if you would, live peaceably. Rather, you must be constrained often to bewail your hard lot, as did the Psalmist;—"Woe is me, that I sojourn in Mesech, that I dwell in the tents of Kedar! My soul hath long dwelt with him that hateth peace. I am for peace; but when I speak, they are for war" (Ps. cxx. 5-7).

Nor is this all. This earth, on which you are to live peaceably, is the very earth of which the Lord himself so emphatically said,—"Think not that I am come to send peace on earth: I came not to send peace, but a sword" (Matt. x. 34).

To keep the peace, then, upon a field of battle; to live peaceably, sword in hand; peaceably to wage war, and that a war which knows no truce or compromise;—such is the practical problem given you to solve. That the solution of it should be ever possible, might seem to be the wonder; not that it should sometimes not be so. You, moreover, are the aggressors in this contest. You, as it were, give the challenge; you provoke the

hostilities. You disturb the world's peace, such as it is.
Your preaching of Christ, your witnessing for Christ, your
living for Christ, all tend to break up men's repose, and
make them uneasy, and therefore angry. The more faithful you are to Christ, and to them, the more must you run
the risk of irritating their pride, and rousing their passions. The spirit that worketh among them, as the children of disobedience, is the serpent; between whose seed
and the seed of the woman the Lord hath put irreconcilable enmity. You go among them as men that would
turn the world upside down. How can you expect them
to live peaceably with you? How can you hope to be
allowed to live peaceably with them?

How but by entering into the spirit of that " Christianized humanity" which the Apostle has been commending?
Let all men see that, underlying the spiritual and heavenly
brotherhood into which you enter with Christ and all
that are his, and hallowed and intensified by it, there
beats strong in your bosom the pulse of a real human
brotherhood with all who bear the human name. You
and they may be on opposite sides in the great battle
between light and darkness, between Christ and Belial,
for which earth finds the arena, and heaven and hell furnish the witnesses and onlookers. In that battle, kindness to them, as well as fidelity to yourselves and to
the Captain of your salvation, will not suffer you to give
them any rest, or to give their principles any quarter.
You must be ever assailing them, and ever pursuing them.
Then, moreover, as to the whole of that inner life which
is the real life of a man, you and they are wide as the

poles asunder. You cannot enter into their secret, or admit them into yours. They and you are, and must be, in the hidden life of your souls and theirs, strangers and adversaries; without common sympathies; dwelling apart;—as it were, in different worlds.

Ah! but on that very account try all the more to live peaceably with them all. And for that end, make it clear and palpable to them, that while you have no common sympathies with them as fellow-believers, you have all common sympathies with them as fellow-men. You have, and will have, no quarrel with them in that character. You do not, on the ground of your Christianity and their opposition to it, elevate yourselves above them; keeping them at a distance; looking upon them with a sort of stern, supercilious pity, and from the height of your own serene composure, sending down your blessing in exchange for that cursing of theirs which, as you take care to let them know, does not reach you. They, for their part, are very apt to conceive of you as occupying such a position towards them; and so conceiving of you, it is not wonderful that they should imagine that the controversy between you and them is a personal one, and that you hold them personally to be your enemies or your inferiors, and the objects of your dislike or your contempt accordingly. The imagination, you feel in your inmost soul, is groundless. See that you so act towards them as to make them also feel that it is groundless. Disarm their suspicion of there being any other sentiments in your bosom towards them than sentiments of warm friendship and entire good-will. You are not

their enemies because you tell them the truth. You recognise them as entitled not only to your good offices
but to your smiles when they rejoice, and your tears when
they weep. There is no such cold distance, or jealous
dread, or stern defiance on your side, as they think. You
love and would live peaceably with them all.

Still there is need of the precept being qualified by
the conditional clauses,—" If it be possible, as much as
lieth in you, live peaceably with all men." You may not
succeed in disarming worldly men's hostility of its bitterness, and conciliating their confidence in your personally
kind dispositions towards them. They may persist in
believing, or affecting to believe, that you mean to treat
them as enemies; and they may be bent on treating you as
enemies. They will not accept your advances in good part;
believing, or affecting to believe, that they are not made
in good faith. They will pick a quarrel with you if they
can; and if they will, they can. They will misunderstand,
or misconstrue, something, no matter what, in whatever
you say or do. They will listen to no explanations. There
can and shall be no mistake. They will not suffer you
to live on even civil and courteous terms with them.

The fault then is not yours. You take the benefit of
the limitations of the statute. They into whose house
you enter, bearing good tidings, will not receive you, or
so much as give you a cup of cold water. You shake
the dust of their threshold from off your feet, as you leave
them with the solemn warning,—" Notwithstanding be
ye sure of this, that the kingdom of God is come nigh
unto you " (Luke x. 11).

But remember; if these limitations and qualifications of the statute are, in one view, a necessary abatement of its strictness; in another view, they deepen the solemnity of its obligation, and they enhance and increase your responsibility under it. For the words are very strong;—" If it be possible, as much as lieth in you." They make a very urgent appeal to your conscience and good faith, as in the sight, not of man, but of God. They throw upon you the burden of saying, in every case in which you would apply them,—I cannot keep the peace as my Lord would have me keep it. It is absolutely impossible.

Will any of you venture lightly to say that, at any time, or with reference to any man? If you are forced to say it, will you say it with a feeling of relief, or with a deep pang of regret; with a contented mind, or in brokenness of spirit? Ah! is it a conclusion in which you can easily and calmly acquiesce, to find a single human being resolutely determined to be on such terms with you, that you cannot hope to be allowed to do him an office of kindness, or speak to him a word in season?

Ah! my friends, you will weigh the matter well before you rest in such a consummation as that. You will not be in haste to give over your fellow-man as inaccessible to your overtures of peace. And if things seem tending in that direction, knowing your own heart, and its deceitfulness, you will be in far less haste to acquit yourself of responsibility and throw all the blame on him.

Only think what your finding it impossible to live peaceably with any individual man implies. It shuts you out, as far as that individual man is concerned, from all hope of participation in that most gracious beatitude, " Blessed are the peacemakers : for they shall be called the children of God " (Matt. v. 9).

For, why would you live peaceably with any man ? What makes it worth while to try to live peaceably with any man ? Why should you bear injuries unavenged, and confer kindness undeserved, and take an infinite deal of trouble to have all needless causes of offence removed, with a view to your living peaceably with any man ? Is it merely for his pleasure, or for your own pleasure ? Is it because you feel it to be painful, and you think he may feel it to be painful too, to be on bad terms with a fellow-creature ? Is it because to live peaceably with your neighbour is decent and seemly, and to quarrel is a shame and scandal ? Surely that is not all.

No, you say, that is not all ; nay, it is not that at all. If that were all, I would give myself little concern comparatively about what he thinks of me, or how he feels towards me. That there should be a decent measure of good understanding between him and me, is so far well. But that is not the end I seek. I long to be a peacemaker, not only between him and me, but between him and my God. Ah ! what matters it that he is willing to accept my proposals of peace ? I would that through my instrumentality he were made willing, in the day of the Lord's power, to accept the proposals of peace which come from the Prince of Peace himself ! Why is it that I am anxious, and take pains, to remove and obviate any prejudice he has taken up against me ? Why do I go about so earnestly to explain what has offended him ? Why am I so eager that everything personal between him and me should be cleared up? Is it that my peace may visit his soul? No. But that,—my peace, if it please God, pioneering the way,—his soul may be visited by that "peace of God, passing understanding, which keeps the heart and mind, through Christ Jesus" (Phil. iv. 7).

Now if it be thus, in this spirit and for this end, that you make it your business, as it is your duty, at least honestly to attempt to live peaceably with all men, can you contemplate without grief the failure of your attempt, even in a single instance? Can you easily make up your mind to say, or to think, There is a man, one man at least, in regard to whom I must now give up the hope of ever being useful to his soul? The state of things between us has now come to be such, that I can never expect him to listen to my voice, or yield to my influence, or profit by my example. He will regard me always with a jaundiced eye. He will look askant at any approach I make to him. He will judge unfavourably of everything I say or do. He will give me no credit for a sincere profession or a consistent walk. He will suspect me as a self-seeker, and brand me as a hypocrite. Ah! how can I win the blessedness of a true peacemaker in connection with him? That privilege I may have in connection with others; and some other brother may have it even in connection with him; but oh! it is sad to lose even a single opportunity of winning so honourable a privilege, so godlike a blessedness,—in connection even with a single soul.

And then when I reflect how his dislike of me, or sus-

picion of me, or prejudice against me, may prejudice him
against other witnesses for Christ, and even against
Christ himself; and how his report of me, or the rumour
of our disagreement, may so work in the minds and
hearts of many as to set them in hostility to true religion
and its professors altogether ;—when I thus realize to myself the evil which my not finding myself able to live
peaceably with that one man, may do to him and to
multitudes besides, and to the cause I love and the name
in which I glory ; I will pause, and re-try the cause, as
between him and me, in the secret chamber of my own
broken heart, and before the tribunal of my quickened
conscience.   Yes, I will ask if I have really exhausted all
the legitimate means of pacification?   Have I in very
truth done all I could do for the preventing or the healing of this breach?   Is there no concession which pride,
under the subtle guise of self-esteem, has hindered me
from making?   Is there no point which I have mistaken
for a principle ; no punctilio on which I have been standing as if it were the very pillar of the truth?   While
not neglecting the things that make for peace, has there
been no lack of peace and love in my bosom, no coldness,
no mere perfunctory performance of what I considered
my duty towards him, with a view rather to the exoner-
ating of myself than to the winning of him ; no restrain-
ing, for him and for myself, of the effectual fervent prayer
of uprightness, which availeth much?

Is it not thus, my friends, that you will feel and act
in every case in which your efforts as peacemakers seem
to be hindered?   Is it not thus that you will deprecate

such a result as a sore evil, in which only after much searching of heart, and deep communing with God, you can ever bring yourselves sorrowfully to acquiesce ? Is it not thus that, " if it be possible, as much as lieth in you, you will live peaceably with all men ?"

The view which I have given of the import and bearing of this precept about peace, may serve to show how fitting a close and climax it is to those precepts which go before. It is in the light of this last commandment that these are all to be regarded. Your great object and aim, in all your dealings with " them which persecute you,"—with men generally in the world,—is to be peace ;—peace, as far as possible, between you and them,—and that in order to peace between them and your God. This is the end which you seek,—the end to which all your good offices of blessing, and sympathy, and a ready mind, and generosity, and honour, are but means. And you are to seek this end hopefully. You may with all confidence seek it. For in seeking it you may plead a special promise, and one which you may now see to be invested with a special and very precious significancy ;—" When a man's ways please the Lord, he maketh even his enemies to be at peace with him " (Prov. xvi. 7).

What a motive does this promise, in the connection in which you must now take it, suggest ! How should it inspire you with a determination to give good heed to it that, by his grace helping you, your ways shall please the Lord ! You know what those ways are towards his

adversaries and yours that are sure to please him. They
are ways, not of compromise, indeed, but of conciliation ;
and of conciliation carried to the utmost length to which,
without compromise, it can be made to go. Let such be
your ways. You need have no apprehension of their
being ways of which you shall ever have cause to be
ashamed ; for you adopt them and make them yours, not
in any mean and ignoble spirit of selfishness,—for the sake
of your own personal safety, or ease, or reputation ; but
with most honourable, high and heavenly aspirations ;—
first, that the Lord whom you love may be pleased ;
next, that, in token of his good pleasure, he may make
your enemies to be at peace with you ; and lastly, that
you, finding it possible, because the Lord makes it
possible, to live peaceably with them, may find it
possible ere long,—the Lord making that too possible,—
to persuade them to come along with you to your Father's
home of peace, and to taste with you the blessedness of
living peaceably with Him.

15

REDRESS AND RETRIBUTION:
ABDICATED BY MAN AND LEFT TO GOD

"Dearly beloved, avenge not yourselves, but rather give place unto wrath: for it is written, Vengence is mine: I will repay, saith the Lord."   —Romans 12:19

THE affectionate appeal with which this verse opens—
"Dearly beloved"—is surely very significant as well as very emphatic. Its full force and propriety may be better seen when the command which it introduces, and especially the reason of the command, have been considered, as brought out in the three closing verses of the chapter. Evidently it points to something more than ordinarily solemn, if not awful, in the position which, according to the representation about to be given, you occupy, as Christians, in the face of a hostile and persecuting world. It marks the relation in which you now stand to those who are your enemies, because they are the enemies of the Lord, as a relation of very peculiar delicacy and difficulty, in which you have need of all the aid and support that the most vivid sense of the love of which you are the objects can afford.

It is assumed that you have exhausted all the means and measures of conciliation that are consistent with fidelity. You have gone as far as you can in the way of manifesting forbearance, and sympathy, and genuine human fellow-feeling, towards all, even the most opposed, to whom you have access. You have felt yourselves and shown yourselves to be upon honour, and have done your best to secure peace. But although some may have been thus won, others continue obdurate. Their enmity is even imbittered by coming in contact with that charity of yours which fails to charm it away. You must make up your mind to this sad result,—that in spite of all your efforts to the contrary, there will be those who relentlessly and remorselessly stand out against you, and do you wrong. How are you to feel and act towards such persons? What frame of mind are you to cherish? What course of conduct are you to pursue? That is the question which, at this stage, is to be met.

It is met, in the first place, by an implied recognition of the reality and the righteousness of the law or principle of retribution; in the second place, by the intimation that it is a law or principle which you are not yourselves to administer or apply; and in the third place, by the assurance that the Lord himself will give effect to it.

I. The law or principle of retribution is recognised as one which, in the last resort, must be brought into operation. It is not obscurely indicated that neither you who suffer wrong, nor He to whom you commit your cause, could in the long run be otherwise satisfied.

There are three different expressions used in this verse to denote the manner of dealing with offenders which is

intended. In the first clause it is, "Avenge not yourselves,"—or more literally and exactly, "Right not yourselves." In the second, the word is "wrath,"—"rather
give place unto wrath,"—a word unequivocally expressing
the sentiment or passion of anger or indignation. In the
third, we have at the beginning, the same form of expression as in the first clause,—"vengeance," or say
rather, the righting of the injured, "belongeth to me;"—
and then, we have a new idea,—"I will repay," or
retaliate, or give back to the wrong-doer what he has
done. In the first place, there would seem to be an
admission that you who suffer injury are entitled to
redress,—that you must be righted,—that a just vengeance, or righteous retribution, must on your behalf be
executed upon your adversary,—that you must be vindicated by his being punished. But then you are told,
secondly, not to take the matter into your own hands and
seek to right yourselves, but rather to "give place unto
wrath." This may mean either that you are to yield and
allow your adversary's wrath to expend itself,—or that you
are to stand back and let an angry God take up the case.
The last is now generally held to be the most accurate
sense; and it is both very relevant and very affecting.
You are wronged; you feel that redress is due; you are
inclined to be your own avenger,—the redresser of your
own wrong. Nay, but rather give place,—withdraw,—
be still. Know that there is One in whose bosom the
wrong done to you awakens holy anger, righteous indignation and wrath. When His anger is kindled on your
behalf, you may well be dumb and silent. To that wrath

you may well give place. For, in the third place, do you not hear his voice, commanding you to leave all to him ? The righting of wrong,—the avenging of the injured upon his adversary,—" belongeth to me." And be sure that in his hands the redress,—the vengeance,—will be complete. " I will repay." I will execute retributive and penal judgment. I will reward and recompense the wrong-doer. And he, and you, and all shall know that " it is a fearful thing to fall into the hands of the living God."

All throughout it is taken for granted that, if there be no relenting on the part of the offender, retribution, pure and simple, is at last inevitable ;—retribution, I say ; not salutary chastisement or corrective discipline, but mere punishment—the penal infliction of suffering for sin. And a threefold ground for such judicial and retributive procedure is found to lie deep down in the essential nature, not of man only, but even of God himself. A sense of equity, a sentiment of irrepressible holy anger, and the demand of legal justice, conspire to establish its necessity. Wrong must be redressed ; righteous anger must be appeased ; and law must be vindicated, and government by law. No intelligent being, of whose moral constitution it is characteristic that, in the first place, he recognises the existence of personal rights ; that, secondly, he has emotional sympathies which throb and thrill in harmony with truth and justice ; and that, in the third place, he owns the majesty of law, purely as law, promulgated by sovereign authority and enforced by absolute power ;—in other words, no rightly balanced mind, true to its own ethical intuitions,—can dispense with the principle of retributive judgment, as a vital element in the administration of the universe.

Partial views, indeed, of benevolence, or of expediency, may incline those who resolve all government into influence, to frame a theory of both worlds,—the present and the future,—that shall have no dark cloud of penal wrath hanging over it, but shall glow with the bright ideal, or pleasing imagination, of evil being always dealt with, now and hereafter, in the interest, as it were, of the evil-doer himself; the very worst severities inflicted on him, however deservedly, being in reality and in the long run visitations for his benefit; and the Divine rule over responsible agents being thus nothing more than the unfolding of a plan, or method, or agency,—administered by a Divine person,—which, by its own pressure upon men and things, is gradually to work sin and misery out of the system, so as ultimately to leave nothing but pure and placid peace everywhere and evermore.

No countenance, however, is given by the Apostle to such a vague and dreamy notion of law and government. Nor is it a notion which commends itself to the unsophisticated moral instinct of mankind. There is in the human bosom a stern and robust sense of justice, which, irrespectively of all calculations of consequences,—and, indeed, of all collateral considerations, of whatever sort,—will not be satisfied unless, by a judicial procedure and in terms of law, injured right is seen to triumph, and the inflicter of wrong is doomed. It insists upon a trial and a verdict. That sense of justice may be deadened and perverted by plausible sophistries, while a man is living contentedly in disregard of the authority and commandment of God. But when the conscience is awakened and the divine law asserts its supremacy, the innate and in-eradicable feeling, or rather faith, as to a righteous government, is quickened into new life. And it is found practically that no plan of saving mercy, and no precept of new obedience, can win acquiescence and approval, which does not recognise and satisfy that principle of mere and simple retribution upon which all righteous government must ultimately rest.

II. But while thus you are permitted and taught to hold fast,—and to hold fast as applicable to your own case,—that sense of wrong and craving for redress,—that con-viction of the reality and the righteousness of retribution,—which is no sinful excrescence upon your human nature, or sinful corruption of it,—but is of the essence of its original constitution, being part and parcel of the very image of God in which man was made ; you are at the same time interdicted from administering or applying it yourselves. You are not to avenge or right yourselves. Rather you are to give place, and, so far as any move-ment of yours is concerned, simply to suffer the wrong. And you are required to act thus, for this most relevant and sufficient reason,—because your case is taken up by another, to whom you may safely leave it.

But for that reason, it might be almost too much to expect that you should not avenge or vindicate yourselves. In a rude and unsettled state of society, when the autho-rity of law is weak and the administration of it precarious, men will not easily be persuaded to surrender the right or privilege of private justice and personal revenge. Individuals and families will hold themselves entitled to take by force what they consider their due, and to inflict violent retribution and retaliation on any who hurt or injure them. But when the ruler comes to be one whom they can trust, and when he undertakes their cause, they are willing to give place, and to resign the function of executing judgment to him and to his ministers. On a somewhat similar ground you are asked to abstain from avenging yourselves ;—because you know that the Lord, who is your God, reigneth in righteousness.

More particularly, you are commanded to " give place unto wrath." Your wrath is to retire, and to make way for his wrath. For in your righting or avenging yourselves, there is apt to be wrath; not merely a calm sense or desire of justice, but an impulse of anger. It may be a holy anger, a justifiable resentment, a feeling of righteous indignation. Still it is a passion which, even at the very best, you must admit to be in you an unsafe motive and guide of conduct. Restrain and regulate it as you may, you cannot trust it, especially in your own cause. Therefore let it retire, and do you, instead of righting yourselves, as your own anger might prompt, rather give place to the anger or wrath of God. In his bosom, and there alone, anger is perfectly pure. He, and he alone, in the strictest and most literal sense, can be angry and not sin. Therefore, leave anger and wrath to him.

Certainly there is something wonderfully fitted to arrest the flow of angry feeling, in this brief and startling summons:—give place to the wrath of God. If his wrath is kindled but a little against the men who hate you for the love you bear to his Son,—what room can there be for yours? You may well stand back,—yourself, and all who have a fellow-feeling with you, in your rising indignation against the "workers of iniquity," who "eat up the Lord's people as they eat bread." Do you look upon them as deserving of your resentment? Ah! that is nothing. See! they are exposed to the wrath of God! Contemplate them in that light; and are you not irresistibly impelled to give place, even with fear and trembling? Is not all your wrath changed into solemn awe?

Nay, when you contemplate these men in that light, if you yourselves know "the power of that anger of God" to which you leave them, will not a sort of terrible compassion begin to possess your souls? The wrath to which you give place is the wrath of the Holy One, the Unchangeable, the Eternal. It is that same wrath which you have felt to be lying upon you; which you have seen to be laid on Christ for you. When you were made to know yourselves as sinners in the hands of an angry God, you were consumed, and became as dead before him. Everything else,—your own anger, as in revenge of your guilt and folly, you were even ready to do execution upon yourselves, —the anger of all saints, and of all the world,—everything gave place to that wrath of God. The one, solitary thought in your spiritual consciousness was that of an angry God. 'Give place to wrath, real and righteous, inevitable and inexorable;' that was still the cry. Then again, as you heard that cry re-echoed, you looked and saw that it was not now you that was pointed at, but another in your stead. 'Give place,' is the voice from heaven, when men and devils have done their worst, and vented all their rage against the Christ of God,—'give place unto wrath. Let wrath,—the holy judicial anger of offended Deity,— have its way. Let all in heaven and earth and hell stand apart. Room! Room for wrath! Room for the wrath of the righteous Father to pour its full and fiery flood upon the bleeding head of Him who beareth sin!'

Do I understand this? Do I really know the power of the anger or wrath of God, in my own miserable case as a sinner, and in the marvellous grace of my Saviour's substitution in my stead? And do I now hear that same voice of awe and terror uttered concerning any poor fellow-sinner who may have wronged me, but not more than I have wronged my Lord,—who may have wronged my Lord even less than I once did, —'Give place unto wrath,—leave him to the anger of God?' Can that voice reach my ear, quickened by the Spirit, without sending a thrill of mingled fear and pity through my whole frame? All my longing for redress,—all my resentment,—all selfish passion,—is gone. The man is to me no longer my adversary or my persecutor; but simply what I once was myself, and but for grace must still have been,—a sinner in the hands of an angry God! As such he is the object of no other feeling on my part but that of earnest sorrow of heart, and intense solicitude for his salvation.

III. The purpose for which the wrath of God is to have place given to it, as it is brought out in the third and last portion of the verse, will be found to enforce the practical lessons already suggested. That purpose is, that the word which is written may be fulfilled;—"Vengeance is mine; I will repay, saith the Lord."

It is not needful to advert to the connection in which this saying stands in the two passages of the Old Testament,—two at least,—in which it occurs (Deut. xxxii. 35; Ps. xciv. 1), or to compare the Apostle's present use of it with his application of it in writing to the Hebrews (x. 30). It is enough to consider it as assigning the ultimate reason of the command, "Avenge not yourselves, but rather give place unto wrath."

The Lord takes vengeance and recompense,—the righting of the injured and retribution upon the wrong-doer,—into his own hands; and keeps it in his own hands. It is a right or prerogative which he claims and challenges as exclusively his own,—to avenge and to repay; to avenge wrong, and to repay, or requite, the wrong-doer. He never delegates it to any creature. He may, indeed, employ, and he does employ, the agency or instrumentality of the creature in carrying his purpose of vengeance into effect. He may ask and require the sympathy of the creature in the carrying of his purpose of vengeance into effect. But the vengeance itself he never delegates, or hands over to another. He reserves it to himself, as an incommunicable attribute of his divine nature and sovereignty.

That he should, when he sees fit, employ his people as the executioners of his vengeance ; and that he should expect them, when called to act in that capacity, not only to obey, but to enter into his mind in obeying; need not surely startle or surprise any who know and believe that the highest perfection of man's nature is to be of one mind with his Maker. Whatever vengeance it may be that is his, I must learn to make mine; as an onlooker, approving and concurring; as an actor, if need be, zealous even to slaying. Still, in the first instance, vengeance is his. It is his vengeance that I must make mine; not my vengeance that I dare ask him to make his.

This last, however, is my natural instinct. I suffer injury in a righteous cause, and for my maintenance of its righteousness. I am vexed, irritated, provoked. It seems to me that I have a right to redress, even at the expense of the injurious party suffering loss and punishment. I do not lift my hand ; but I would have God to put forth his hand, and make my vengeance his.

Now there is doubtless a sense in which I may ask and expect God to enter into my cause, and to take it up as his own. The Lord Jesus in that sense " committed himself to Him that judgeth righteously" (1 Peter ii. 23). In the same sense you are commanded to give place unto wrath. But what is that sense ? What does it imply ?

Does it mean that you ask or expect God to be the executioner of your wrath, or vengeance, or judgment ? Taking "wrath" and "vengeance," as the terms here occur, to denote, not angry passion, but a calm sense of wrong, and of the necessity of redress, are you first to make up your mind upon your own case; and then, having come to the conclusion that you ought to be righted and to be avenged, to call a halt, and say within yourself: ' No!

I will take no step, I will guard against even the desire
to take any step, in the way of righting or avenging
myself. I will leave all to Him who says, " Vengeance
is mine?" ' Is it not plain that in so saying, or so feeling, I do not really hand over to God, and leave in God's
hands, the vengeance; but only the execution of it? The
vengeance is still mine ; what is to be God's is simply
the fixing of the time when, and the manner how, the
vengeance is to be carried into effect.

Such an interpretation, or application, of the saying,
—"Vengeance is mine, I will repay,"—is by no means
contrary to nature. It is rather, in truth, but too
natural,—by far too natural.

You may see it to be so, if you listen to the impreca-
tions, the horrid and blasphemous curses, in which the
madness of anger is too often vented. What is that
coarse and ribald malediction which, coming from these
infuriated lips, sends a thrill of horror through your
frame? Is it not, on thy part, O thou wretched and
profane taker of God's name in vain,—in so far as it is
anything at all,—is it not a prayer, a wish, that God
would follow out thy vengeance, to the end and to the
extent which thou desirest? The vengeance is thine.
Thou huggest it to thy bosom, all burning as it is with
self-destroying venom. What thou askest God to do is
to act for thee, as thou wouldst act thyself, if, having a
devil's malignity, thou hadst a God's omnipotence to
work it out.

That, of course, is an extreme case. But it may serve
to illustrate the distinction between these two states of

mind; the consenting, on the one hand, that the vengeance itself should be the Lord's; and the mere desire,
on the other hand, that the Lord would make the
injured man's own vengeance practically effectual,—or,
which perhaps he would like still better, give him the
means of making it practically effectual himself.

In a much more subtle form, there is room for self-deception. When I am crossed and thwarted in my lawful
calling; when I am injured and insulted in my neigh-
bourly and friendly approaches to my fellow-men; when
I am opposed and persecuted in my efforts to do good; I
do not curse or swear; I do not call down fire from
heaven. No. I am silent. I keep my mouth with a
bridle. I am meek and uncomplaining. And yet behind,
or within, this quiet demeanour, there may lurk, almost
unconsciously, a sense or persuasion of my having a claim
on God for reparation and redress; ay, all the more on
account of my own forbearance. The vengeance is in me
still. It is mine. It may affect to be,—it may really, in
some measure, be,—vengeance of the right, even of the
righteous sort; not the mere animal instinct of revenge,
but the longing which every rightly constituted mind has
to see justice done and injustice punished. I take it to
be so. And, taking it to be so, I cherish it all the more
readily. And still it is mine. It is my own judgment in
my own cause. I think that it is sound; that God will
ratify it, and will ere long show and give significant
proof that he ratifies it. But it is, after all, my act,
my decision, my wish or will. God is to set his seal to
my verdict, and practically carry out my volition. In his

own way, and at his own time, no doubt, he is to do so. Thus far I leave the matter to him. But really no further. As to the actual essence and inner spirit of the transaction, the vengeance is not his, but mine.

Alas! how readily do I deceive myself here! How apt am I, when I suffer wrong, and abstain from vindicating my own cause, to take to myself a secret compensation and reward in the thought that God will do me justice and avenge me! And how insidiously, under such a cover, do feelings of self-righteous complacency in my own meekness and forbearance,—and feelings also of vindictiveness or uncharitableness towards my offending neighbour,— continue to find harbour in my bosom!

And if I can but advance a step beyond this, and persuade myself that God, making my vengeance his, means me to be the agent in giving effect to it, now that it has become his,—am I not ripe and ready for the holy office of the Inquisition? Could a Philip, or a Dominic, desire a fitter instrument or tool?

It cannot surely be in any such spirit as this that the souls under the altar cry, "How long, O Lord, holy and true, dost thou not judge and avenge our blood on them that dwell on the earth?" (Rev. vi. 10.) That certainly is the complaint, the ejaculatory prayer, not of the martyrs in the agony of their trial, asking the Lord to make their natural and human vengeance his; but of the spirits of the martyrs, their trial being over, waiting and intensely desiring to know and see what that vengeance is which the Lord says is his. No doubt they are themselves personally concerned. It is with immediate reference to themselves, and their own earthly history, that they desire to know and see what that vengeance is. But it is as the Lord's vengeance, and not their own, that they desire to see and know it. For themselves they have abdicated; they have wholly surrendered and given over to God; not the executing merely of the vengeance, but the vengeance itself. They learned that lesson long before they came to be "souls under the altar." They learned it in the fiery furnace; in the lions' den; under the tyrant's sword; amid the shower of stones; upon the rack, and at the stake. All their own vengeance went out of them. Not in thought or in heart, any more than in act, did they avenge themselves. Not for a moment did they dream of ascribing to the Lord anything in the least analogous to their own vengeance,—the vengeance natural to them as fallen men. Nay, take vengeance in its highest and purest sense; as it may dwell in the breast of men redeemed and renewed; purged of all malice and personal thirst for revenge; become the holy instinct of a just nature, that hates wrong in itself and on its own account, and not selfishly, but in the interests of everlasting truth and righteousness, demands redress. Still I say, these men, of whom the world was not worthy, did not dare or venture,—they did not wish,—they absolutely refused,— to make the Lord the executioner of their vengeance, even in that view of this vengeance. They shrunk from the very idea of judging for the Lord. He must judge for himself. The whole of the vengeance is entirely and exclusively his. It belongs to him alone to repay.

Is there, then, no natural human feeling in that cry of the souls under the altar? Am I not to be honestly indignant when I read the Book of Martyrs? May I not espouse warmly the cause of injured innocence? Shall I learn to be passive and unmoved when a brother beloved of the Lord suffers wrong; or when I myself even, because I am a brother beloved of the Lord, suffer wrong?

Not so. I would not empty my soul of that feeling which the sight, or the sense, of wrong done is fitted to awaken. Only, in the first place, I would have the feeling in my soul to be the same that it is in the bosom of my God. And, secondly, instead of planning for myself, even in idea, any way, in any instance, of giving the feeling vent, I would wait always to see how God will satisfy it. Let me mark well these two conditions :—

1. Vengeance in me is to be what it is in God. It is not my vengeance that I am to ask God to make his; it is God's vengeance that is to become mine. I am to ascend into heaven, and enter into the mind and heart of the great Father, the righteous Judge of all; and there and thus learn what, and of what sort, that vengeance is which, as he says himself, belongeth to him.

Or if I may not ascend into heaven, I may betake myself to Him who came down from heaven. I may ask that patient sufferer, that bleeding Lamb of God, what this vengeance is. I may get the answer in his cross!

It is real; it is terrible. It is real and terrible resentment of wrong. It is real and terrible judicial wrath, against every one personally, against any one, upon whom wrong is chargeable. Yes! against every one; against

any one. Even when it is his own beloved Son upon
whom the guilt of wrong-doing is chargeable,—vengeance
is even then real and terrible; all the more so, because
he who is the object of it is so dear to him whose vengeance it is. Personal vindictiveness it cannot be. No
element of selfish irritation or passion,—the irritation or
passion of wounded self-esteem,—can be in it. On that
very account it is unappeasable. Wounded self-esteem
may be soothed by concession, and the irritation or
passion which it causes may pass away. But the vengeance of which Calvary witnessed the execution knows no
relenting. It is the unalterable demand of justice in the
bosom of the everlasting God, that wrong done in his
universe shall be redressed; and that the doer of it shall,
either in his own person, or in the person of a worthy
substitute whom he voluntarily accepts in that character,
give full and adequate satisfaction.

That is the vengeance which the Lord says is his.
And I must make it mine. I must be brought to
sympathize with him, and be of the same mind with him,
in that very vengeance of his.

First, for the saving of my own soul I must do so. I
must apprehend that vengeance,—that sort of vengeance,
—as directed against me, and lying upon me. I must
know and feel that the God with whom I have to do is
the God to whom, in that sense, vengeance belongeth.

To know and feel this, is very terrible. I might be far
more easy if I had to deal with a vindictive Deity; with
one whose vengeance was of the nature of a sudden impulse, or even of a settled purpose of deliberate personal

revenge. But it is law and justice, the Lawgiver and
the Judge, that I have to meet. That is the vengeance.
Can I face that? Do I understand the nature of it? Am
I reconciled to the necessity of it? Am I saved,—do I
look for salvation,—not through any compromise or
surrender of it, which is impossible, but through the
great Atonement which has been made in terms of it?
If not, let me fairly face the only other issue. Can I
" dwell with the devouring fire? " Can I "dwell with
everlasting burnings? " (Isa. xxxiii. 14.)

Then, secondly, if I am thus exercised, as regards my
own case; my being exposed to this vengeance; accepting
of it; accepting of it as,—in so wonderful and terrible a
way,—made to be consistent with my being saved even
in terms of it ;—can there be room in my mind for any
other sort of vengeance, towards any one, than I now see
that God challenges as his own? I must have sympathy
with him in that. I cannot be more tolerant of wrong,
or more indulgent to the wrong-doer, than He is who
says, " Vengeance is mine; I will repay." But I dare
not cherish a feeling in my breast that I would shrink
from ascribing to my God. No vengeance can be mine
that is not first his. I must needs learn to regard
offences as he regards them; and to regard also the
punishment of them as he regards it ;—if I accept the
punishment of my offences in Christ suffering for me ;—
and if I believe, further, that, when he sitteth in judgment, I am to sit on his throne along with him.

2. But there is a second condition that must be fulfilled in order to my full acquiescence in the Lord's

saying, " Vengeance is mine." Even supposing that the feeling or moral instinct of vengeance in me is now of the same nature and character with the attribute of vengeance which is in God,—I am to leave, not in act only, but in wish or desire, the execution of it, or its practical accomplishment, to him. Here, I would again say, is my chief temptation. I try to get into the mind of God. I begin to think that I have got into it. I resent injury as done, not to me, but to God. I am angry ; not because I personally am wronged ; but because wrong is done against him, and done in his sight. And this very freedom of mine, real or supposed, from selfish passion, may prove a snare to me. I am not now, as I think, judging in my own cause, but in the interests of my Master, when, in righteous indignation and holy wrath, I would call down fire upon the Samaritans, who will not give him and me passage, on our journey of heavenly love towards Jerusalem.

Alas ! I know not what spirit I am of. The vengeance which makes my soul thus burn within me, and my hand as if instinctively grasp the sword, is not really of the same sort as the vengeance which belongeth to God. For if it were, I would be but too happy to leave the objects of it altogether in his hands, and to let him determine when and how he is to repay.

Ah ! let me repeat,—if I enter into the meaning of that vengeance of God which hangs over the enemies of his people and of himself ; if with any measure of insight and sympathy I grasp that truth, " God is angry with the wicked every day ;" if from my own experience I know

the terror of the Lord ; if I have felt what it is to have
his anger kindled against me,—and then turned away
from me, because turned in upon the head of my gracious
Surety on the cross ;—if I realize the fact that it is this
anger that is upon the crucifiers of the Lord of glory ;
how will my heart bleed, even when the sense of righteousness within me most loudly calls for redress and
retribution ! "O Lord, how long? How long, O Lord?" I
may be constrained to cry, when I see wrong and tyranny,
and Antichristian falsehood and profane ungodliness, tri-
umphant ; and the Lord's cause oppressed; and his poor
ones trodden under foot. "Arise, O Lord; let not man prevail;"—"It is time, Lord, for thee to work ; for men have
made void thy law;"—so I must often, if I am on the
Lord's side, and on the side of his law, feel and pray.
Yes ! And my soul, if it is righteous, if it is in the
interests of righteousness, cannot but rest with complacency on the prospect of that day when all the Lord's
ways shall be vindicated and justified, and it shall be
made clear that however long he waiteth to be gracious,
he is at the last a God who judges righteously. Without that prospect, I could not reverence and fear, I could
not trust and love, the God of my salvation. I know
that vengeance belongeth unto him, and he will repay ;
and that knowledge stills my bosom when it swells with
indignation at the sight of wrong.

I wait thy time, O Lord ; most willingly I wait thy
time ; content meanwhile to be assured that there shall
not be impunity always ; that there shall not be impunity
long. And I ask thee, O Lord, to help me to be more

and more of one mind, of one heart, with thyself, who, while the impunity of forbearance lasts, "wouldst have all men to be saved, and to come unto the knowledge of the truth" (1 Tim. ii. 4).

Let me remember also, always, that as regards these thine enemies and mine, a twofold vengeance belongeth to thee : in a twofold sense thou canst repay. If they will but look now on Him whom they are piercing,— his blood is the vengeance ; in the answer to his prayer on their behalf, " Father, forgive them ; for they know not what they do," thou wilt repay. Lord, do thou thus avenge me of my adversary. Let him be one of those on whom thy vengeance falls innocuous ; falling upon him in Christ ; upon Christ for him. Avenge me, by making him who holds my clothes when I am stoned the very chiefest of thine apostles.

Let me ever have this spirit within me as I mourn for them that oppose themselves. And when I think of the doom of the ungodly, let it be as Jesus beheld the city, and wept over it, and cried,—" O Jerusalem, Jerusalem, thou that killest the prophets, and stonest them which are sent unto thee, how often would I have gathered thy children together, even as a hen gathereth her chickens under her wings ; and ye would not ! " (Matt. xxiii. 37.)

16

GOOD OVERCOMING EVIL:
THE SOLEMN ISSUE OF WEAL, OR WOE

"Therefore if thine enemy hunger, feed him; if he thirst, give him drink: for in so doing thou shalt heap coals of fire on his head. Be not overcome of evil, but overcome evil with good." —Romans 12:20, 21

THE precept here,—" If thine enemy hunger, feed him; if he thirst, give him drink,"—is plain enough.   It is the opposite of "avenging yourselves."   And it is a fair inference from your not avenging yourselves, that you are to do what is the reverse of avenging yourselves.   You are not to treat those who are opposed to you and to your Lord as they deserve to be treated.   " Therefore," you are to treat them in a way exactly the contrary of that.

The precept has annexed to it first, a reason,—" For in so doing thou shalt heap coals of fire on his head ;" and secondly, an explanation of the reason, in the form of a higher and more generalized commandment,—" Be not overcome of evil, but overcome evil with good."

As to the reason assigned for the precept,—there is an ambiguity, giving room for a serious doubt or question. The heaping of coals of fire upon any one's head may be for one or other of two opposite ends, and may produce one or other of two opposite effects.   It may be meant and fitted to melt, to subdue, to assimilate or incorporate; as when, in the language of the poet,——

> "—Artists melt the sullen ore of lead,
> By heaping coals of fire upon its head."

Or it may be meant and fitted to burn and consume; as when wood or stubble is subjected to the process. Coals of fire, heaped on the head of any object, will do one or other of these two things ; they will either soften or destroy. Which of these two results are you to have in view, when you load your enemy with benefits? Are you to be influenced, in showing him kindness, by the hope that he may be moved to relent? Or are you to be reconciled to your so treating him by the consideration that, failing to melt, your gifts will burn ;——that if not in a way of grace, then in a way of judgment, it will turn out in the long run that, in his history and experience, your conduct has had fruit?

No right minded and right hearted follower of Christ will for a moment hesitate as to his reply ;——it is solely for the purpose of melting my poor fellow-sinner, if that be possible, that I heap coals of fire upon his head. And he will rejoice to find, that as it stands in that passage of the Old Testament which the Apostle is quoting, the proverb, or proverbial saying, naturally bears this interpretation ;—— "If thine enemy be hungry, give him bread to eat ; and if he be thirsty, give him water to drink : for thou shalt heap coals of fire upon his head, and the Lord shall reward thee" (Prov. xxv. 21, 22). The addition there of the promise, "And the Lord shall reward thee," would seem plainly enough to indicate that it can be with no ill design,—with no wish to aggravate your enemy's guilt and doom,—no complacency in that being possibly the effect of your generosity,—that you are to relieve and feed him. Anything approaching to a vindictive spirit,—the doing of good, as the misanthropist may affect to do good, because he anticipates that they to whom he does it will only abuse it, and be the worse for it ;—such a temper never can meet with acceptance or gracious recompense at the hands of the God of love.

At the same time, even as it occurs in the Book of Proverbs, the statement does not imply that in showing kindness to an evil-doer you exclude from your view what may possibly be the result or issue of your doing so,—its being ultimately not for his benefit, but for his hurt. The promise is a general encouragement. Grudge not to expend your resources on those who may prove themselves to be not only undeserving of them, but incapable of being affected by them to any good purpose. Suppose even that all your benefactions are apparently in vain, and, instead of saving your enemy, only tend to his destruction,—still you have no cause of regret. These benefactions are not lost ; they will redound to your advantage ;—" The Lord shall reward thee."

It would seem, therefore, that while, in heaping coals of fire upon your enemy's head, your " heart's desire and prayer" for him must be that they may melt him, you are not to shut your eyes,—as indeed you cannot shut your eyes,—to the other side of the alternative,—that so far from melting, they may only tend to burn and to consume him. You must face either issue, if you would be in a condition to comply with the comprehensive commandment which closes this high argument.

It is a fitting close. The commandment brings out a vital principle, and one which, if rightly apprehended, makes your "heaping of coals upon your enemy's head" truly Godlike ;—" Be not overcome of evil, but overcome evil with good." Either evil overcomes you, or you overcome evil ; which you can do only with good ; —for good alone can overcome evil. It is a great antithesis ; an awful choice. You and evil ;—the evil that thwarts and mars the good ; Satan's evil, as antagonistic to God's good ; you and this evil are close grappled, in a hand-to-hand fight. It is a mortal strife, —a deadly duel. Either this evil overcomes you, or you overcome it. How ? With good ; with the good ; by becoming yourself one with the good ; with Him whose is the good,—who is himself the good ;—for " there is none good but God." Not otherwise can you overcome the evil, or escape being overcome by it.

The position, therefore, which you are now seen to occupy with reference to a hostile world,—with special reference to those who, in spite of all your earnest advances of benevolence and sympathy, on the one hand, and in spite of all your anxious and persevering endeavours, on the other hand, to avoid or obviate offence and live peaceably with them, still insist on being your enemies,—is a very high and holy one. You are to identify yourselves and make common cause with Him whose good is pitted, if I may so say, against Satan's evil. In this view, let us consider, in the first place, what His procedure is, as here virtually described ; and then, secondly, what ought to be your procedure, as moulded and directed after the model of his.

I. It is the prerogative of God to overcome evil. It is the special prerogative of God in Christ to overcome evil with good. God, absolutely considered, must overcome evil. He cannot be overcome of evil. So far from that, evil cannot touch him. It cannot mar the pure peace and joy of his holy nature. It cannot arrest the flow of that stream of holy love which would diffuse everywhere, and always, the joy of his own holy nature among all beings capable of holy fellowship with himself. Evil, however it may be introduced into his created universe, cannot frustrate the tendency of his nature and the purpose of his will. Whatever may happen among the different orders of free and responsible intelligences whom he calls into being ;—and in whatever manner, whether by spontaneous impulse from within, or by temptation from without, evil, the evil of insubordina-- tion and a refusal to be subject to his law, comes in and unfolds itself;—still he is master over it, not it over him. He is not taken aback. He is not overtaken by surprise. The evil, however it may come in, does not reduce him to the necessity of any accommodation, on his part, to its force or to its wiles. It does not dictate to him any terms of surrender or of compromise. That would be equivalent to a confession of defeat ; and therefore it cannot be. He is not, and cannot be, as regards either his character or his government, overcome of evil. On the contrary, it is a necessity of his very nature that he should, and that he must, overcome evil.

But a question occurs. Is it always with good? Can evil be always overcome with good? What is the good meant? Is it that indicated in the text,—"If thine enemy hunger, feed him ; if he thirst, give him drink ?" Is that the way in which, when the matter is in the hands of God himself, evil is always overcome with good?

Nay, the overcoming of evil with such good as that, on the part even of God himself, is a more serious, and, if one may so say, a more difficult matter than may at first sight appear.

For one thing, it implies the recognition of voluntary choice. The evil to be overcome is, on the part of those responsible for it, voluntary. It should seem, therefore, that the overcoming of it with good must be voluntary too. Hence the necessity of all plans for thus overcoming this evil being based upon an appeal to the free will of those who are under its influence. And hence also the necessity of reckoning upon some rejecting, while others comply with the appeal. Even on the part of God, therefore, and as regards his dealings with free intelligences, this overcoming of evil with good must be a movement of moral persuasion ; not merely of physical power. It must, of necessity, contemplate the possibility of failure. Evil, after all, may remain. Nay, we are certainly taught to believe that, as one result of such a movement, evil will remain. For there is a decree of election ; there is a sovereign work of the Spirit. Were there not both, nothing but evil after all would remain.

How the evil which remains is to be overcome,—how it is to be overcome with good, and with what sort of good,—that is a dark and dismal problem. The good now revealed and working, the good of the gospel of Jesus Christ, overcomes evil, in terms of the election of grace and by the sovereign agency of the Spirit of grace, by making a people willing in the day of the Lord's power. But there is, alas! a large remainder or remnant of evil to be otherwise overcome. That it will be overcome, and overcome with good,—that the final and everlasting overcoming of the evil that is not overcome by the means and agencies of good now at work, will still be an overcoming of evil with good,—is most certain. It will be the triumph of good over evil; the vindication of good against evil. It will be good overcoming evil;—in a dispensation, however, not of mercy, but of judgment.

Meanwhile the immediate practical question for us is, How is God overcoming evil with good now?

Even thus put, it must be observed, the question is still too wide. For, even in this world, and in his present dealings with this world, God is, at least upon some occasions, seen and felt to be overcoming evil with good judicially. His judgments are abroad on the earth. Nay, it may be said that everywhere, and always, he is overcoming evil with good judicially, by judgments more or less apparent,—of which not a few signal instances are recorded in history, both sacred and profane. And these are only specimens. The great day will disclose many more, and will make it plain that even the present providence of God is, to a large extent, retributive.

336 The Christian's Relationship/Hostile World (12:20, 21)

But it is not in the retributive aspect of it that the providence of God is a rule or an example of duty to us. In that view, " vengeance belongeth to God ;—he will repay." We are not judges; we are ourselves obnoxious or liable to judgment. We are not ministers or instruments of justice, unless it be in the same sense in which all the powers and elements of nature are so. As regards our own free choice, our voluntary and spontaneous action, we have nothing to do with the pronouncing, or with the executing, of judicial sentences. The Lord alone is judge. We may, indeed, and must, be called to look on and acquiesce when God inflicts his righteous judgments, —possibly through our agency. But the judgments are his. We are simply asked to behold, and wonder, and adore ; to " be still, and know that he is God."

Nevertheless, if our manner of overcoming evil with good is to be analogous to that of God, it must have in it the element, if not of judgment, at least of acquiescence in judgment. I must have sympathy with God. I must enter into his mind. And therefore I must clearly understand and feel, that every act of kindness which I do in his name carries in it a possible sting and curse for him who is the object of it. I must do the act of kindness under this terrible impression.

How, let me ask, with special reference to myself and my own case,—how does God heap coals of fire on my head, in order to overcome my evil with his good ?

That in any way, and in any sense, and to any effect he may do so, he first, in more than a literal meaning of these fiery words, heaps coals of fire on the head of his Son

as my surety. Thus far there is no room for any milder
interpretation of the figure. The coals of fire to which
he must be subjected, for me, are of a burning heat, to
destroy, to consume. Into the thrice hotly heated
furnace of judicial wrath my Saviour is cast. Blessed
be God that thus it becomes possible for him, the just
and holy one, as the God of love, to heap coals of fire
on my head, with the other side of the alternative open ;
namely this,—that, in virtue of my union with Christ, all
the scorching and scathing fierceness being exhausted on
the head of Christ, as my substitute, the melting, mollify-
ing, moulding influence alone shall remain behind for me!

Still it is but an alternative. It is coals of fire, after
all, that God heaps on my head. His mercies, which are
" new to me every morning, and fresh every moment of
my life ;" his benefits, with which " he loads me as the God
of my salvation ;"—all the means, and influences, and
opportunities of grace,—are coals of fire. They have a use
of terror as well as a use of tenderness. If they fail to
subdue me in mercy now, they will silence and slay
me in judgment hereafter. So the Apostle emphatically
testifies when he puts the solemn question,—" Despisest
thou the riches of his goodness, and forbearance, and
long-suffering ; not knowing that the goodness of God
leadeth thee to repentance ? But, after thy hardness and
impenitent heart, treasurest up unto thyself wrath against
the day of wrath and revelation of the righteous judgment of God" (Rom. ii. 4, 5). So the Lord himself
taught in burning words when he " began to upbraid the
cities wherein most of his mighty works were done, be-

cause they repented not. Woe unto thee, Chorazin! woe unto thee, Bethsaida! for if the mighty works, which were done in you, had been done in Tyre and Sidon, they would have repented long ago in sackcloth and ashes. But I say unto you, It shall be more tolerable for Tyre and Sidon at the day of judgment, than for you. And thou, Capernaum, which art exalted unto heaven, shalt be brought down to hell: for if the mighty works, which have been done in thee, had been done in Sodom, it would have remained until this day. But I say unto you, That it shall be more tolerable for the land of Sodom in the day of judgment than for thee" (Matt. xi. 20-24). And so again, with a most solemn and affecting reference to his own evangelistic ministry, and its momentous issues, the Apostle announces the law or principle upon which the whole divine economy of forbearance and grace is now conducted;—" We are unto God a sweet savour of Christ, in them that are saved, and in them that perish. To the one we are the savour of death unto death; and to the other the savour of life unto life: and who is sufficient for these things?" (2 Cor. ii. 15, 16).

II. Now, for us to enter into this plan and purpose of God, in his present dispensation of forbearance and of grace, and in the full view of its alternative issue of life or death eternal; for us to be, in this way, "heaping coals of fire on the heads" of evil-doers, in order to the overcoming of evil with good,—not always, or necessarily, in the turning of the evil-doers to good,—but often, alas! in the aggravation of their guilt, and in their heavier doom;—this, surely, is a very holy calling. It is a very awful calling. We may well ask, "Who is sufficient for these things?" And we can be sustained only when we are enabled to add, "Our sufficiency is of God;"—of that God who has so dealt with us as he would have us to deal with our fellow-men and fellow-sinners.

We must therefore always remember that the good with which we have to overcome evil consists of "coals of fire." It is a solemn thought; but we cannot, we dare not, put it aside. We must keep it always before us, when we feed the hungry and give drink to the thirsty. Whatever office of courtesy or kindness we are discharging towards any one of those who oppose themselves, not to us merely, but to our Lord and his cause;—whether it be a common household service; or, along with that, a more direct and express Christian benefit, such as an attempt to speak a word in season;—we must have full in view the consideration that it is a new "heaping of coals of fire upon his head."

What a consideration is this! In what a light does it present to you the person, however hostile, however estranged, however vile, who is the object of your benevolence and beneficence! In what a relation do you now feel that you stand to him! He is to you what you are to God; nay more,—he is to you what he is to God. You deal with him, in a real and important sense, as God deals with you; as God deals with him. But that dealing is of a very serious and critical nature. It is the "heaping of coals of fire upon his head," under the inexorable condition of a most momentous alternative of life or death.

Bring your enemy, whoever he may be, and for whatever cause your enemy, face to face, before you. Go visit, or summon into your presence, any one of your neighbours or acquaintances whom, with all your charity, you cannot but regard as unfriendly to your Lord. Let him be one also at whose hands, when you would fain be doing him good, and have been trying to do him good, you have experienced cruel discouragement and disappointment; perhaps, also, ill-usage or contempt. You cannot get rid of him; you cannot be neutral to him. How are you to treat him?

Harshly, severely, vindictively? In that case you heap coals of fire, in no ambiguous or alternative sense, not on his head, but on your own: for "with what judgment ye judge, ye shall be judged; and with what measure ye mete, it shall be measured to you again" (Matt. vii. 2).

But it is not so that you deal with him. On the contrary, you load him with benefits. You lavish favours and kindnesses upon him. So far good. But do you feel, all the while, that these favours and kindnesses are coals of fire?—that in lavishing them upon him, and loading him with them, you are heaping coals of fire upon his head? Do you look on him as a patient whom your physic must either kill or cure? Do you lay to heart the thought that your treatment of him must tell, as God's treatment of him, as well as of you, must tell, either for his weal or for his woe, eternally?

Ah! there is room again for self-deception here! I may practise forbearance and meekness; forgiveness of injuries, and a large and liberal bountifulness in returning good for evil. But it may be altogether out of a sense of what I owe to myself personally, and to the relation in which I stand personally to my God. I feel that it would be most unseemly and unbecoming in me,— a monstrous and unnatural inconsistency,—to refuse to show such mercy to my enemy as I trust God is showing to me. I count it unworthy of my prayer to be forgiven, to withhold forgiveness from my adversary. I consider myself bound, on the contrary, to prove the sincerity of my forgiveness of him by doing him all the good I can. Still it may be to myself that I am really looking, all the while; to my own character and standing; to my own duty merely; to what may be expected or required of me. The probable bearing of my treatment of him upon the object of my forgiveness and my liberality, may not be before my mind at all; or it may be a very subordinate and inoperative consideration. To acquit myself, to clear my own conscience, to purge my soul of malice, may be with me the main thing. To feed my enemy, if hungry ; to give him drink, if thirsty; may thus be with me very much a sort of *opus operatum ;*—a good work done and finished, and complete in itself ; a duty discharged ; a load taken off my mind ; and little if anything more.

But all such insidious self-righteousness or self-complacency, in reference to this great command of love to my enemy, is wholly shut out, when I am called to consider, not how my treatment of him may become me, but how it may tell on him ! Especially when I am called to face the terrible alternative of its telling upon him, either as coals of fire tell on the precious metal which they melt, or as they tell on the stubble which they consume !

Ah ! when this alternative is before me ; when I see my poor brother,—for he is my brother, be his suspicious dislike of me ever so strong, and the offence he has given me ever so aggravated ; when I see him going on to the eternal world, as I cannot but fear, unprepared for its eternal awards ; when I feel the very wrong he has done me, not so much as an injury or insult to me, but as a sad, sore proof of his unbelief in God, and his unfitness to die ; and when, with heart thus full of concern, not for myself, but for him, I think how the word I speak to him, or the bread with which I feed him, or the cup of cold water I give him, may prove to him,—nay, must prove to him,—either a blessing or a curse ; there is indeed an end of self,—of every selfish thought or feeling. To me personally, what I do is nothing. How it may tell on him—that is everything.

Thus, and only thus, do you overcome evil with good after the manner of God; when, in dealing with an enemy, you not merely return good for evil, but do so with a clear and full recognition of the position which you are called to occupy with regard to him,—the position, namely, of one "heaping coals of fire upon his head." Otherwise the evil overcomes you. For you may be overcome of evil in more ways than one ;—not merely when the evil moves you to resentment, retaliation, and revenge ; but even when, your angry passions being restrained, policy, or decency, or fear, or a sense of honour, or supercilious indifference, or a sort of contemptuous pity and affectation of superior dignity, may prompt some measure of forbearance and some offices of beneficence. The evil overcomes you when you feel and act under its influence at all, as bearing upon yourself ; when you suffer it to affect you in any manner ; whether you give way to its pressure, or aim at rising above it.

You overcome the evil with good only when you cease altogether from contemplating the evil in a personal point of view ; when you shut out of your mind and keep out of sight the personal offence and injury to yourself; when the wrong-doer stands before you simply as a fellow-immortal, on whom you are to bring to bear a ministry of faithfulness, and kindness, and love ;—a ministry which, as you have ever before your eyes, must have issues for him, for weal or for woe, reaching throughout the ages of eternity.

Look at him in that light. It is the light in which God looks at you, when he would overcome your evil with his good. You are in his sight, not an enemy, giving him personal offence, and affording him an opportunity of displaying magnanimity and generosity by doing you good notwithstanding. He sees in you a poor, lost, sinful soul. He deals with you most graciously, most liberally, most bountifully. He plies you with all agencies and influences of good, and pleads with you to let them move and melt you. And oh ! how earnestly does he plead with you! because he knows that they are indeed " coals of fire " which he is " heaping on your head ;" coals that, if they melt not, must burn ; for " even our God is a consuming fire " (Heb. xii. 29).

So God regards and treats you, who are his enemy. So he would have you to regard and treat your enemy. Every human being before you, every son and every daughter of Adam, every member of the human family, be his conduct to you what it may, is to you an immortal spirit, to whom you are called to apply a discipline of Christian kindness, and gospel truth and love, that cannot leave him as it finds him ;—that must either move and melt, or consume and burn.

How solemn the thought ! With what a sacredness does it invest every individual man ! How is it fitted to empty your soul of every selfish consideration, either of resentment or, if I may say so, of non-resentment! How Godlike does your position become ! And what a responsibility is yours !

Surely it is with good meaning and effect that the Apostle thus sums up his teaching on the subject of your intercourse with those who are the Lord's enemies and yours ;—" Be not overcome of evil, but overcome evil with good." Even as the Lord himself closes his great lesson on the same theme ; " Be ye therefore merciful, as your Father also is merciful" (Luke vi. 36) ; " Be ye therefore," as regards this whole matter of doing good, as God does good, to the evil and the unthankful,—" Be ye therefore perfect, even as your Father which is in heaven is perfect" (Matt. v. 48).

17

FORCE OF THE APPEAL: "DEARLY BELOVED"

"Dearly beloved."   *—Romans 12:19*

THIS mode of address—" Beloved," or " Dearly beloved,"—may seem to have in it nothing very worthy of
note. It may be simply a matter-of-course and common-
place sort of interjection or invocation, such as a speaker
or writer is apt occasionally to use when he warms with
his subject, without any special meaning, for the most part,
beyond a kind and complimentary acknowledgment of
the " brethren " or "friends " whom he has in his eye.
I am persuaded, however, that it is not thus at random,
and as a mere customary and formal usage, that the
expression occurs in the Apostolic Epistles. I find it
generally where some difficult duty, or high attainment,
or precious privilege, of Christian faith or Christian
fellowship, is the subject of discourse; and where, as I
think most readers will feel, so tender and affectionate
an appellation is fitted to have a spirit-stirring and
heart-stirring effect.

' I speak to you,' the writer may be supposed to say,
' as " beloved " ones, " dearly beloved ;"—not beloved of
me only, or my beloved, as the phrase is sometimes

qualified ;—but without any term of limitation,—beloved ;—I say not of whom beloved ;—you know that right well yourselves ;—you are conscious who they are that dearly love you. I appeal to you as dearly beloved ones ; I appeal to that dear love of which you are the objects ; and by that love I beseech you to give heed to what I say, as they who are the objects of such dear love may be fairly asked and expected to do.'

Is there not a touching emphasis in a call like that? Is it not fitted powerfully to carry home any lesson to which it refers to the best affections of the soul?

In the present instance, the precise place at which it is introduced in the series of precepts regulating your treatment of offenders, as well as the nature of these precepts themselves, may be regarded as contributing to make the appeal at once seasonable and significant ; and accordingly it will fall to be considered, for practical purposes, in both of these points of view.

I. The address or appeal—" Dearly beloved "—breaks in two the series of precepts in the midst of which it stands ; it separates the five preceding verses (14–18) from the three which close the chapter (19–21). And the division is a true and right one ; not forced or fanciful, suggested by an incidental phrase, but substantial and of real practical importance.

Run your eye over the successive commandments of the first part, and observe how the first four,—to bless, to sympathize, to lay mind alongside of mind, to be generously forbearing, and tender of your neighbour's honour and your own,—are all in the line of the fifth, and fitted to make the keeping of it hopeful;—" If it be possible, as much as lieth in you, live peaceably with all men." If you fairly carry out the course of conduct sketched, you may warrantably look for some considerable success in your vocation of peacemakers. At all events, it is in that character that you are acting; it is peace, in the highest and best sense, that you keep steadily in view as the end at which you aim in your dealings with mankind. It is in the capacity of peacemakers that you go among the most hostile, seeking to disarm their jealousy and conciliate their confidence, if by any means they may be persuaded to accept, not only your peace, but your Master's.

It is this consideration, indeed, which ennobles and hallows the sort of treatment of your persecutors and adversaries which is here recommended; elevating it immeasurably above the tame patience of a mean spirit, and the plausible patience of a worldly spirit, both of which are sometimes confounded with it. For mere cowardice on the one hand, or policy on the other, may move a man to go great lengths in the way of truckling to pride and power, and so to study the arts of accommodating flattery and feigned courtesy, as to become a proficient in what may pass with many for Christian meekness and good-will. But the genuine grace is to be distinguished from all spurious counterfeits by the stamp upon it of Heaven's mint,—the divine seal of unselfishness and disinterestedness. If, as the Psalmist counsels (xxxiv. 14), "departing from evil and doing good, you seek peace and pursue it," you make it plain that it is not for your own sakes only or chiefly, but for the sake of those, the unquiet restlessness of whose troubled spirits, at universal war with you, and with themselves, and with all things in earth and heaven, you cannot contemplate unmoved. It is the pacifying of the uproar of their dark souls, over whose stormy waves you would fain invoke the spell of the Divine word, "Peace, be still," that you desire and seek. It is with a view to that result that you make advances to them; and are willing to concede and ready to be accommodating; and careful not to irritate any resentful, or wound any honourable, feeling; and with the reservation only of principle, which you cannot compromise, anxious to be yourselves nothing, and to consult simply for them,—if by any means you may so live peaceably with them as not to hinder, but to help, their coming to have peace with God.

Thus far the task or work assigned to you should be felt to be in itself not unpleasant; and, as regards the encouragement you have to look for success, not unpromising. They with whom you have to do are persecutors, no doubt, more or less; opposed to the truth, and not slow to injure its champions. But as yet you are not required to regard the case of any of them as desperate. You are at liberty to look, not upon the dark and gloomy, but upon the bright and hopeful side of the picture. Nay, it is your duty to do so. You do not exaggerate their perverseness. Rather you make allowances, and search for what may be pleaded in palliation, and what may be turned to account for good. What they do they do ignorantly, misled by prejudice, or blinded by unbelief. But they are not utterly hardened, or given over by the Spirit as reprobate. You may, therefore, go about the business of dealing with them cheerfully; not anticipating failure or defeat, but rather cherishing a good assurance that, with a goodly number, your following after peace will, by God's blessing on your prayers and pains, not be in vain. It is in this buoyant and sanguine frame of mind that you are to bless, and not curse ; that you are to rejoice with them that do rejoice, and weep with them that weep ; that, being neither high-minded nor selfishly-minded, you are to let your mind frankly meet with other minds ; that, not rendering evil for evil to any, you are to feel and show yourselves to be upon honour with all ; and that, finally, you are to live with all men as peaceably as they will let you. Such a temperament of charity, thinking no evil, hoping all things, is the only habit of soul that is in harmony with those broad and genial sentiments of natural humanity, genuine human kindness, the simple kindness of man to man, which alone, divesting your benevolence of whatever might give it a stiff or studied air of artificial condescension, will win for it confidential access into the warm recesses of many a thankful and many a broken heart.

But there comes to be a point,—a stage,—in the course of your dealings with your fellow-men, at which you cannot but apprehend that your position is changed. You are forced to look the sad fact of failure in the face, and see too many upon whom all your charity is expended in vain. Your conciliatory efforts are exhausted

upon them, and, as it would appear, to no purpose ; you
are for peace, but they are for war.   You are forced,
therefore, now to contemplate an issue or result of your
kindly dealing less favourable than that the prospect
of which has hitherto cheered you.

It is not that even yet you abandon all hope, and
acquiesce in the conclusion that all of those with whom,
in spite of all your endeavours, you have found it impossible to live peaceably, must be given over as impracticable subjects, on whom no gracious impression can
be made.   So far from that, you continue to ply them
with all Christian and gentle influences, and will rather
redouble your exertions than contentedly abandon them
to their fate.   You remember well how, in the Lord's
dealings with yourself, there was a crisis,—nay, more
than one,—at which, according to all ordinary calculations of probability, your case might have been pronounced
irremediable, and the Spirit might have ceased to strive
with you, and the awful sentence might have gone forth
against you, "Ephraim is joined to idols; let him alone."
But instead of that, the Lord's language concerning you was
the language, not only of most patient long-suffering, but
of most affectionate relenting ;—" How shall I give thee
up, Ephraim ? how shall I deliver thee, Israel? How shall
I make thee as Admah ? how shall I set thee as Zeboim?
Mine heart is turned within me, my repentings are
kindled together.   I will not execute the fierceness of
mine anger, I will not return to destroy Ephraim ; for I
am God, and not man" (Hos. xi. 8, 9).   So the Lord
persevered in loading you with his benefits, and bringing

to bear upon you the means, and overtures, and influences of his grace, even when your carnal enmity of mind and evil heart of unbelief, having resisted advances fitted to break in pieces the very stones, might have been held to be beyond the reach of cure. In the same long-suffering spirit you will persist, in the face of all discouragements, in discharging the blessed office of peacemaker, even towards those who are most obstinately and inveterately set against your good offices.

Nevertheless, you cannot help feeling that you occupy a position towards them very considerably different from that in which you were when you began the work of reconcilement. You cannot shut your eyes now to the dread alternative under the pressure of which you labour. You are forced to face the law which is the inexorable condition of whatever kindness you show to an enemy;— that it must either melt or burn.

Doubtless that law is in full force all along, as a law universally applicable. Your blessing them which persecute you; sympathizing with them when they rejoice or weep; being of one mind with them; demeaning yourself courteously and honourably towards them; seeking peace and pursuing it;—all these methods of amiable and friendly approach fall under the same stern and inexorable rule. In every instance of your acting according to any of these methods, your conciliatory conduct tells for evil on the object of it, if it does not work him good ; you are to him either "a savour of life unto life or of death unto death." That is a responsibility of which you cannot get rid. Still, it is when the limit is reached of that conditional command, " If it be possible, as much as lieth in you, live peaceably with all men ; "—it is when you apprehend and realize the failure of your attempts to make peace ;—it is then chiefly,—then for the first time fully,—that you apprehend and realize also the nature of the weapon which you are wielding ; the double power of the coals of fire which you are heaping on the enemy's head.   Then it is that you are called to quit the merely human platform from which you have been moving towards him, and to plant your foot on one that is divine.   Hitherto, you have felt yourself to be dealing with him simply as man with man ; now you feel that you deal with him even as God himself does. Hitherto, you have been holding out to him the olive branch, just as one who has himself found safety in the Ark would desire to have a fellow-sinner and fellow-sufferer brought into the same blessed refuge ;—now you sit with God who is over all, as the Avenger as well as the Deliverer ; and there is present to your mind, what is ever present to his, the solemn and awful truth, that what you are doing,—that the holding out of the olive-branch,—may kill as well as cure ; may destroy, as well as save ; nay, in the long-run, must destroy and kill, if it do not save and cure.

Now it is at the precise point, or stage, at which you pass from the simple doing of good with a view to peace, to the clear and vivid realization of the terrible fact that if it does not make for peace, the good you do is as a consuming fire ; it is when, renouncing all idea of righting or avenging yourself, you stand back, and give way before the burning wrath of God,—and are called to feed your enemy with this dread issue full in view, that, by the judgment of that God of vengeance, the food you give, if it does not heal him, must prove his bane and poison ;—it is at such a crisis that the affectionate appeal comes in so very opportunely,—"Dearly beloved."

Yes! it is most opportune, and you will own it to be so, if you have any sympathy with the Apostle in the cry that was wrung from him, under an overwhelming sense of his preaching being, to every one of his hearers, a savour either of death or of life,—" Who is sufficient for these things ? " You would need to be as God himself, to be able calmly to contemplate this alternative issue of whatever good he does to his enemy, and whatever good he moves you to do to yours. That doing of good now becomes, in your eye, an infinitely more serious and awful affair than you may have been apt to imagine, when you knew not thoroughly the terror of the Lord and the power of his anger. You see your enemy,—one who is your enemy for Christ's sake,—not in your own hands, in which case you might have some discretion as to what should come of your kind treatment of him and his ill requital of it ; but you see him in the hands of an angry God,— to whose wrath you give place ; and you have to feed him and give him drink with this awful handwriting of God himself on the wall before you,—that, not by your choice, but by his ordinance, the food and the drink are coals of fire heaped on the man's unsheltered head, either to melt his heart or to scath and slay his soul. Surely for such a momentous ministry as that,—if you really take in

the great fact on which it rests, and the meaning of it,—
you need to be nerved and braced with no common
strength ; you must have some firm and yet tender stay
on which you may fall back and lean. And have you
not such a stay in the deeply-rooted memory, or sense, of
all the divine affection, and all the intimate, endearing,
and confidential divine fellowship, to which the Apostle,
or rather the Lord himself, emphatically appeals, when he
hails you and salutes you with the simple address of
home-familiarity—" Beloved,"—" Dearly beloved ?"

II. What there is in the address itself, as coming in at
this stage and in this connection, to give it point and
power, is to be felt rather than described. If one does
not, as by a sort of spiritual and yet natural instinct, discern and grasp the charm of it, there is great difficulty
in making it plain and palpable. Perhaps an illustration
may best bring out what I take to be the charm of it,—
the spell lying in this one little word of endearment,
" Dearly beloved."

Let me suppose that I go out from a loving household,
of which I have been a loved and cherished member.
My home is all perfect harmony and pure peace ; and I
have been a favourite at home. Father, mother, brothers,
sisters, friends, companions, all have loved me dearly.
From such a quiet nest I suddenly pass into a very
different world. Sin and strife are rampant all around
me. Idleness, frivolity, jealousy, and envy,—or else sordid
covetousness, selfishness, and mean ambition,—reign
everywhere paramount. The men and women I meet

are wearying themselves and one another with their vain
rivalries and angry passions. And yet my business is
with them. I am sent to tell them of my home, and my
Father, and my Elder Brother, and all the inmates who
conspire to make it happy,—if by any means these men
and women may be persuaded to come with me that I
may show them good. Alas ! they will not understand
or give heed to what I say. They are irritated, and
resolved to pick a quarrel with me. They study how
they may best wound and vex me, by maligning the Head
and members of the family I belong to, and treating all
that I have to testify concerning it with indifference, or
incredulity, or scorn. I find it hard to keep my temper,
and to persevere in treating them courteously and kindly.
And when I see that all my courtesy and kindness is not
only lost upon so many of them, but is, in fact, only
putting them so much more in the wrong, and inten-
sifying the bitterness of their opposition, and increasing
their hard-heartedness, and aggravating their guilt ;—
ah! I exclaim, why must I continue to be buffeted by so
perverse a crew, to whom my well-intended good offices
are at least as likely to prove a curse as a blessing ; or
rather, indeed, far more so ? It is a position too trying
for me ; I cannot stand it.

But what is that sound which I hear ; wafted as on the
wings of some soft spice-laden gale ; "redolent of joy and
youth ;" fresh from my Father's dwelling ;—"Beloved ;
dearly beloved!" It "gives me pause." What ! shall I,
the child of love, and of such love as is mine in my
Father's dwelling, shrink from the post at which that

Father has placed me! Is it for me, who bask in the sunshine of a home full of love, to dream of leaving these unloved and unloving ones alone? Rather let my heart yearn over them the more, the more their sad enmity frets and rages. Let the thought of what they are, forlorn and lost, and of the risk of their case becoming daily worse, under the daily ministry of kindness with which they are plied, stir in me a new intensity of deep concern for their distress and keen desire for their deliverance. And let the very love of which I am the object, brought so vividly to mind by that startling word of awakening appeal as well as of endearing tenderness,—Dearly beloved one,—put me once more on the alert, as I feel myself adjured by all the love that is mine so richly, to be true to my loving Father, and true to those poor outcasts whom, if they will but be persuaded, even at the eleventh hour, my loving Father would fain have to be partakers of that very love of his which he delights to lavish upon me.

Some such force and emphasis, I apprehend, you are to recognise and appreciate when, in the midst of your close conflict with evil, and your earnest striving to overcome it with good, you hear yourselves affectionately saluted, as by a familiar voice from home,—" Dearly beloved." It is a voice that not only falls gently and sweetly, like an evening hymn, on your soul disquieted with vexing thoughts, but rings, like a trumpet call summoning you to work and war. And all the more is it thus powerful, because it reminds you of all that your being thus saluted implies. It carries your thoughts back

to what your sad case was, when you were yourselves
wanderers and outcasts in that far country, in which so
many are still wasting their substance in riotous living,
or else perishing with hunger. Who has made you to
differ now? In what manner, and by what means? Ye,
believers, were but yesterday what they are to-day.
Now you are beloved, dearly beloved. Love, divine
love, is the air you breathe. You dwell in love, because
you dwell in God. How has this blessedness become
yours? It is not that you have loved; but that you
have been and are beloved. The love which is of God,
the love wherewith the Father loveth the Son, has, by
the power of the Spirit, reached you. The Father loveth
you even as he loveth the Son. You are well-beloved,
as the Son is well-beloved. And you are the beloved of
all of whom the Son is the beloved. You therefore are in
the world as the Son was in the world. The voice which
hails you from heaven,—for it is a voice from heaven coming through the mouth or pen of one moved by the Holy
Ghost,—the voice hailing you as "beloved," is the very
voice which hailed him when he was in Jordan's stream;
—"This is my beloved Son, in whom I am well pleased!"
It is as hearing still evermore that voice from heaven,
that you now, like Him who heard it then, "go about
doing good" on the earth. It is the echo of that voice
in your bosom that not only stills the rising sense of ill-
usage when the good you do is ill-requited, but enables
you to accept, as he did, the solemn alternative and condition on which alone good can be done to any one here below,—that it is the "heaping of coals of fire upon his head."

For, let me be allowed to say, in drawing the discussion of this whole subject to a close, nothing can be more mistaken than the view on which a certain class of writers delight to expatiate,—grave theologians some of them, as well as authors of light literature catching and spreading the strain,—as to the frame of spirit in which, they think, one humbly confident of his own salvation by grace, must look abroad upon a world, of whose inhabitants, alas! but too many may be doomed ultimately to perish. Of course, every fair reasoner will protest against such a consideration being allowed any weight whatever, in the argument respecting the future and eternal condition of mankind. Whether all the race, or only a portion, is to be ultimately rescued from perdition, is a question to be determined upon its own proper evidence, by an appeal to Scriptural statements and representations. It is illogical to infer, from the supposed effect upon certain minds of a particular doctrine concerning the future state, that the doctrine must be false. And it is alike unfair and uncharitable to impute odious sentiments to those who conscientiously hold that a particular doctrine on this subject is a part of revelation, merely because one who denies or doubts it chooses to think that, if he believed the doctrine, it would awaken such sentiments in him. Let the truth be sought and ascertained, without regard at all to considerations such as these. Let the inquiry be impartially prosecuted, upon this issue ;—Does God so deal with men as absolutely to insure that all shall in the end be saved ?—or does he deal with them in such a way as to raise the dread alternative, that either they are saved, or are, by his very method of dealing with them, the more irretrievably lost? If this last idea of the divine government shall appear to be the only one warranted either by the providence or by the word of God;—if it shall turn out to be a great and awful fact, that light having come into the world, men may still to the last persevere in loving darkness rather than the light, and that they who do so must on that account fall under the heavier condemnation;—of what avail is it to say that this may tempt me, as one of the saved, to exult over my perishing neighbour,—hugging myself in my own security, and coolly consigning him to his doom? Rebuke my pride and malice by all means. But let God be true; charge not him foolishly.

I protest, however, for my part,—so will every child of God most energetically say, having in him the Spirit of Christ,—I protest against the imputation. With one voice we all unite in protesting against the imputation. You who make it little understand us. Because we realize, as it is our duty to do, our own blessed position as the Lord's friends, on the one hand; and the precarious and perilous position of all who are not his friends, on the other hand; you imagine that we must be ever dwelling on the contrast with mingled emotions of self-complacent exultation and either gratified vindictiveness or contemptuous pity. In the first place, you do our faith more than justice when you conceive of it as so easy a thing for us, or so much a matter of course, to take in the fact of so many of the men and women around us

360 · The Christian's Relationship/Hostile World (12:19)

who are living without God, being so miserably without
hope as they are. We have acquaintances and friends
among them, of whom and of whose prospects we would
fain think favourably ; and even strangers and enemies,
our indolence is ever prompting us to fancy, may not be
in such danger that we must put ourselves very much
about to help them. The real and actual difficulty with
us is all on the side of our being sufficiently alive to the
terrible risk which they among whom we dwell are
running. And then you do less than justice to the love
by which faith works. For we can confidently assure
you, that just in proportion as our faith is strong and
vivid in Him who " is set for the fall and rising again of
many in Israel" (Luke ii. 34) ; who " unto them which
believe is precious, but unto the disobedient a stone of
stumbling and a rock of offence" (1 Peter ii. 7, 8) ;—in
the same proportion does our love burn ; both as a love
of most self-abasing gratitude to Him who makes us to
differ; and as a love also of such self-sacrificing anxiety
as that which breaks out in these utterances of Paul ;—
" I say the truth in Christ, I lie not, my conscience also
bearing me witness in the Holy Ghost, that I have great
heaviness and continual sorrow in my heart. For I
could wish that myself were accursed from Christ for
my brethren, my kinsmen according to the flesh" (Rom.
ix. 1-3) ; " Brethren, my heart's desire and prayer to
God for Israel is, that they might be saved" (Rom. x. 1).

" We know that we are of God, and the whole world
lieth in wickedness ;"—such assured faith, apprehending
the sharp line which severs us in Christ from our fellow-

sinners who are out of Christ, the beloved Apostle John would have us to cherish ;—" We know that we are of God, and the whole world lieth in wickedness " (1 John v. 19). He is not speaking of the world to come,—the state in which the line is unchangeably determined. How the blessed ones who, like Lazarus in Abraham's bosom, behold the torments of the condemned in hell, between whom and them there is a great gulf fixed, impassable, everlasting ; how they behold the terrible sight and give glory to God while beholding it, we may not now inquire. It is to this present world that John is pointing. And in this present world the line is not determined, the gulf is not fixed.

This, indeed, is the very consideration that stamps upon our treatment of those we meet with in the world a character of deepest interest. They are " lying in wickedness ;"—not, however, hopelessly ; for there is brought to bear upon them, on the part of God, a ministry of forbearance, and kindness, and mercy, that is designed and fitted to deliver them. In that ministry we are called to be fellow-workers with God. Our acts and expressions of good-will form a part of that ministry of his. We regard our acts and expressions of good-will in that light, and therefore we seek to abound in them. But we know the condition which is attached to the ministry as a whole, and to every particular instance of it. If not graciously effectual to save, it is infallibly powerful to destroy.

And who am I, each one of us is ready to exclaim, that I should be in this way, in any sense and to any extent,

instrumental, however unintentionally, and even unconsciously, in influencing or determining another's destiny,
not in time merely, but perhaps for eternity? And who
is he? Let me isolate myself and him together. Here
am I, like Daniel—shall I say?—" a man greatly
beloved." There is he,—a man who, as I cannot but
apprehend, is still " in the gall of bitterness and the
bond of iniquity." My home, how blessed! His exile,
how dreary! And why is my case not his, and his case
not mine ; his the blessed home, mine the dreary exile?
Can I regard him with cold indifference, can I ever dream
of avenging any wrong he may do me in his blindness,
with that question ringing in my ears continually? Can
I nestle in my own warm nest, under affection's wing,
when he is starving outside? When I am hailed by a
whole chorus of harmonious, heavenly voices,—" Beloved,"
" Dearly beloved,"—is he to be left shivering in the cold
blast of earth's unkindness, and on the verge of the
fathomless pit of despair? I must be ministering to
him. I do minister to him. It is an anxious service.
My neighbour, my friend, whom I would fain have for
my brother, is in a critical position. It is, as I may
say, life or death with him ; now or never. I see his
fate trembling in the balance. How is he taking my
advances and assiduities? What impression is my word or
deed of Christian solicitude making ; my word in season,
my well-intended deed of kindness and good-will? I watch
with intense concern. Is he relenting? Are there signs
of jealousy allayed, suspicion lulled, some spark of confidence kindled? Is there some faint indication of the

hard heart becoming soft, and the sealed fountain of gracious tears being opened ? Is there anything like the bruised reed, or the smoking flax ? Or, alas ! is there only increasing sullenness and gloom ; the impatience that will not let its wound be probed, the anger that will not have its misery interfered with ? How eagerly do I note every sign ! Now, it seems as if my dealing were doing him good. Again, I shudder to see that it is only irritating and vexing him. All the while I have full in view the issue that may be more or less dependent on my movement. I am handling coals of fire. I cannot help it. Through me, through my agency and instrumentality, he is undergoing a process that cannot leave him as it finds him. He is the better or the worse for it. And it is I who am at this moment practically shutting the question up to this issue. I cannot be calm, as if I were conducting a common experiment upon unconscious matter. If I know anything of Heaven's love, and of Heaven's wrath,—the love of which I, once a child of wrath, am now the object,—the wrath hanging in suspense over him ;—so hanging over him that the very next step he takes, in consequence of my interposition, may, for anything I can tell, decide whether its winged and fiery thunderbolt is to give place to the same love that has reached me, or to fall on his head for ever ;—if, I repeat, I know anything of Heaven's love, and of Heaven's wrath ;—then by all that love,—the love with which Christ dying for me loveth me ; the love with which the Holy Ghost, shutting me up into Christ, loveth me ; the love with which the Father, giving me his dear

Son and all things else in him, loveth me; the love with which all saints and holy angels love me;—by the dear love of my Father's house where now I dwell;—I cannot but be moved with most thrilling intensity, as I hang over yonder yawning gulf,—and hold out my hand to catch, to feed, to rescue, my poor famished brother sinking in the pit,—and with tearful eagerness strain my eyes to see if he will let me help him;—since, if he will not, full well I know, and it is full terrible to know, that all that I am doing on his behalf must make his case the worse! Knowing this,—feeling that it may be for him salvation or destruction,—I dare not draw back; I must hold on and persevere. No ingratitude can cool me; no injury provoke me; no obstinacy weary me. Tasting for myself the free and full love of my Father in heaven, and of all his heavenly household, I cannot but persist in heaping coals of fire on the head of every foe, if by any means,—I would it were not in a way of judgment, but in a way of grace,—I may have a share in my Father's great and glorious work of " overcoming evil with good."

Additional Resources for Your Study of the Book of Romans:

COMMENTARY ON ROMANS   **Robert Haldane**
One of the most authoritative expositions ever to appear on this epistle. It offers exhaustive exegesis on every sentence in Romans, emphasizing scholarship, theological reflection, and spiritual insight. Special attention is given to the glorious doctrine of justification by faith. Clearly refutes critical attacks on the words and doctrines communicated by Paul.

0-8254-2865-3	754 pp.	paperback
0-8254-2862-9	754 pp.	deluxe hardcover

EXPOSITORY AND EXEGETICAL STUDIES   **A. F. & F. J. A. Hort**
(5 vols. in 1.) Includes: *Prolegomena to Romans and Ephesians, The Epistle of St. James, The First Epistle of St. Peter, The Apocalypse of St. John 1-3* by F.J.A. Hort and *The Gospel According to St. Mark* by A. F. Hort.

0-8254-5127-2	896 pp.	dexuxe hardcover

ROMANS: WHERE LIFE BEGINS   **Roy L. Laurin**
Part of the "Life" Commentary Series. Laurin writes in a rich and exciting style. This devotional commentary is neither dry nor technical, but rather full of vibrant life. Billy Graham says, "Many of the thoughts I use in my preaching have come from this great preacher's writings."

0-8254-3130-1	540 pp.	paperback

OUTLINE STUDIES IN ROMANS   **Robert Lee**
A unique guide to discovering the riches of God's Word. Expositional outlines, practical notes, illustrations, and teaching helps provide students, teachers, and preachers with building blocks for studying and communicating this important epistle.

0-8254-3142-5	128 pp.	paperback

COMMENTARY ON ROMANS   **Martin Luther**

Here is Luther's most famous exposition of the epistle he loved most. The preface to this commentary was instrumental in the salvation of John Wesley.

0-8254-3119-0   224 pp.   paperback

NOTES ON ROMANS   **Arthur Pridham**

This treatment not only deserves a place in the library of every serious Bible student, but, once there, will become a much used resource.

0-8254-3519-6   462 pp.   hardcover

STUDIES IN ROMANS   **Thomas Robinson**

Features the leading notes and comments from major commentators and examines the great doctrinal themes found in this epistle. A masterpiece for expositors. "Worth any amount to preachers." - C. H. Spurgeon

0-8254-3625-7   908 pp.   hardcover

SALVATION AND BEHAVIOR.   **William Scroggie**

Romans 1–8 and 12–15 are practically taught and applied.

0-8254-3735-0   104 pp.   paperback

STUDIES IN ROMANS   **W. Leon Tucker**

The main doctrinal themes are examined and fully alliterated in this unique study.

0-8254-3827-6   112 pp.   paperback

**Available from your favorite
Christian bookstore or:**

KREGEL Publications

**P.O. Box 2607
Grand Rapids, MI 49501**